Moodle 1.9
E-Learning Course Development

A complete guide to successful learning using
Moodle 1.9

William H. Rice IV

PUBLISHING

BIRMINGHAM - MUMBAI

Moodle 1.9

E-Learning Course Development

First published: June 2008

Production Reference: 1230608

Published by Packt Publishing Ltd.
32 Lincoln Road
Olton
Birmingham, B27 6PA, UK.

ISBN 978-1-847193-53-7

www.packtpub.com

Cover Image by Vinayak Chittar (vinayak.chittar@gmail.com)

Credits

Author

William H. Rice IV

Reviewers

Michelle Moore

Mark Bailye

Acquisition Editor

Rashmi Phadnis

Technical Editors

Mithun Sehgal

Arnab Chakrabarty

Editorial Team Leader

Mithil Kulkarni

Copy Editor

Sumathi Sridhar

Project Manager

Abhijeet Deobhakta

Project Coordinator

Abhijeet Deobhakta

Indexer

Hemangini Bari

Proofreader

Camillie Guy

Production Coordinator

Shantanu Zagade

Cover Work

Shantanu Zagade

About the Author

William Rice is a software training professional who lives, works, and plays in New York City. His indoor hobbies include writing books and spending way too much time reading sites like slashdot and 43folders. His outdoor hobbies include orienteering, rock climbing, and edible wild plants (a book on that is coming someday).

William is fascinated by the relationship between technology and society—how we create our tools, and how our tools in turn shape us. He is married to an incredible woman who encourages his writing pursuits, and has two amazing sons.

For Lisa, who inspires me to be more than I thought I could be.

About the Reviewers

Michelle Moore discovered Moodle five years ago, while completing her MS in Instructional Design and Technology. Michelle's thesis explored quality alternatives to expensive course management systems.

Michelle first used Moodle with her middle school math students. Soon she was sharing and supporting Moodle within her school district. Today, as the Director of Training for Moodle Partner Remote-Learner.net, Michelle assists teachers and trainers across the United States as they implement and integrate Moodle.

In my work with Moodle, I have learned from and been assisted by many individuals, three of whom deserve special acknowledgment. First, I owe thanks to Martin Dougiamas, the creator of Moodle, for his vision, passion, and desire to design an LMS that makes a difference. Second, I thank Bryan Williams, CEO of Remote-Learner. net, for seeing my potential and providing me opportunities to grow and learn. Finally, I thank my husband, Jonathan, for his continuous encouragement and support.

Mark Bailye describes himself as a developer, teacher, and learner. He has wide-ranging industry experience in software and online learning development, and with using information and communication technologies as educational tools. Mark is passionate about medical education, and has developed a wide variety of online solutions aimed at enhancing, engaging, and enriching the learner's experience. Mark has a proven track record in online and face-to-face education and training, and is always keen to develop, pilot, and be involved in projects that have an e-learning focus based on the latest technologies.

I would like to thank PACKT Publishing, and in particular, Rashmi, for giving me the opportunity to review another book.

Table of Contents

Preface

This book shows you how to use Moodle as a tool to enhance your teaching. Initially, it will help you to analyze your students' requirements, and understand what Moodle can do for them. After that, you'll see how to use different features of Moodle to meet your course goals.

The social constructionist learning philosophy is at the heart of Moodle: we all *construct* knowledge through interaction with one another and with learning materials in a social way. This book will show you how to add static learning material, interactive activities, and social features to your courses so that students reach their learning potential.

Whether you want to support traditional class teaching or lecturing, or provide complete online and distance learning courses, this book will prove a powerful resource throughout your use of Moodle.

What This Book Covers

Chapter 1 introduces you to the basics of Moodle. It takes you on a guided tour of a Moodle site.

Chapter 2 guides you through installing and configuring Moodle.

Chapter 3 explains how to make changes to your site's configuration, so that it helps to create the kind of learning experience you want for your students.

Chapter 4 helps you create courses and organize those courses into categories.

Chapter 5 teaches you how to add static course material, such as text pages, web pages, links, directory views, and labels, to a course, and how to make best use of them.

Chapter 6 teaches you how to add interactive course material, such as assignments, journals, lessons, quizzes, and surveys, to your course.

Chapter 7 teaches you how to add social course material, such as chats, forums, and wikis, to a course, and how to make best use of them.

Chapter 8 helps you to customize your Front Page, which includes customizing your site's logo, header, footer, icons, and strings.

Chapter 9 describes several features that Moodle offers to the teachers to assess their students' progress.

Chapter 10 covers adding new modules, duplicating courses on your site, and importing course material from other Moodle sites. Finally, it shows how Moodle uses roles to determine who can do what on your site.

What You Need for This Book

To make the most of this book, you need access to a Moodle site where you have at least the rights to create course material. It would be even better if you have administrator rights to the Moodle site, but this is not needed. Also helpful is an enthusiasm for learning, teaching, and using the Web to reach out and make a difference in your students' lives.

Who is This Book For

This book is written for anyone who wants to get the most from Moodle. Beginners to the software will get a thorough guide to how the software works, and some great ideas for getting to a good start with their first course. More experienced Moodlers will find powerful insights into developing more successful and educational courses.

Conventions

In this book, you will find a number of styles of text that distinguish between different kinds of information. Here are some examples of these styles, and an explanation of their meaning.

There are three styles for code. Code words in text are shown as follows: "ID number of user is a unique identifier for the user.".

A block of code will be set as follows:

```
$string['addanewdiscussion'] = 'Add a new discussion topic';
$string['addanewtopic'] = 'Add a new topic';
$string['advancedsearch'] = 'Advanced search';
```

When we wish to draw your attention to a particular part of a code block, the relevant lines or items will be made bold:

```
$string['addanewdiscussion'] = 'Add a new discussion topic';
$string['addanewtopic'] = 'Add a new topic';
$string['advancedsearch'] = 'Advanced search';
```

New terms and **important words** are introduced in a bold-type font. Words that you see on the screen, in menus or dialog boxes for example, appear in our text like this: "Moodle offers a variety of ways to authenticate users. You'll find them under **Site Administration | Users | Authentication**.".

 Warnings or important notes appear in a box like this.

Reader Feedback

Feedback from our readers is always welcome. Let us know what you think about this book, what you liked or may have disliked. Reader feedback is important for us to develop titles that you really get the most out of.

To send us general feedback, simply drop an email to feedback@packtpub.com, making sure to mention the book title in the subject of your message.

If there is a book that you need and would like to see us publish, please send us a note in the **SUGGEST A TITLE** form on www.packtpub.com or email to suggest@packtpub.com.

If there is a topic that you have expertise in and you are interested in either writing or contributing to a book, see our author guide on www.packtpub.com/authors.

Customer Support

Now that you are the proud owner of a Packt book, we have a number of things to help you to get the most from your purchase.

Downloading the Checklist for the Book

Visit http://www.packtpub.com/support/3537_Checklist.zip, and select this book from the list of titles to download the checklist for this book. The file available for download will then be displayed.

Errata

Although we have taken every care to ensure the accuracy of our contents, mistakes do happen. If you find a mistake in one of our books—maybe a mistake in text or code—we would be grateful if you would report this to us. By doing this you can save other readers from frustration, and help to improve subsequent versions of this book. If you find any errata, report them by visiting http://www.packtpub. com/support, selecting your book, clicking on the **let us know** link, and entering the details of your errata. Once your errata are verified, your submission will be accepted and the errata are added to the list of existing errata. The existing errata can be viewed by selecting your title from http://www.packtpub.com/support.

Questions

You can contact us at questions@packtpub.com if you are having a problem with some aspect of the book, and we will do our best to address it.

1
Introduction

Moodle is a free learning management system that enables you to create powerful, flexible, and engaging online learning experiences. I use the phrase 'online learning experiences' instead of 'online courses' deliberately. The phrase 'online course' often connotes a sequential series of web pages, some images, maybe a few animations, and a quiz put online. There might be some email or bulletin board communication among the teacher and students. However, online learning can be much more engaging than that.

Moodle's name gives you insight into its approach to e-learning. From the official Moodle documentation:

> *The word Moodle was originally an acronym for* **Modular Object-Oriented Dynamic Learning Environment***, which is mostly useful to programmers and education theorists. It's also a verb that describes the process of lazily meandering through something, doing things as it occurs to you to do them, an enjoyable tinkering that often leads to insight and creativity. As such, it applies both to the way Moodle was developed, and to the way a student or teacher might approach studying or teaching an online course. Anyone who uses Moodle is a* **Moodler***.*

The phrase 'online learning experience' connotes a more active and engaging role for the students and teachers, as in:

- Web pages that can be explored in any order
- Courses with live chats among students and teachers
- Forums where users can rate messages on their relevance or insight
- Online workshops that enable students to evaluate each other's work
- Impromptu polls that let the teacher evaluate the students opinion on a course's progress
- Directories set aside for teachers to upload and share their files

All these features create an active learning environment, full of different kinds of student-to-student and student-to-teacher interaction. This is the kind of user experience that Moodle excels at, and the kind that this book will help you create.

Who is This Book for?

This book is for anyone who wants to make the most of Moodle's features to produce an interactive online learning experience. If you're an educator, corporate trainer, or just someone with something to teach, this book can guide you through the installation, configuration, creation, and management of a Moodle site. It is suitable for people who perform the task of creating and setting up the learning site, and for those who create and deliver courses on the site. That is, it is for site administrators, course creators, and teachers.

A Plan for Creating Your Learning Site

Whether you are the site creator, or a course creator, you can use this book as you would use a project plan. As you work your way through each chapter, the book provides guidance on making decisions that meet your goals for your learning site. This helps you create the kind of learning experience that you want for your teachers (if you're the site creator) or students (if you're the teacher). You can also use this book as a traditional reference manual. But its main advantages are its step-by-step, project-oriented approach, and the guidance it gives you about creating an interactive learning experience.

Moodle is designed to be intuitive to use, and its online help is well written. It does a good job of telling you how to use each of its features. What Moodle's help files don't tell you is, when and why to use each feature, and what effect it will have on the student experience. These are exactly the topics discussed in this book.

The appendix contains a checklist of the major steps for creating a Moodle site and populating it with courses. The steps are cross-referenced to the relevant sections of this book. Download this checklist from the Packt Publishing website (`http://www.packtpub.com/support/3537_Checklist.zip`), print it, and keep it handy while creating your Moodle site.

Step-By-Step—Using Each Chapter

When you create a Moodle learning site, you usually follow a defined series of steps. This book is arranged to support that process. Each chapter shows you how to get the most from each step. The steps are listed here, with a brief description of the chapters that supports the step.

As you work your way through each chapter, your learning site will grow in scope and sophistication. By the time you finish this book, you should have a complete, interactive learning site. As you learn more about what Moodle can do, and see your courses taking shape, you may want to change some things you did in the previous chapters. Moodle offers you this flexibility. And this book helps you determine how those changes will cascade throughout your site.

Step 1—Learn about the Moodle Experience (Chapter 1)

Every Learning Management System (LMS) has a paradigm, or approach, that shapes the user experience and encourages a certain kind of usage. An LMS might encourage sequential learning by offering features that enforce a given order on each course. It might discourage student-to-student interaction by offering few features that support it, while encouraging solo learning by offering many opportunities for the student to interact with the course material. In this chapter, you will learn what Moodle can do and what kind of user experience your students and teachers will have, while using Moodle. You will also learn about the Moodle philosophy, and how it shapes the user experience. With this information, you'll be ready to decide how to make the best use of Moodle's many features, and to plan your online learning site.

Step 2—Install and Configure Moodle (Chapter 2)

Most of the decisions you make while installing and configuring Moodle will affect the user experience. Not just students and teachers, but course creators and site administrators are also affected by these decisions. While Moodle's online help does a good job of telling you how to install and configure the software, it doesn't tell you how the settings you choose affect the user experience. Chapter 2 covers the implications of these decisions, and helps you configure the site so that it behaves in the way you have envisioned it.

Step 3—Create the Framework for Your Learning Site (Chapter 3)

In Moodle, every course belongs to a category. Chapter 3 takes you through creating course categories, and then creating courses. Just as you chose site-wide settings during installation and configuration, you choose course-wide settings while creating each course. This chapter tells you the implications of the various course settings so that you can create the experience you want for each course. Finally, Chapter 3 takes you through the usage of the various blocks, each of which adds a well-defined function to the site or to the course. After creating the categories and courses, and deciding which blocks to use, you've created a framework for your site. Then, you're ready to fill your courses with learning material, which you'll do in Steps 4 through 6.

Step 4—Add Basic Course Material (Chapter 4)

In most online courses, the core material consists of web pages that the students view. These pages can contain text, graphics, movies, sound files, games, exercises, and so on. Anything that appears on the World Wide Web can appear on a Moodle web page. Chapter 4 covers adding web pages to Moodle courses, plus other kinds of static course material such as plain-text pages, links to other websites, labels, and directories of files. This chapter also helps you determine when to use each of these types of materials.

Step 5—Make Your Courses Interactive (Chapter 5)

In this context, 'interactive' means interaction between the student and teacher, or the student and an active web page. Student-to-student interaction is covered in the next step. This chapter covers activities that involve interaction between the student and an active web page, or between the student and the teacher. Interactive course material includes:

- Surveys posed by the teacher
- Journals written by the student and read by the teacher
- Lessons that guide students through a defined path based upon their answers to review questions and quizzes

Chapter 5 tells you how to create these interactions, and how each of them affects the student and teacher experience. You'll need this information to help you manage Moodle's interactive features.

Step 6—Make Your Course Social (Chapter 6)

Social course material enables student-to-student interaction. Moodle enables you to add chats, forums, and wikis to your courses. These types of interactions will be familiar to many students. You can also create glossaries that are site-wide and specific to a single course. Students can add to the glossaries. Finally, Moodle offers a powerful workshop tool, which enables students to view and evaluate each other's work. Each of these interactions makes the course more interesting, but also more complicated for the teacher to manage. Chapter 6 helps you make the best use of Moodle's social features. The result is a course that encourages students to contribute, share, and evaluate.

Step 7—Create a Welcome for New and Existing Students (Chapter 7)

Previous chapters covered the many features that you can add to a Moodle course. The same features can be added to the Front Page of your Moodle site. The Front Page can be anything from a simple welcome message to a full-fledged course of its own. This chapter helps you create a public face for your Moodle site. You can show a Login Page or the Front Page of your site. The content and behavior of the login and Front Pages can be customized. You can choose to allow anonymous users, require students to be registered, or use a combination of Guest and registered access. Each of these options affects the kind of welcome that new and existing students get, when they first see your site. Chapter 7 helps you determine which options to use, and how to combine them to get the effect you desire.

Step 8—Use Teacher's Tools to Deliver and Administer Courses (Chapter 8)

Moodle offers several tools to help teachers administer and deliver courses. It keeps detailed access logs that enable teachers to see exactly the content that the students accessed, and when they did it. It also enables teachers to establish custom grading scales, which are available site-wide, or for a single course. Student grades can be accessed online, and also downloaded to a spreadsheet program. Finally, teachers can collaborate in special forums (bulletin boards) reserved just for them.

Step 9—Extend Moodle (Chapter 9)

As Moodle is open source, new modules are constantly being developed and contributed by the Moodle community. The modules that are part of Moodle's core distribution are covered in this book. Additional modules extend Moodle's capabilities. While this book cannot cover every module available, it can cover the process of installing and integrating new modules into your site. One of the modules included with the core distribution is a **PayPal** module. Chapter 9 covers how this module is used for pay sites. This chapter also covers backing up and restoring the entire site, individual courses, and components within a course.

The Moodle Philosophy

Moodle is designed to support a style of learning called *Social Constructionism*. This style of learning is interactive. The social constructionist philosophy believes that people learn best when they interact with the learning material, construct new material for others, and interact with other students about the material. The difference between a traditional class and the social constructionist philosophy is the difference between a lecture and a discussion.

Moodle does not require you to use the social constructionist method for your courses. However, it best supports this method. For example, Moodle enables you to add five kinds of static course material that a student reads, but does not interact with:

- Text pages
- Web pages
- Links to anything on the Web (including material on your Moodle site)
- A view into one of the course's directories
- A label that displays any text or image

However, Moodle enables you to add six types of interactive course materials. This is the course material that a student interacts with, by answering questions, entering text, or uploading files:

- Assignment (uploading files to be reviewed by the teacher)
- Choice (a single question)
- Journal (an online journal)
- Lesson (a conditional, branching activity)
- Quiz (an online test)
- Survey (with results available to the teacher and/or students)

Moodle also offers five kinds of activities where students interact with each other. These are used to create social course materials:

- Chat (live online chat between students)
- Forum (you can have none or several online bulletin boards for each course)
- Glossary (students and/or teachers can contribute terms to site-wide glossaries)
- Wiki (these are a familiar tool for collaboration to most younger students and many older students)
- Workshop (these support peer review and feedback of assignments that the students upload)

So far, we have listed five kinds of static course materials, and eleven kinds of interactive course materials. In addition, some of Moodle's add-on modules add more types of interaction. For example, one add-on module enables students and teachers to schedule appointments with each other.

The Moodle Experience

As Moodle encourages interaction and exploration, your students' learning experience will often be non-linear. Conversely, Moodle has few features for enforcing a specific order upon a course. For example, there is no feature in Moodle that would require a student to complete Course 101 before allowing the student to enroll in Course 102. Instead, you would need to manually enroll the student in each course. Also, there is no Moodle feature that would require a student to complete Topic 1 in a course before allowing the student to see Topic 2. If you wanted to enforce that kind of linear course flow, you would need to manually place the student into the group that is authorized to view Topic 1, and then upon completion, place the student into the group that is authorized to view Topics 1 and 2, and so on.

As a site administrator or teacher, enforcing a linear path through a course catalog, or through the material in an individual course, often requires manual intervention. However, if you design your site with Moodle's non-linear style in mind, you will find that it offers you great flexibility and the ability to create engaging online courses.

As Moodle becomes more popular, there is more demand for features that enforce a linear flow through a course. Modules are being developed to lock and open activities based upon a student's performance in previous activities. Check the Moodle.org news, roadmap, and modules pages for the status of these efforts.

In this section, I'll take you on a tour of a Moodle learning site. You will see the student's experience from the time the student arrives at the site, enters a course, and works through some material in the course. You will also see some student-to-student interaction, and some functions used by the teacher to manage the course. Along the way, I'll point out many features that you will learn to implement in this book, and how the demo site is using those features.

The Moodle Front Page

The Front Page of your site is the first thing most visitors will see. This section takes you on a tour of the Front Page of my demonstration site. Probably the best Moodle demo site on the Web is `http://demo.moodle.org`.

Arriving at the Site

When a potential student arrives at the demonstration learning site, the student sees the Front Page. Later in this book, you'll learn to control what an anonymous visitor to your learning site sees on the Front Page. You can require the visitor to register and log in before seeing any part of your site, or allow the visitor to enter with a Guest account. Like most sites, my demonstration site allows anonymous visitors to see a lot of information about the site on the Front Page:

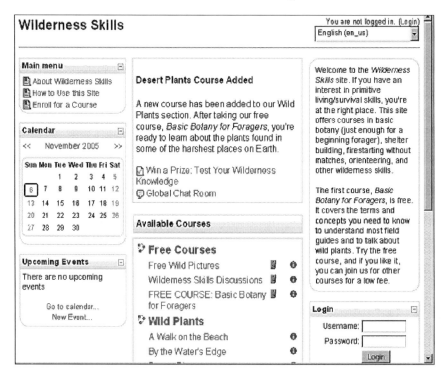

One of the first things a visitor will notice is the announcement at the top and center of the page, **Desert Plants Course Added**. Below the announcement are two activities: a quiz, **Win a Prize: Test Your Wilderness Knowledge**, and a chat room, **Global Chat Room**. Selecting either of these activities will require the student to register with the site.

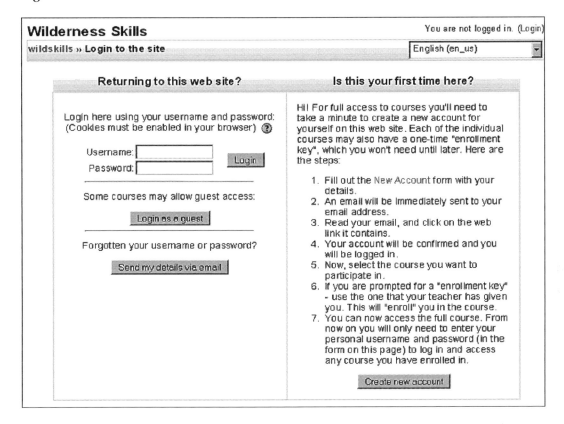

Anonymous, Guest, and Registered Access

Note the line **Some courses may allow guest access** in the middle of the page. You can set three levels of access for your entire site, and for individual courses:

Anonymous access allows anyone to see the contents of your site's Front Page. Note that there is no Anonymous access for courses. Even if a course is open to Guests, the visitor must either manually log in the user as Guest or the site must automatically log in a visitor as Guest.

Guest access requires the user to login as Guest. This enables you to track usage, by looking at the statistics for the user Guest. But as everyone is logged in as the user Guest, you can't track individual users.

Registered access requires the user to register on your site. You can allow people to register with or without email confirmation, require a special code for enrolment, manually create their accounts, import accounts from another system, or use an outside system (like and LDAP server) for your accounts. There's more on this in Chapter 2.

The Main Menu

Returning to the Front Page, notice the **Main menu** in the upper left corner. This menu consists of three documents that tell the user what the site is about, and how to use it.

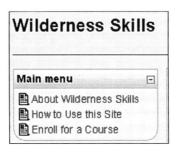

In Moodle, icons tell the user the kind of resources that will be accessed by a link. In this case, the icon tells the user these are web or text pages. The course materials that a student observes or reads, such as web or text pages, hyperlinks, and multimedia files are called **Resources**. In Chapter 4, you will learn how to add Resources to a course.

Blocks

There is a **Calendar** and the **Upcoming Events** below the **Main menu** . These are blocks, which you can choose to add to the Front Page, and to each course individually.

Other blocks display a summary of the current course, a list of courses available on the site, the latest news, who is online, and other information. In the lower right of the Front Page you can see the **Login** block. Chapter 3 tells you how to use these blocks.

You can add these blocks to the Front Page of your site because the Front Page is essentially a course. Anything that you can add to a course—such as resources and blocks—can be added to the Front Page.

Site Description

On the right side of the Front Page you see a **Site Description**. This is optional. If this were a course, you could choose to display the **Course Description**.

Welcome to the *Wilderness Skills* site. If you have an interest in primitive living/survival skills, you're at the right place. This site offers courses in basic botany (just enough for a beginning forager), shelter building, firestarting without matches, orienteering, and other wilderness skills.

The Site or Course Description can contain anything that you can put on a web page. It is essentially a block of HTML code that is put onto the Front Page.

Available Courses

You can choose to display available courses on the Front Page of your site. In the Demonstration site, I've created a category for **Free Courses** and another for **Wild Plants**. **Free Courses** allow Guest users to enter. Courses in other categories require users to register.

Free Courses
- Free Wild Pictures
- Wilderness Skills Discussions
- FREE COURSE: Basic Botany for Foragers

Wild Plants
- A Walk on the Beach
- By the Water's Edge

Clicking on the information icon ❶ next to each course displays the **Course Description**. Clicking on a course name takes you into the course. If the course allows anonymous access, you are taken directly into the course. If the course allows Guest access, or requires registration, you are taken to the Login screen.

Inside a Course

Now let us take a look inside the course.

Breadcrumbs

In the next screenshot, the user has logged in as **Guest** and entered the **Basic Botany** course. We know this from the breadcrumbs trail at the top left of the screen, which tells us the name of the site and of the course. In the upper right, we see a confirmation that the user has logged in under the name **Guest**.

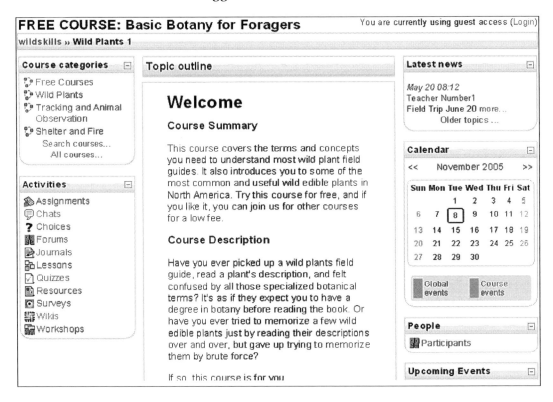

Blocks

Similar to the Front Page, this course displays the **Calendar** and **Upcoming Events** blocks. It also displays blocks for the **Latest news, People, Activities**, and **Course categories**. The **Activities** block lists all of the types of Activities and Resources that are available in this course. Clicking on a link will display that type of activity. For example, clicking **Quizzes** displays this screen:

wildskills » Wild Plants 1 » Quizzes			
Topic	**Name**	**Quiz closes**	**Best grade**
2	Life Cycles of Plants	Thursday, November 9 2006, 04:50 AM	
3	Leaf Types and Shapes	Saturday, July 8 2006, 04:15 PM	

Note that the breadcrumbs at the top now indicate the site name, course name, and also indicate that you are viewing the quizzes in the course. The course is organized by **Topic**, and the number of each **Topic** is displayed in the left column. As the user is logged in as Guest, and many users can use that ID, the **Best grade** column is not meaningful here. It indicates only the highest grade for everyone who has ever attempted this quiz with Guest access. Clicking on the name of a quiz takes the user to that quiz. In the breadcrumbs at the top of the page (the navigation line), clicking on **Wild Plants 1,** takes the user back to the course.

Earlier, I commented on the non-linear nature of many Moodle courses. Note that even though the user has not completed Topic 1, the quizzes for Topic 2 and 3 are open to the user. Also, looking at the **Activities** block, you can see that all the resources for this course are available to the user at all times. Later, we'll discuss features that enable you to selectively hide and show different activities.

Topics

Moodle also enables you to organize a course by week, In that case, each section is labeled with a date, instead of a number. Or, you can choose to make your course a single, large discussion forum.

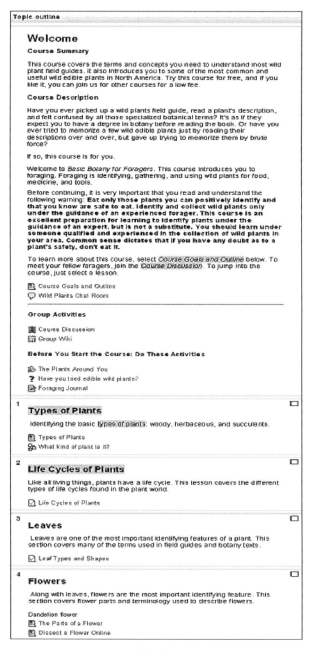

Most courses are organized by **Topic**. Note that the first topic, which I've labeled **Welcome**, is not numbered. Moodle gives you a Topic 0 to use as the course introduction.

Teachers can hide and show topics at will. This enables a teacher to open and close activities as the course progresses.

Topics are the lowest level of organization in Moodle. The hierarchy is: **Site | Course Category | Course Subcategory (optional) | Course | Topic**. Every item in your course belongs to a topic, even if your course consists only of Topic 0.

Join a Discussion

Clicking on **Course Discussion**, under **Group Activities**, takes the student to the course-wide forum. Clicking on the topic line opens that thread. You can see in this screenshot that the teacher started with the first post. Then **William Rice** left a **test** message, and a student replied to the original post:

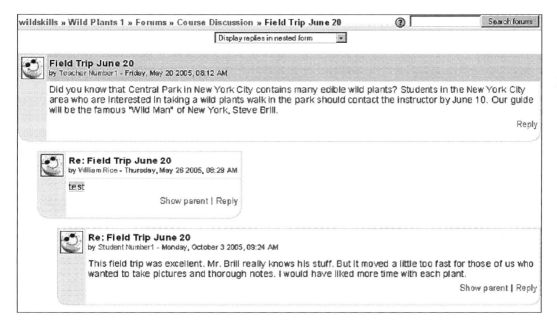

That **test** message doesn't serve our students. Fortunately, the teacher has editing rights to this forum. So he or she can delete posts at will. The teacher can also rate posts for their relevance, as shown in the following screenshot:

As Moodle supports an interactive and collaborative style of learning, students can also be given the ability to rate forum posts and materials submitted by other students. You'll find out more about forums in Chapter 6.

Complete a Workshop

Next, the student will enter a workshop called **Observing the Familiar**.

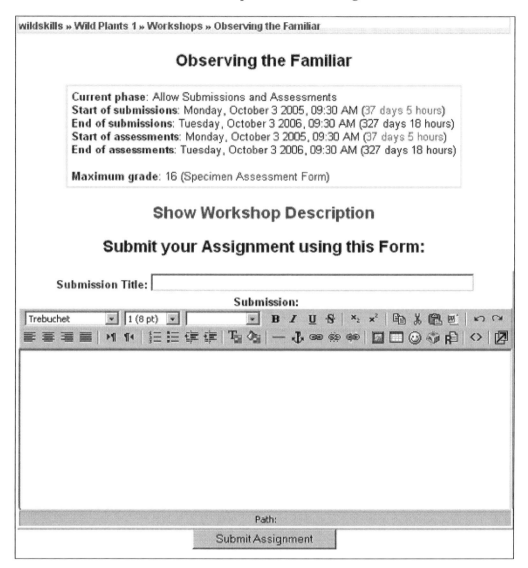

In this workshop, the student writes and updates some defined observations. These observations are then rated by other students in the course. When the student first enters the workshop, he or she sees directions for completing the workshop:

Workshop Directions

You might want to print out these directions for reference.

1. Choose three or four plants from your everyday environment. They don't need to be edible wild plants. We're at the beginning of the course, so you probably can't identify many edible plants yet, anyway! However, they should be as different as possible from one another. For example, you might choose a vine, a low-growing weed, a tree and a flower.
2. In this topic, you will see a wiki called "Observing the Familiar." Enter the wiki, and start a subsection with your name for the title. Use the style *Heading 2* for the section head.
3. Create a sub-section, using the style *Heading 3* for the heading. Name the section today's date.
4. Enter observations about the plant's appearance, texture, smell, etc. **Do not taste the plant unless an experience, qualified forager has confirmed it is edible. Wash your hands after handling it.** Also record your observations about the area immediately around the plant: the soil, nearby plants, shade and sun..
5. Over the next few weeks, return to the workshop every few days to record changes on the plants and their immediate environment. Especially, record your observations after a significant weather event: rain, a dry spell, an unseasonable change in temperature, etc.

Continue

After reading these directions, the student continues to the workshop submission form (shown at the right).

Note the online word processor that the student uses to write the assignment. This gives the student basic WYSIWYG features. The same word processor appears when course creators create web pages, or when students write online Assignment entries, and at other times when a user is editing and formatting text.

At the top of the page, you can see that this workshop has opening and closing dates for submissions, and for assessments. It also has a maximum point value of 16. When the students assess each others' work, they will see the evaluation criteria and how many points each criterion is worth.

If you're able to read Step 5 in the workshop directions above, you can see that the student should return to this workshop every few days to update this assignment. To enable this, the course creator used a feature that allows students to resubmit workshops. The course creator could have chosen to allow a single submission, instead.

Assessing Other Students' Work

In the previous subsection, you saw how a student submits an assignment to a workshop. After each of the students submits an assignment, the student is given a chance to assess other students' work. In the following screenshot, **Student Number2** has just submitted an assignment, and now can assess the work of Student 1. Student 2 would begin the assessment by clicking on the **Assess** link.

Current phase: Allow Submissions and Assessments
Start of submissions: Monday, October 3 2005, 09:30 AM (37 days 12 hours)
End of submissions: Tuesday, October 3 2006, 09:30 AM (327 days 11 hours)
Start of assessments: Monday, October 3 2005, 09:30 AM (37 days 12 hours)
End of assessments: Tuesday, October 3 2006, 09:30 AM (327 days 11 hours)

Maximum grade: 16 (Specimen Assessment Form)

Show Workshop Description
Please assess these Student Submissions

Submission Title	Action	Comment
Chamomile Growing in the Cracks of the Sidewalk	Assess	

Your assessments of work by your peers
No Assessments Done
Your Submissions

Submission Title	Action Submitted	Assessments
Edible Weeds in my Lawn	Wednesday, November 9 2005, 09:59 PM	0

You are logged in as Student Number2 (Logout)

Under **Your assessments of work by your peers**, you can see that this user has not yet assessed anyone else's work. Under **Your Submissions**, you can see the title of this user's submission, and also note that no one has assessed the submission yet.

The **Specimen Assessment Form** at the top of the page displays the form that the student will use to assess others' work. However, it is a sample form. So it does not affect anyone's assessment.

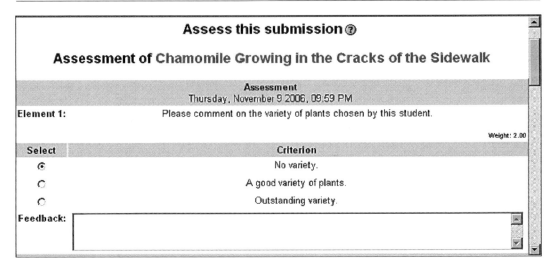

Clicking the **Assess** link brings up the assessment form for Student 1's workshop submission. The current user, Student 2, uses this form to assess the work. The teacher will have the opportunity to grade Student 2's assessment of Student 1's workshop. So not only does Moodle give you the ability to grade students' work, but also the ability to grade their assessments of other students' work. Because Moodle emphasizes collaborative effort, there are several places where a teacher can grade students on the quality of their collaboration.

Editing Mode

Let us see what happens when you turn on the editing mode to make changes.

Normal Versus Editing Mode

When a Guest user or a registered student browses your learning site, Moodle displays pages normally. However, when someone with course creator privilege logs in, Moodle offers a button for switching to the Editing mode:

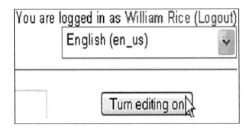

Clicking **Turn editing on** puts Moodle into the **Editing mode**:

Normal Mode   Editing Mode

Let's walk through the icons that become available in editing mode.

The Editing Icon

Clicking the Edit icon ✎ enables you to edit the content that precedes the icon. In this example, clicking the Edit icon that follows the paragraph enables you to edit the announcement:

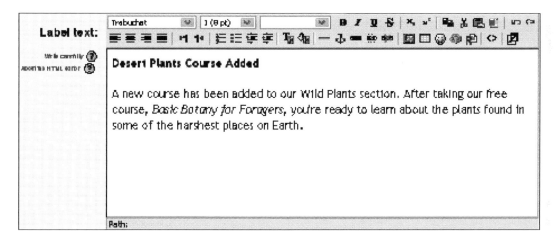

Clicking the Edit icon next to the quiz, **Win a Prize,** takes you to the editing window for that quiz. In that window, you can create, add, and remove quiz questions, change the grading scheme, and apply other settings to the quiz.

The Delete Icon

Clicking the Delete icon ✗ deletes the item that precedes the icon. If you want to remove an item from a course, but you're not sure you'll want to use it later, then don't delete the item. Instead, hide it from view. Hiding and showing content is explained below.

The Hidden/Shown Icons

I call these the Hidden/Shown icons ⚊ / ⚊ instead of Hide/Show because the icons indicate the current state of an item, and not what will happen when you click on them. The Hidden icon indicates that an item is hidden from the students. Clicking it shows the item to the students. The Shown icon indicates that an item is shown for the students. Clicking it hides the item from the students.

If you want to remove an item from a course while keeping it for later use, or if you want to keep an item hidden from students while you're working on it, hide it instead of deleting it.

The Group Icons

These ⚊ ⚊ ⚊ icons indicate the Group mode that has been applied to an item. Groups are explained in a later chapter. For now, you should know that you can control access to items based upon which group a student belongs to. Clicking these icons enables you to change that setting.

Resources and Activities

Course material that a student observes or reads, such as web or text pages, hyperlinks, and multimedia files, are called resources. Course material that a student interacts with, or materials that enable interaction among students and teachers are called activities. Now let us see how to add some resources and activities to your Moodle site.

In the Editing Mode, you can add resources and activities to a course. Moodle offers more activities than resources, such as **Chat**, **Forum**, **Journal**, **Quiz**, **Wiki**, and more.

Adding Resources and Activities

You add resources and activities using the drop-down menus that appear in the
Editing Mode:

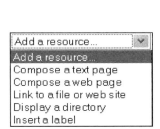

Selecting an item brings you to the Editing window for that type of item. For
example, selecting **Link to a file or website** displays the window to the right. Note
that you can do much more than just specify a hyperlink. You can give this link
a user friendly name, and a summary description. You can also open it in a new
window, and do much more.

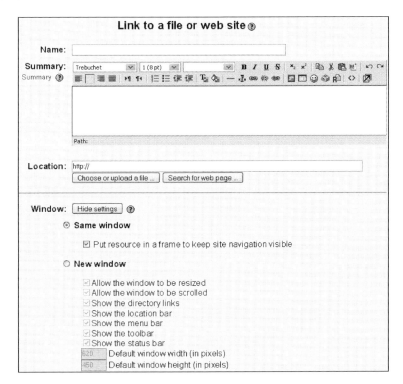

Almost every resource and activity that you add to Moodle has a **Summary**. This **Summary** appears when a student selects the item. Also, if the item appears in a list (for example, a list of all the resources in a course), the **Summary** is displayed.

While building courses, you will spend most of your time in the Editing window for the items that you add. You will find their behavior and appearance to be very consistent. The presence of a **Summary** is one example of that consistency. Another example is the presence of the Help icon ⑦ next to the title of the window. Clicking this icon displays an explanation of this type of item.

The Administration Block

All the contents of the **Administration** block are displayed only when someone with administration, or course creator privileges has logged in. Students see a much more limited view of this block. The following screenshot shows the student's view of the **Administration** block on the left, and the teacher's on the right:

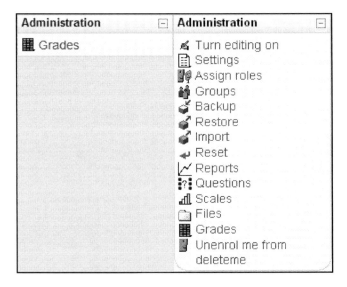

The choices on this block change depending on whether you are viewing the Front Page or a course, and the privileges that you have.

Choices in this block affect only the current course. For example, selecting **Logs** from the Front Page displays a page where you can view logs for all site activity, while selecting it from the course displays logs just for that course.

And Much More

This short tour introduced you to the basics of the Moodle experience. The following chapters take you through installation of Moodle and creation of courses. If you work through those chapters in order, you will discover that many features are not mentioned in this tour. And, as Moodle is open source, new features can be added at any time. Perhaps, you will be the one to contribute a new feature to the Moodle community.

The Moodle Architecture

Moodle runs on any web server that supports the PHP programming language, and a database. It works best, and there is more support, when running on the Apache web server with a MySQL database. These requirements, Apache, PHP, and MySQL are common to almost all commercial web hosts, even the low-cost ones.

The Moodle learning management system resides in three places on your web host:

- The application occupies one directory, with many subdirectories for the various modules.
- Data files students and teachers upload, such as photos and assignments submitted by students, reside in the Moodle data directory.
- Course materials that you create with Moodle (web pages, quizzes, workshops, lessons, and so on), grades, user information, and user logs reside in the Moodle database.

The Moodle Application Directory

The following screenshot shows you my Moodle application directory. Without even knowing much about Moodle, you can guess the function of several directories. For example, the admin directory holds the PHP code that creates the administrative pages, the lang directory holds translations of the Moodle interface, and the mod directory holds the various modules:

Location: /www/moodle/moodle

Select	Type	Permission	User	Group	Size	Date	Filename
«BACK							..
☐	📁	drwxr-xr-x	williamr	williamr	4096	Sep 05 22:05	admin
☐	📁	drwxr-xr-x	williamr	williamr	4096	May 24 02:03	auth
☐	📁	drwxr-xr-x	williamr	williamr	4096	Sep 29 22:05	backup
☐	📁	drwxr-xr-x	williamr	williamr	4096	Sep 29 22:05	blocks
☐	📁	drwxr-xr-x	williamr	williamr	4096	Sep 29 22:05	calendar
☐	📁	drwxr-xr-x	williamr	williamr	4096	Sep 23 22:05	course
☐	📁	drwxr-xr-x	williamr	williamr	4096	Jun 18 22:11	doc
☐	📁	drwxr-xr-x	williamr	williamr	4096	Sep 29 22:05	enrol
☐	📁	drwxr-xr-x	williamr	williamr	4096	May 24 02:04	error
☐	📁	drwxr-xr-x	williamr	williamr	4096	Sep 29 22:05	files
☐	📁	drwxr-xr-x	williamr	williamr	4096	Sep 29 22:05	filter
☐	📁	drwxr-xr-x	williamr	williamr	4096	Sep 27 22:05	grade
☐	📁	drwxr-xr-x	williamr	williamr	4096	Sep 29 22:05	lang
☐	📁	drwxr-xr-x	williamr	williamr	4096	Sep 29 22:05	lib
☐	📁	drwxr-xr-x	williamr	williamr	4096	Sep 23 22:05	login
☐	📁	drwxr-xr-x	williamr	williamr	4096	Sep 07 22:04	message
☐	📁	drwxr-xr-x	williamr	williamr	4096	Oct 19 14:47	mod
☐	📁	drwxr-xr-x	williamr	williamr	4096	May 24 02:07	pix
☐	📁	drwxr-xr-x	williamr	williamr	4096	Sep 29 22:05	rss
☐	📁	drwxr-xr-x	williamr	williamr	4096	Aug 01 22:25	sso
☐	📁	drwxr-xr-x	williamr	williamr	4096	Sep 29 22:05	theme
☐	📁	drwxr-xr-x	williamr	williamr	4096	Sep 28 22:04	user
☐	📁	drwxr-xr-x	williamr	williamr	4096	May 24 02:07	userpix
☐	PHP	-rw-r--r--	williamr	williamr	15087	Jul 04 22:13	config-dist.php
☐	PHP	-rw-r-----	williamr	williamr	724	Sep 30 13:24	config.php
☐	PHP	-rw-r--r--	williamr	williamr	5931	Jul 12 22:16	file.php
☐	PHP	-rw-r--r--	williamr	williamr	4893	May 24 02:03	help.php
☐	PHP	-rw-r--r--	williamr	williamr	7529	May 24 02:03	index.php
☐	PHP	-rw-r--r--	williamr	williamr	23503	May 24 02:03	install.php
☐	📄	-rw-r--r--	williamr	williamr	943	May 24 02:03	README.txt
☐	📄	-rw-r--r--	williamr	williamr	2923484	Jul 06 02:09	tags
☐	PHP	-rw-r--r--	williamr	williamr	515	Sep 10 22:05	version.php

The `index.php` file is the Moodle Home Page. If a student were browsing my Moodle site, the first page the student would read is the `http://moodle.williamrice.com/index.php` file.

In my site, the free course **Basic Botany for Foragers** happens to be course number 4. Only the Moodle system knows it as course number 4. We know it as **Basic Botany for Foragers**. When a student enters that course, the URL in the student's browser reads `http://moodle.williamrice.com/moodle/course/view.php?id=4`. In the previous screenshot, you can see that `/course` is one of the directories in my Moodle installation. As the user navigates around the site, different `.php` pages do the work of presenting information.

As each of Moodle's core components and modules is in its own subdirectory, the software can be easily updated by replacing old files with new ones. You should periodically check the `http://www.moodle.org` website for news about updates and bug fixes.

The Moodle Data Directory

Moodle stores the files uploaded by the users in a data directory. This directory should not be accessible to the general public over the Web. That is, you should not be able to type in the URL for this directory and access it using a web browser. You can protect it either by using an .htaccess file, or by placing the directory outside the web server's documents directory.

In my installation, the previous screenshot shows you that the web document directory for `moodle.williamrice.com` is `/www/moodle`. Therefore, I placed the data directory outside `/www/moodle`, in `/www/moodledata`:

Location: /www							
Select	Type	Permission	User	Group	Size	Date	Filename
	🗀	drwxrwxr-x	root	williamr	4096	Oct 24 14:45	moodle
	🗀	drwxrwxr-x	williamr	williamr	4096	Jul 11 16:45	moodledata
	🗀	drwxrwxr-t	williamr	williamr	4096	Mar 28 2005	www
	📄	-rw-rwxr--	williamr	williamr	24	Aug 22 2003	.bash_logout
	📄	-rw-rwxr--	williamr	williamr	191	Aug 22 2003	.bash_profile
	📄	-rw-rwxr--	williamr	williamr	124	Aug 22 2003	.bashrc
	📄	-rw-rwxr--	williamr	williamr	3511	Aug 22 2003	.screenrc

On my server, the directory `/www/moodledata` corresponds to the subdomain `www.moodledata.williamrice.com`. This subdomain is protected from open access by a .htaccess file. The directory `/www/www` corresponds to the root domain, `www.williamrice.com`.

The Moodle Database

While the Moodle data directory stores files uploaded by students, the Moodle database stores most of the information in your Moodle site. The database stores objects that you create using Moodle. For example, Moodle enables you to create web pages for your courses. The actual HTML code of these web pages is stored in the database. Links that you add to a course, the settings, and content of forums and wikis, quizzes created with Moodle are all examples of data stored in the Moodle database.

The three parts of Moodle—**application**, **data directory**, and **database**— work together to create your learning site. Chapter 9 talks about backing up and disaster recovery, which is an obvious application of this knowledge. However, knowing how the three parts work together is helpful while upgrading, troubleshooting, and moving your site between servers.

Summary

Moodle encourages exploration and interaction among students and teachers and also between them. As a course designer and teacher, you will have the most tools at your disposal if you work with this tendency and make your learning experiences as interactive as possible. Creating courses with forums, peer-assessed workshops, journals, surveys, and interactive lessons is more work than creating a course from a series of static web pages. However, it is also more engaging and effective, and you will find that it is worth the effort to use Moodle's many interactive features.

While teaching an online course in Moodle, remember that Moodle enables you to add, move, and modify course material and grading tools on-the-fly. If it is permitted by your institution's policies, don't hesitate to change a course in response to the students' needs.

Finally, learn the basics of Moodle's architecture, and at least read over the 'installation' and 'configuration' in Chapter 2. Don't be afraid of the technology. If you can master the difficult art of teaching, you can master using Moodle to its full potential.

2

Installing and Configuring Moodle

The title of this chapter makes it sound as if it applies only to the person who installs Moodle. If your system administrator or webmaster has installed Moodle for you, you might be tempted to skip this chapter. Well, *don't* do that.

Many of the configuration choices that are made during and after the installation process affect the student and teacher experience in Moodle. These are found on the **Site Administration** menu, which becomes visible when you log in with Administrator privileges. These configuration settings affect your students' and teachers' experience when they use the site. This chapter's focus is on helping you create the user experience you want by making the right configuration choices. While someone else may have installed Moodle and made these configuration choices for you, the settings under **Site Administration** can always be changed.

Go Ahead, Experiment

While this chapter describes the effects of different configuration choices, there is no substitute for experiencing them yourself. Don't be afraid to experiment with different settings. You can try this method:

1. Install two different browsers in your computer. For example, **Internet Explorer** and **Firefox**.

2. In one browser, log in as an administrator. Go to the **Site Administration** menu, and experiment with the settings that you read about here.

3. In the other browser, go to your site as a user—an anonymous visitor, student, or teacher. Each time you change a configuration setting, refresh the user's browser and observe the change to your site.

4. Sometimes when I'm configuring a site, I use three browsers at once (**Internet Explorer**, **Firefox**, and **Opera**), and log in as a site administrator, teacher, and student. Then I can immediately see the effects of my configuration choices on the teacher and student experiences.

Using This Chapter

Even if you did not install Moodle, I encourage you to read the configuration sections in this chapter. If you want, work with your system administrator to select the settings you want. Your administrator can create a site administrator account that you can use for this.

Moodle's online installation instructions provide a good step-by-step reference for installing Moodle. However, they do not cover the implications of the choices you make while configuring Moodle. This chapter covers the effects of the:

1. Technical and configuration choices you make while installing Moodle
2. Configuration choices that you are prompted to make immediately after installing Moodle
3. Configuration choices that you can make anytime

Installing Moodle

Installing Moodle consists of:

1. Obtaining space and rights on a web server that has the capabilities needed to run Moodle
2. Creating the subdomains and/or directories needed for Moodle and its data
3. Getting and unpacking Moodle, and uploading it to your web server
4. Creating the data directory
5. Creating the Moodle database
6. Activating the installation routine and specifying settings for your Moodle site
7. Setting up the cron job

Each of these is covered in the following sections.

The publisher and the author of this book contribute Moodle installation instructions to installationwiki.org. On this site, you will find the latest installation instructions for Moodle and many other open-source applications.

Installation Step 1—The Web Server

Moodle is run from a web server. You upload or place Moodle in your directory on the server. Usually, the server is someone else's computer. If you are a teacher, or you are in the corporate world, your institution might have their own web server. If you are an individual, or have a small business, you will probably buy web-hosting services from another company. In either case, we are assuming that you have an account on a web server that offers Apache, PHP, and MySQL.

If you must install your own Apache web server and MySQL software, the easiest way to do so is to use another open-source tool: XAMPP from http://www.apachefriends.org. Apache Friends is a non-profit project to promote the Apache web server. XAMPP is an easy, all-in-one installer that installs Apache, MySQL, PHP, and Perl. It is available for Linux, Windows, Mac, and Solaris. If you would like to create a test environment for Moodle, then installing XAMPP onto your computer will install the web server with the components required to support a Moodle installation.

How Much Hosting Service Do You Need?

With only a few dozen students, Moodle runs fine on a modest web-hosting service. At this time, many hosting companies offer services that can run a small Moodle installation for less than $10 a month. Make your decision based on the factors discussed here:

Disk Space

A fresh Moodle installation will occupy about 55MB of disk space, which is not much. Most of the space will be occupied by content that is added while users create and take courses. Make your decision based on how much space you need for the kinds of courses you plan to deliver. You'll need less space if the courses contain mostly text and a few graphics than for music or video files. Also, consider the disk space occupied by the files that the students will upload. Will the students upload small word processing files, large graphics, or huge multimedia files? While determining how much disk space you need, consider the size of the files that your courses will serve and your students will submit.

Bandwidth

Moodle is a web-based product, so course content and assignments are added over the Web. Whenever a reader or user connects to a website, they're using bandwidth. When a user reads a page on your Moodle site, downloads a video, or uploads a paper, he or she uses some of your bandwidth. The more courses, students, activities, and multimedia that your Moodle site has, the more bandwidth you will use. Most commercial hosting services include a fixed amount of bandwidth in their service.

If your account uses more bandwidth than allowed, some services cut off your site's access. Others keep your site up, but automatically bill you for the additional bandwidth. The second option is preferable in case of unexpected demand. While deciding upon a hosting service, find out how much bandwidth they offer and what they do if you exceed that limit.

Memory

If you're using a shared hosting service, your account will be sharing a web server with other accounts. All accounts share the memory, or RAM, of that server. In times of high demand, very little memory will be available for each account. In times of low demand, your account may be able to use more memory.

Moodle runs fine on most shared hosting services. However, when you have a large number of courses, or large courses, Moodle's automated backup routine often fails on shared hosts with low memory limits. Site administrators get around this limitation by manually backing up their site, one course at a time, or by moving to a different host.

If your site is likely to have more than a few courses or any course whose size is measured in tens of megabytes, and you want to use automated backup, research your web host. Especially search the forums on Moodle.org to find out if any other customers of that host have complained about automated backups failing due to lack of memory. In general, Moodle's automated backup routines are inefficient, and you might want to consider alternatives for a large site.

What You Should Do Now

Check with your hosting service to ensure that you will be given the following minimum prerequisites:

1. Enough **disk space** for the Moodle software, your course material, and the files that the students will upload.
2. Enough **bandwidth** to serve your course files, and for students to upload their files.
3. **PHP**.
4. The ability to create at least one MySQL **database**, or to have it created for you.
5. The ability to create at least one MySQL database **user**, or to have it created for you.
6. Enough shared or dedicated **memory** to run Moodle's automated backup routines. You might not know how much that is until you've tried it.

When you confirm that you have those items, you are ready to proceed with the installation.

Many hosting services also offer automated installation of Moodle. Search for hosting services using the terms 'fantastico' and 'moodle', or 'one-click install' and 'moodle'. These are usually shared hosting services. So, you will have the same performance limitations as that of installing Moodle on a shared host. However, they simplify the installation and thus provide a fast, inexpensive way to get a Moodle site up and running.

You should also research the services offered by the official Moodle Partners. You can find out more about Moodle partners on moodle.com (notice the "dot com" and not "dot org" address).

Installation Step 2—Subdomain or Subdirectory?

A subdomain is a web address that exists under your web address, and acts like an independent site. For example, my website is `www.williamrice.com`. This is a standard website, not a Moodle site. I could have a subdomain, `http://www.moodle.williamrice.com`, to hold a Moodle site. This subdomain is like an independent site. However, it exists on the same server, under the same account, and they both count towards the disk space and bandwidth that I use. Inthe following screenshot, note that I have one subdomain, in addition to my normal website:

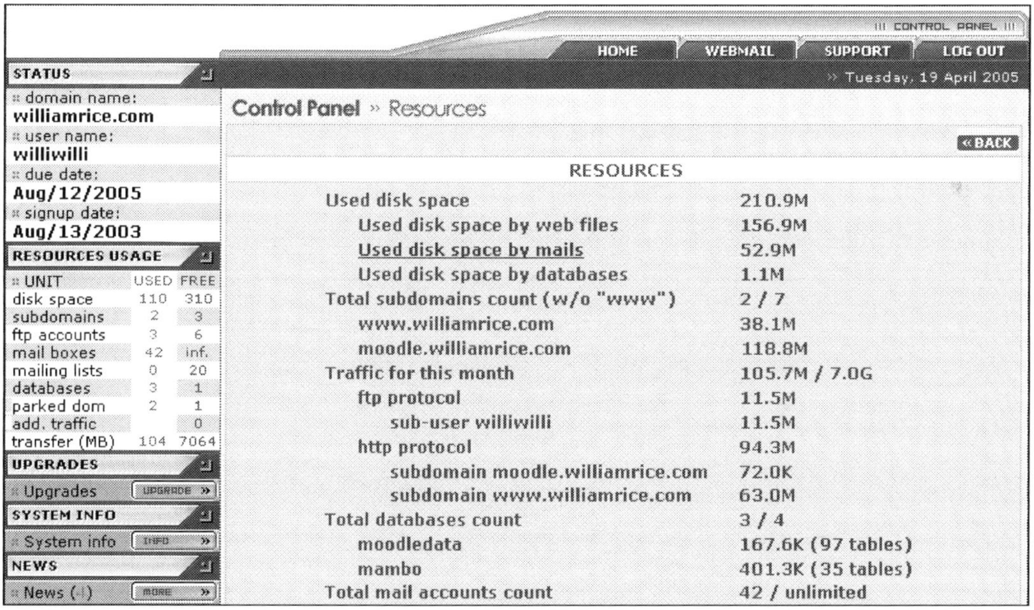

	HOME	WEBMAIL	SUPPORT	LOG OUT

STATUS

|| | Tuesday, 19 April 2005 |

:: domain name:
williamrice.com
:: user name:
williwilli
:: due date:
Aug/12/2005
:: signup date:
Aug/13/2003

Control Panel » Resources

« BACK

RESOURCES

Used disk space	210.9M
Used disk space by web files	156.9M
Used disk space by mails	52.9M
Used disk space by databases	1.1M
Total subdomains count (w/o "www")	2 / 7
www.williamrice.com	38.1M
moodle.williamrice.com	118.8M
Traffic for this month	105.7M / 7.0G
ftp protocol	11.5M
sub-user williwilli	11.5M
http protocol	94.3M
subdomain moodle.williamrice.com	72.0K
subdomain www.williamrice.com	63.0M
Total databases count	3 / 4
moodledata	167.6K (97 tables)
mambo	401.3K (35 tables)
Total mail accounts count	42 / unlimited

RESOURCES USAGE

:: UNIT	USED	FREE
disk space	110	310
subdomains	2	3
ftp accounts	3	6
mail boxes	42	inf.
mailing lists	0	20
databases	3	1
parked dom	2	1
add. traffic		0
transfer (MB)	104	7064

UPGRADES

:: Upgrades UPGRADE »

SYSTEM INFO

:: System info INFO »

NEWS

:: News (·) MORE »

In this example, Moodle is installed in the subdomain `http://www.moodle.williamrice.com`. Using a subdomain offers me several advantages. As you can see, I can manage them both from the same interface. Second, I can use a subdomain as a test site for my Moodle installation. I can install and test Moodle in the subdomain, and then copy it over to my main site when it's ready. Having a site to test updates and add-ons may be helpful if uninterrupted service is important to you. Later, you'll see how easy it is to copy a Moodle installation to a different location, change a few settings, and have it work. If you want to do this, make sure the hosting service you choose allows subdomains.

If you want to keep things simpler, you can install Moodle into a subdirectory of your website, for example, `http://www.williamrice.com/moodle` or `http://www.info-overload.biz/learn`. In the next step, you will see how Moodle can automatically install itself into a subdirectory called `/moodle`. This is very convenient, and you'll find a lot of websites with Moodle running in the `/moodle` subdirectory.

What You Should Do Now

Decide if you want to install Moodle into a **subdirectory** or a **subdomain**. If you choose a subdomain, create it now. If you choose a subdirectory, you can create it later, while uploading the Moodle software.

Installation Step 3—Getting and Unpacking Moodle

Get Moodle from the official website, `http://www.moodle.org/`. Go to the **Download Moodle** page and select the version and format that you need:

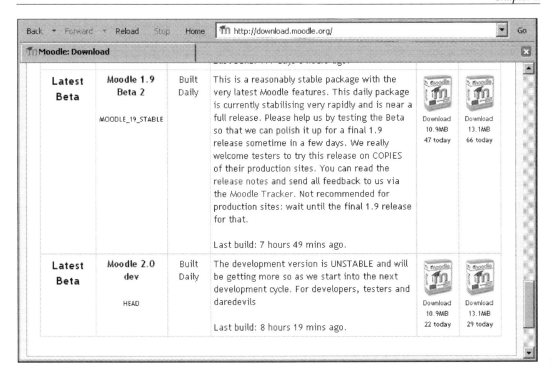

Which Version?

For a new installation, the **Latest Stable Branch** is usually your best choice. The **Last build:** information tells you when it was last updated with a bug-fix or patch. This is usually irrelevant to you; the version number determines which features you get, not the build time.

The Quick Way—Upload and Unzip

Moodle is downloaded as a single, compressed file. This compressed file contains many small files and directories that constitute Moodle. After downloading the compressed file, you could decompress (or unzip) the file. Unzipping it on your local PC will extract many files and directories that you must place on your server.

If you're using a hosting service which has the ability to decompress the file on the server, you can just upload the entire zip file and tell the server to decompress it. Now, all your Moodle files will be in place. This is much faster than decompressing the zip file on your computer and uploading the many files that it creates.

Upload and Decompress the Zip File on the Server

1. Go to `http://www.moodle.org/` and download the Moodle package (ZIP or TAR file) to your local hard drive.

2. Upload the file to your hosting service. My hosting service uses the popular cPanel control panel. So, uploading a file looks like this:

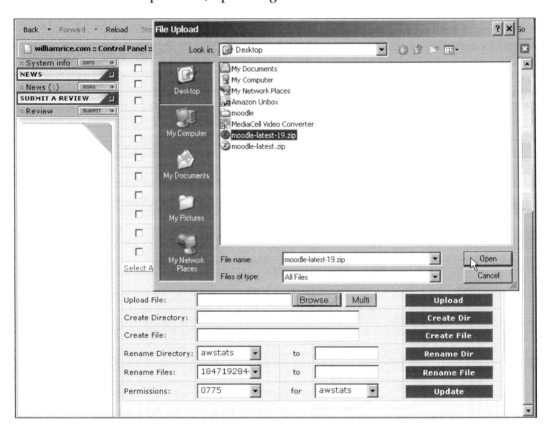

3. In your hosting service's control panel, select the compressed file. If you're given a choice to unzip the file, then you can use this method. In the following example, I have selected the compressed file, **moodle-latest-19.zip**. My control panel then showed the following screen. If I click the **Next** link, the file will start decompressing:

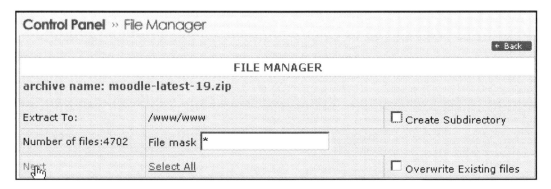

4. If your hosting service gives you the option to create a new directory for the unzipped files (**Create Subdirectory** in the previous example), you can select not to. Moodle's compressed file will automatically create a subdirectory called `moodle` for the unzipped files.

The Long Way—Decompress the Zip File Locally and Upload Files

If you cannot decompress the Zip file on the server, you must decompress the file on your PC, and then upload the extracted files to the server. If you're using a hosting service, you will probably:

1. Download the Moodle package (ZIP file) to your local hard drive.

2. Decompress or unzip the package. This will extract many files from the package. In this example, you can see from the title bar that I'm using the freeware program **ZipGenius** to unzip the package. Each file will be extracted to a specific directory.

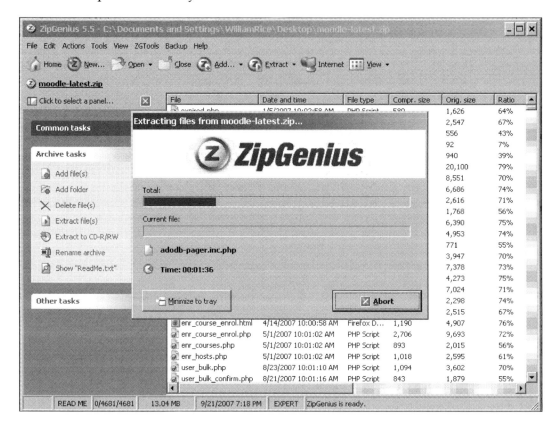

3. Upload the files to your web server. You'll need to use an FTP program to upload the files.

Whether you're using Windows, Mac, or Linux personal computer, you can find a decompression program that will unzip .zip files. If your system doesn't have a decompression program that works with .zip files, and you're using Windows, try http://www.nonags.com for freeware unzip programs. If you're using a web page editor such as Dreamweaver or Microsoft FrontPage, your program has the ability to upload files to the server. If you're not using a web page editor that can upload files, you'll need an 'FTP client'. Again, try http://www.nonags.com for freeware FTP clients.

If your school or company has given you space on their web server, you might have access to the directory just as if it were another folder on your PC. In that case, you can download the `.tgz` file, put it into your directory on the web server, and then decompress it. Tell the system administrator who gave you access what you want to do, and ask how to decompress a file in your directory.

What You Should Do Now

1. Go to `http://moodle.org` and download the version of Moodle that you want to install. You will download a compressed file, in either `.zip` or `.tgz` format.

2. Upload the compressed file to your hosting service.

3. Using the control panel that your host gives you, select the compressed file. If it automatically decompresses, you're in luck. Go ahead and decompress it in place. Or decompress the file on your local PC, and upload the resulting files to your hosting service.

Installation Step 4—The Moodle Data Directory

When you run the Moodle install script, the installer asks you to specify a directory in which to store course material. This is the Moodle data directory. It holds material that is uploaded to the courses. You will need to have this directory created before you run the install script. That is what you will do in this step.

For security, the Moodle data directory should be outside the main Moodle directory. For example, suppose you are creating a learning site called www.info-overload.biz/learn. You will install Moodle into /learn, and create the Moodle data directory somewhere outside of /learn. Preferably, you will put the data directory in a place where it is not accessible over the Web. For example, on my hosting service, my directory name is /williamr. In that directory is a subdirectory, /williamr/www. Anything that I put into /williamr/www is served to the Web. However, if I create another directory under /williamr, such as /williamr/moodledata, that directory is not served by my hosting service. You should check with your hosting service technical support to see if you can create a directory that is not accessible to the Web.

In the following screenshot, I am installing Moodle on my local server. That simply means that instead of the server being at the other end of a web connection, I am accessing the server directly, as if I were sitting in front of it. In fact, this server is my desktop PC. You can tell this server is local to me because the **Web Address** begins with `localhost`.

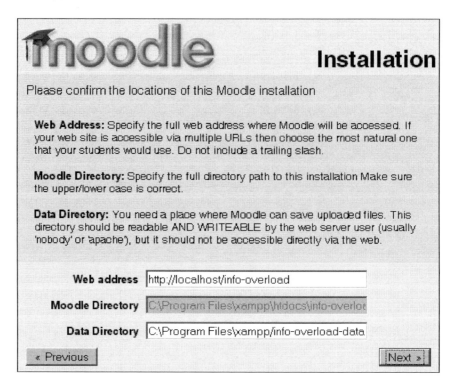

In the preceding screenshot, look at the field **Moodle Directory**. You can see that the Moodle software is being put into the directory `xampp/htdocs/info-overload`.

The directory `xampp` is where my Apache web server is installed. In a standard Apache web server, the directory `/htdocs` contains web pages that are served to the world. So anything put into `xampp/htdocs` appears on the Web. That is, the contents of `http://www.info-overload.biz` will be the same as in `/htdocs` on my server.

The Moodle data will be stored in the directory, `xampp/info-overload-data`. Note that this is **not** under the `/htdocs` directory. That means the contents of `/info-overload-data` are not served as web pages, and are not accessible over the Web. This is what you want for your Moodle data directory.

What You Should Do Now

On your server, create a directory to hold the Moodle data. This can be a directory outside the Moodle directory, or a subdirectory.

Installation Step 5—Creating the Moodle Database and User

While the Moodle data directory stores files uploaded by students, and some larger files, the Moodle database stores most of the information in your Moodle site. By default, the installer uses the database name `moodle` and the username `moodleuser`. Using these default settings gives any hacker a head start on breaking your site. When creating your database, change these to something less common. At least, make the hackers guess the name of your database and the database username.

You should also choose a strong password for the Moodle database user. Here are some recommendations for strong passwords:

- Include at least one number, one symbol, one uppercase letter, and one lowercase letter.
- Make the password at least 12 characters long.
- Avoid repetition, dictionary words, letter or number sequences, anything related to your usernames, and anything based on biographical information about yourself.

You will need to create the Moodle database, and database user, before you run Moodle's installation routine. In the following screenshot, you can see that I am specifying the type, location, and name of the Moodle database.

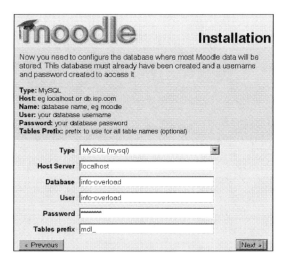

Before you begin the installation routine, you must have created the database and database user, and know the settings shown in the preceding screenshot. Otherwise, when you reach that screen during the installation routine, it will be too late!

Creating the Database

Moodle can use several types of databases. The recommended type is MySQL. There are many ways to create a database. If you are using a shared hosting service, you might have access to phpMyAdmin. You can use this to create the Moodle database and database user.

The following is a screenshot of creating the database using **phpMyAdmin**.

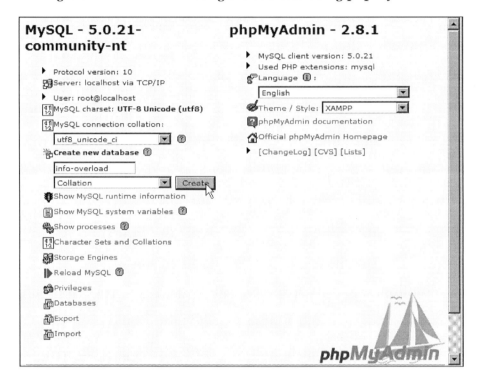

This process will create a blank database. Moodle will add the necessary database tables during the installation routine. So unless the installation routine fails, you don't need to do anything more to the database.

Creating the Database User

Whatever username you choose, that user will need the following privileges for the Moodle database: **SELECT, INSERT, UPDATE, DELETE, CREATE, DROP, INDEX,** and **ALTER**. In the following screenshot, I've created the database user, and am specifying the user's privileges with **phpMyAdmin**.

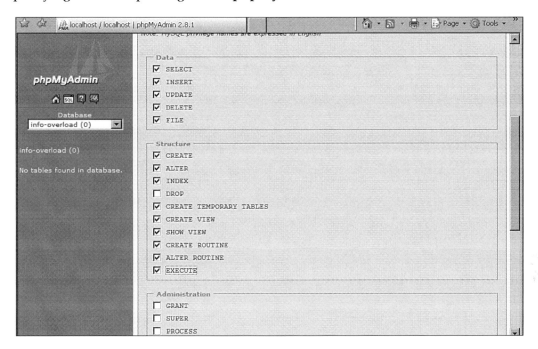

During the installation routine, you will enter the name of the database, the database user, and the database user's password. If you're not creating these yourself, you will need to get them from your system administrator or any other person who creates them.

What You Should Do Now

1. Create the Moodle database. Moodle works best with a MySQL database, but you have a variety of choices.

2. Take note of the name of the server that holds your database. If the database and Moodle are on the same server, this will probably be localhost. If they are on different servers but in the same institution, it will probably be an IP address. If you're not sure, ask your system administrator for the path that your Moodle software would use to access the database server.

3. Create a database user with the privileges listed above. Take note of the user's password.

Installation Step 6—The Installer Script

At this point, you have:

1. Uploaded the Moodle software to your web server
2. Created a data directory outside of the directory that Moodle is served from
3. Created a database for Moodle to use
4. Created a user for the Moodle database

You are now ready to run the installation routine. Moodle's installer script walks you step-by-step through setting some of the configuration settings, and the creation of Moodle's database tables. But first, some background information:

Configuration Settings and config.php

Configuration variables are settings that tell Moodle where the database is located and what it's called, the name of the database user and password, the web address of the Moodle system, and other necessary information. All these configuration settings must be correct for Moodle to run. They are stored in a file called `config.php`, in Moodle's home directory.

Stepping through the install routine creates `config.php`, among other things. Here's the `config.php` for www.info-overload.biz/learn:

```php
<?php  /// Moodle Configuration File

unset($CFG);

$CFG->dbtype    = 'mysql';
$CFG->dbhost    = 'localhost';
$CFG->dbname    = 'info-overload';
$CFG->dbuser    = 'info-overload';
$CFG->dbpass    = 'badpassword';
$CFG->dbpersist =  false;
$CFG->prefix    = 'mdl19_';


$CFG->wwwroot   = 'http://info-overload.biz/learn';
$CFG->dirroot   = '/home/info-overload/www/learn';
$CFG->dataroot  = '/home/info-overload/www/info-overload-data';
$CFG->admin     = 'admin';


$CFG->directorypermissions = 00777;  // try 02777 on a server in Safe
Mode
```

```
require_once("$CFG->dirroot/lib/setup.php");
// MAKE SURE WHEN YOU EDIT THIS FILE THAT THERE ARE NO SPACES, BLANK
LINES,
// RETURNS, OR ANYTHING ELSE AFTER THE TWO CHARACTERS ON THE NEXT
LINE.
?>
```

This site uses a `mysql` database. On most servers, the hostname is `localhost`. In a previous subsection we discussed the creation of the Moodle database, which in our example we called `info-overload`. We created a user, also called `info-overload`, with the proper privileges. Note that the configuration file stores the password for the Moodle database, which in this example is `badpassword`.

Database Tables

Database tables are sections of your database similar to miniature databases. Each table in your database stores information that has a different purpose. For example, the table `user` stores the names, passwords, and some other information about each Moodle user. The table `wiki_pages` stores the name, content, date modified, and other information about each wiki page in your system. A standard Moodle installation creates over 200 tables in the database.

By default, the prefix `mdl_` is added to the beginning of each table that Moodle adds to your database. I changed this to `mdl19_` because I'm using version **1.9**. If I upgrade to version **2.0**, I want to be able to use the same database. You could use the same database for Moodle and something else, or for two Moodle installations, if each program uses its own tables with its own prefix. The different prefixes would prevent the two programs from becoming confused and reading each other's tables. If you're running more than one copy of Moodle, you might consider using the same database and different tables. You could back up the data for both copies by backing up one database.

Now, in the following subsections, I will walk you through the Moodle installation routine.

Step 6a—Run install.php

In the Moodle directory, a script called `install.php` creates the Moodle configuration file when it is run. You run the script by just launching your browser and pointing it to wherever you've placed the Moodle software. The script creates `config.php`, which holds the configuration settings for your Moodle installation.

In the following screenshot, I've pointed my browser at the Home Page of my Moodle installation. I'm working on a local host, so the address bar says `http://localhost/info-overload`. If I was doing this over the Web (such as when using a shared hosting sevice), the address bar would be a web address, such as `http://www.info-overload.biz/learn`:

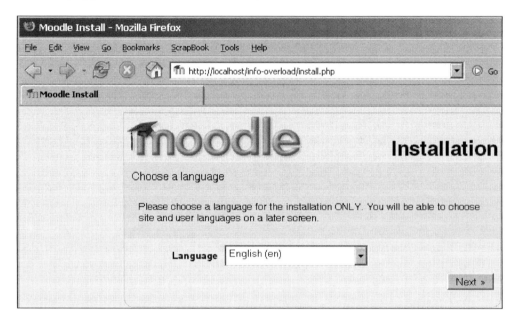

Also note that even though I pointed my browser at `http://localhost/ info-overload`, I was redirected to `install.php`.

The first thing I'm asked to do is select the language for the installation. This is the language that the installer script will use. It is not the language that my site will use. I can specify that later.

Step 6b—Checking PHP Settings

Moodle is written in a programming language called PHP. PHP is installed on your web server. Some of PHP's capabilities are turned off and on using settings that you, or your system administrator, control. Moodle's installation routine will check some of these settings to ensure that they are compatible with Moodle.

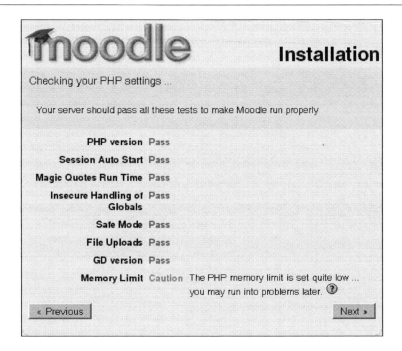

In the preceding screenshot, you can see that I have received a common warning message. The memory that PHP is allowed to use on my server is set too low. When the message states that I **may run into problems later**, it isn't kidding. This installation failed because PHP did not have enough memory to finish it. This is a common cause of the installation 'hanging' or 'stalling'. If you get this message, you may have to cancel the installation and fix the situation right away.

The PHP installed on your server uses a file called php.ini to store its settings. The memory limit that caused the warning above is set in php.ini. If you have your own server, you can edit php.ini to increase this limit. On my server, I changed this limit to 64 megabytes by editing this line in php.ini:

```
memory_limit = 64M
```

If you're using someone else's server, you need to contact support and find out how to increase the limit. Sometimes, this will be to put a file in your Moodle directory call .htaccess, and include the following line in that file:

```
php_value memory_limit = 64M
```

For more information, start by searching http://moodle.org for the terms 'php memory limit'. Usually, 32 megabytes works fine. Start with that setting and increase it, if needed.

Whether you're using your own or someone else's server, I recommend that you fix the situation before continuing the installation.

Step 6c—Specify the Web Address and Directories

Next, the installation routine asks for the **Web Address** of your Moodle system, and the names of the directories for the software and data.

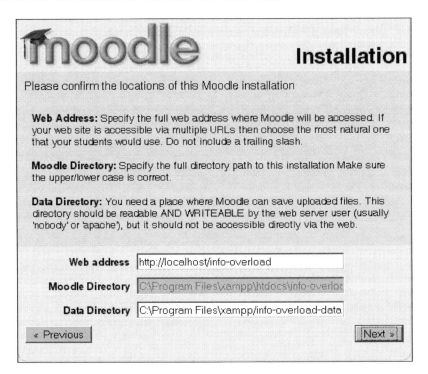

The **Web address** is the URL that browsers use to access Moodle. The **Moodle Directory** is filled in for you. This is the directory on your server, to which you uploaded the software. You created the **Data Directory** in Step 4.

Fill in these values, and continue to the next step.

Step 6d—Specify Database Settings

In this step, you specify the **Database** that Moodle uses.

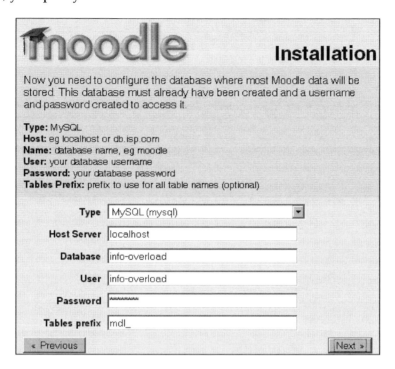

The **Host Server** is the address of the computer that serves the database. On most servers, the hostname will be `localhost`. Think of it this way: Moodle and its database are on the same server, so they are 'local' to one another. So from Moodle's point of view, the database server is a local host. If the database existed on another server, you would enter the IP address or web address of that server.

The **Database**, **User**, and **Password** you created in Step 5.

The **Tables prefix** will be added to the beginning of the name of every table that Moodle creates. If you use the same database for Moodle and something else, you can easily spot the tables used by Moodle from their prefix (`mdl_user`, `mdl_courses`, and so on). Also, if you upgrade Moodle, you can use the same database for the old and new versions by using different prefixes for their tables (for example, `mdl19_user` versus `mdl20_user`).

Step 6e—Database Tables Created by install.php

After stepping through a few more screens, `install.php` creates the tables in your Moodle database. You don't need to do anything during this part of the installation except click to see the next screen. The installation script tells you when this is complete:

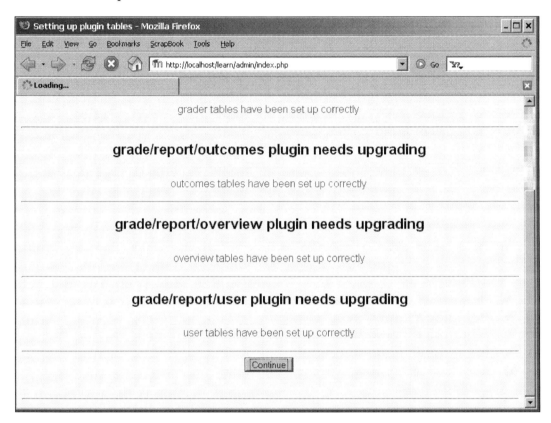

What You Should Do Now

Launch your browser and point it to the Home Page of your Moodle installation (where you uploaded the software). Step through the installation, using the subsections in the chapter as a guide. If you have all the information ready to enter, it will probably take less than 15 minutes.

Summary

When the installation is finished, you will see your Moodle Home Page:

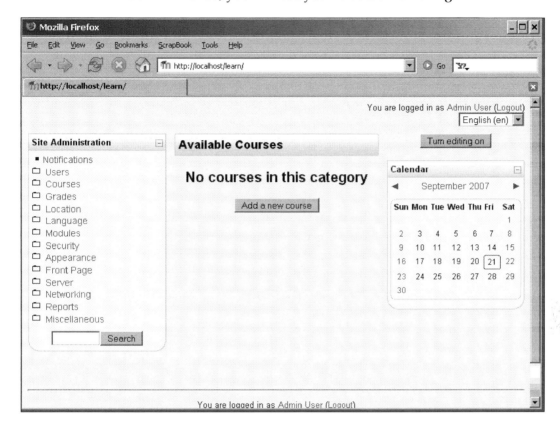

From here, you can continue with any, or all of the following:

1. Configure your site
2. Set up your site's Front Page
3. Create user accounts
4. Create courses

You can do these in any order, but I usually use the order presented here. And don't be intimidated into thinking that you must get all of these *correct* or *right* the first time. They can be changed and edited at any time. So start with something you are most comfortable with, develop some momentum, and build your learning site.

3
Configuring Your Site

Many of the configuration choices that are made after the installation process affect the student and teacher experience in Moodle. These configuration settings affect the experience of the students and teachers, when they use the site. This chapter focuses on helping you create the user experience you want by making the right configuration choices.

Many of the configuration choices you make will be easy to decide upon. For example, will you allow your users to select their own time zones? Other configuration choices are not so obvious. You could spend a lot of time trying different settings to see what effect a setting has on your user's experience. These are the settings that I will focus on, in this chapter. My goal is to save your time by showing you the various effects that your configuration choices will have on your site.

If your system administrator or webmaster has installed Moodle for you, you might be tempted to just accept the default configuration and skip this chapter. Don't do that! Even if you did not install Moodle, I would encourage you to read the configuration sections in this chapter. If you wish, you can also work with your system administrator to select the settings you want. Your administrator can create a site administrator account that you can use for configuring Moodle.

Go Ahead, Experiment!

Although this chapter describes the different effects of the various configuration choices, there is no substitute for experiencing them yourself. Don't be afraid to experiment with different settings. You can try the following method:

1. Install two different browsers in your computer. For example, **Internet Explorer** and **Firefox**.

2. In one of the browsers, log in as an administrator. Go to the **Site Administration** menu, and experiment with the settings that you will read about here.

3. In the other browser, go to your site as a user—an anonymous visitor, student, or teacher. Each time you change a configuration setting, refresh the user's browser, and observe the change to your site.

4. Sometimes when I'm configuring a site, I use three browsers all at once (**Internet Explorer**, **Firefox**, and **Opera**), and log in as a site administrator in one, as a teacher in another, and as a student in the third. Then, I can immediately see the effects of my configuration choices on the teacher and student experiences.

The Site Administration Menu

After installing Moodle, I would like to set some basic configuration options. Some of these settings determine how the site functions, such as how users are authenticated, what statistics the site keeps, and which modules are turned on and off. Other settings just affect the user experience, such as which languages are available, the color scheme, and what is displayed on the Front Page. All these settings are available through the **Site Administration** menu, which by default appears on the Front Page of your site.

The complete **Site Administration** menu has these options:

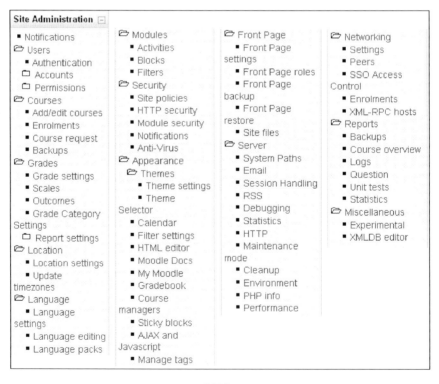

In this chapter, which is about configuring your site, we'll cover some of these settings. Others will be covered as we build our courses, teach, calculate grades, and update our site. The important idea here is this: unlike many other applications, in Moodle, the Site Administration menu isn't something that you 'set and forget'. You keep returning to the configuration settings as you work with your site, and as it develops.

Accessing the Site Administration Menu

To access the Site Administration menu:

1. Log in to Moodle with an administrator account.

2. By default, the **Site Administration** menu is displayed on the left side column of your site's Home Page. It displays only for users who have administrator privileges:

3. If you log in, and you don't see the **Site Administration** menu on the Home Page, it means that either you don't have administrator privileges, or your site administrator has hidden the menu. In your browser's address bar, enter the URL of your site and add /admin (for example, info-overload. biz/learn/admin). If you have access to the menu, it will display the **Site Administration** page:

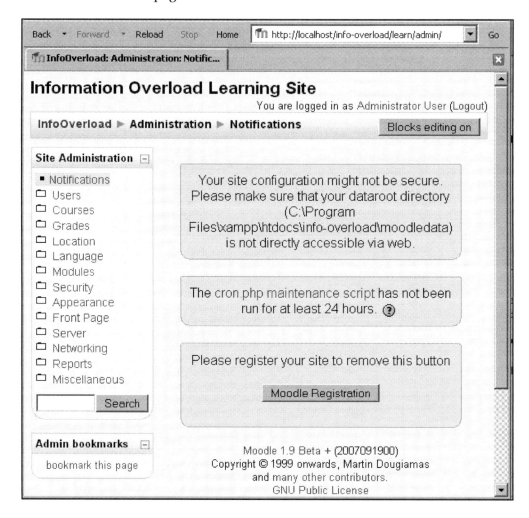

On most of my sites, I use the Site Administration menu the most while developing them. After that, I return to the Site Administration occasionally, but not frequently. After the initial site development, I like to hide the menu. It saves space on the Home Page and makes it look more like what my teachers and students see. When I want the Site Administration menu, I just go to the /admin page.

Later in this chapter, we'll go through the settings you use to configure your site for the kind of user experience you want to create.

Authentication

Authentication and login are different. Authentication happens when a new user signs up for your site, and creates a new Moodle account. Login happens when an authenticated user logs into Moodle.

Moodle offers a variety of ways to authenticate users. You'll find them under **Site Administration | Users | Authentication**. Each of the options is briefly explained by clicking on **Settings** for that option:

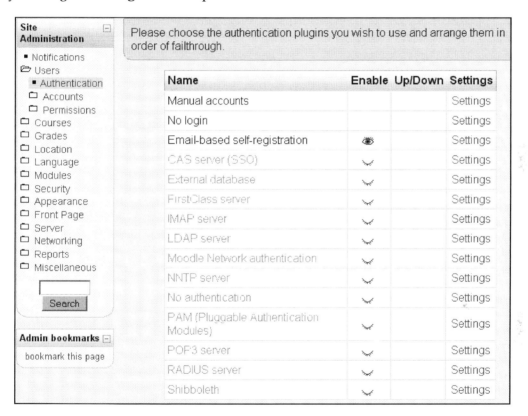

This subsection will fill in some key information to make it easier for you to work with these authentication methods.

Authenticating Against an External Database or Server

In the previous screenshot, you can see that **External database** is one of your choices for authenticating users. This is the choice you would use if the users are stored in a **database** outside of Moodle. An external database is not the same as an external server. For example, Moodle can authenticate users against these servers: **CAS server**, **FirstClass server**, **IMAP server**, **LDAP server**, **NNTP server**, **POP3 server**, **RADIUS server**, and **Shibboleth**. These are not just external databases known by different names. Authenticating your users against an external server enables you to do certain things that you cannot do while authenticating against an external database.

When you authenticate users with an external database, you can handle passwords in two ways:

- You have the option of making Moodle copy over the password from the external database into Moodle's internal database. From then on, when the user logs into Moodle, it uses Moodle's internal database to check the username and password. There is no live link between the external database and Moodle's user database. This means that if the user changes his or her username and password in the external database, the username and password in Moodle are not changed.

- You can have Moodle check the external database for the password every time the user logs in. Moodle will not store the password in Moodle's database. And, Moodle cannot change the user's password. If the user wants to change his or her password, it must be done in the external database.

When you authenticate users with an LDAP server, you can allow them to change their passwords through Moodle. You can also make Moodle use the LDAP server's password expiration feature, forcing users to change their passwords periodically. These are the two features that you get while authenticating against LDAP. But, you don't get these while authenticating against an external database. Each type of server offers unique advantages and disadvantages.

If you are authenticating against an external database or server, it is usually because your corporation or school requires you to do so. In that case, you usually don't have a choice about the type of database or server you must use. For example, if your school says that you must use their LDAP server for authenticating Moodle users, the decision is made for you.

Manual Accounts and No Login Methods

In the screenshot showing the authentication methods, note that there are two methods that cannot be disabled—**Manual accounts** and **No login**. These methods are always available to the site administrator.

Manual accounts enables the administrator to create user accounts. These users are stored in Moodle's database. If you are authenticating against an external database, you can still use this method to create users. For example, suppose that your company or school uses Moodle, and authenticates against your organization's IMAP email server. As everyone at your organization has an email account, this ensures that your colleagues, and only your colleagues, have accounts in Moodle. However, what if you have a Guest or consultant to teach one of your courses? If your organization doesn't want to give that person an official email address at your organization, then the Guest teacher won't have an entry into the IMAP server. In that case, you can manually create the Guest's account in Moodle. Their account will exist only in Moodle, and will not be written back to the IMAP (or other) server.

No login enables the administrator to suspend a user's account. While authenticating against an external server, the server can suspend a user's account. The **No login** plug-in enables the administrator to suspend a user's account manually. Suspending a user takes away that person's ability to log in, but retains their data in the system, such as their blog and **My Moodle** workspace. Deleting a user removes the account and the user's data. To suspend a user's account, edit the user's profile, and for the authentication method, select **No login**:

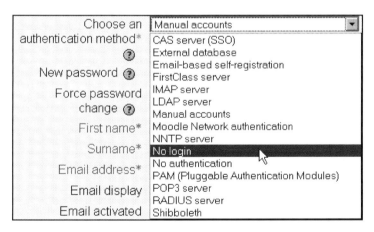

Enrolment Choices

Enrolment is different from authentication. In authentication, you confirm a user's membership to your site. In enrolment, you grant or confirm a user's access to a course. That is, authentication answers the question, 'Are you a member of this site?' Enrolment answers the question, 'Are you enrolled in this course?'

You have several options for managing student enrolment. They are found under **Administration | Courses | Enrolments**:

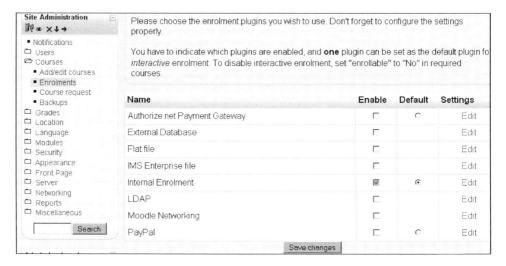

Notice the column labeled **Default**. At first, you would think this is for choosing the default enrolment method. But, you can choose only one of three methods as the default. The other five methods are not available. If this seems curious, here's why: **Default** is not for choosing the default enrolment method. It is for choosing the default **interactive** enrolment method. Interactive means that the student can enrol himself or herself into a course. **Authorize.net Payment Gateway**, **Internal Enrolment**, and **PayPal** are the only interactive methods in that list; the other five are not. You would use **Internal** if your courses are free, such as in a school or corporation. You would use **Authorize.net Payment Gateway** and **PayPal** if you charge for enrolment.

The other non-interactive enrolment methods are external databases or servers that are managed outside Moodle.

Internal Enrolment

This is the default form of enrolment. When this is selected, there are two ways to enrol a student in a course.

A teacher or administrator can enrol the student. From within the course, the teacher selects **Assign roles,** and is taken to the **Assign roles** screen. The user then selects the role that he or she wants to assign, in this case, **Student**:

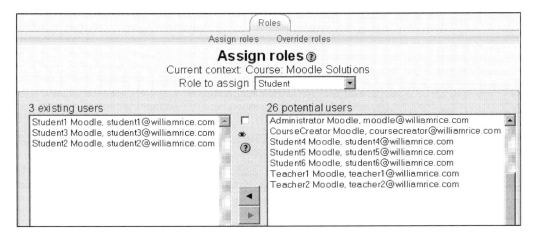

The administrator or teacher then selects a user from the right, and clicks the left-facing arrow to assign that user the **Student** role.

Alternatively, the prospective student can be supplied with an **Enrolment key**. Using this key, the student can enrol in the course:

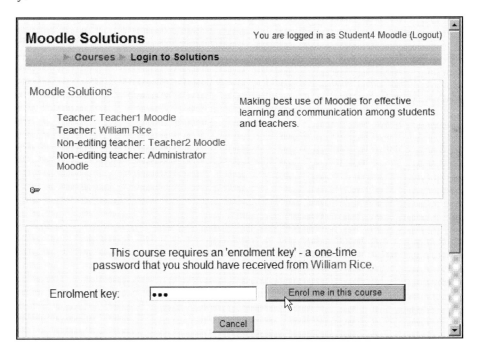

Flat File

The flat file method of student enrolment causes Moodle to read in a text file, or 'flat file', and use that as the source for enrolment information. The flat file method is especially useful if you need to enrol a large group of people who have records in another system.

For example, suppose that all the nurses at your hospital need to be trained in patient privacy laws. We can assume that these people have records in the hospital's human resource or payroll system. Or, suppose all the teachers in your school need to be trained on new educational standards. These people will probably have records in the school's email or human resource system. If you can get a flat file, or text file, containing a list of everyone who needs to be trained, and that file contains their ID numbers, you are well on your way to enrolling them all at once.

The File

The flat file has this format:

```
operation, role, ID number of user, ID number of course
```

...where:

- `operation` is `add` or `del`, which respectively enrol and unenrol the user from the course.
- `role` is role, or function, the user has in the course such as, student, teacher, or administrator.
- `ID number of user` is a unique identifier for the user.
- `ID number of course` is a unique identifier for the course.

Moodle periodically reads this file, and modifies its enrolment data according to what the file says. For example, the line `add, student, 007, EM102` will add the student with the **ID number** of **007** to the course with the **ID number** of **EM102**.

Place this file in a directory that is accessible to your web server. For example, you can put it inside the data directory.

Student ID Number Required

Before you can enrol a person into a course, that person needs to be a member of your site, that is, the person needs to be authenticated. In this case, your first step is to authenticate the users using one of the methods discussed in the section on *Authentication*.

If you use a flat file to enrol students in a course, the file will identify each student by his or her ID number. Whatever method you use to authenticate your users, it should include a unique ID number for each student. This number should consist only of digits, and can be up to ten characters in length. In the user profile page, you can see that **ID number** is an **Optional** field:

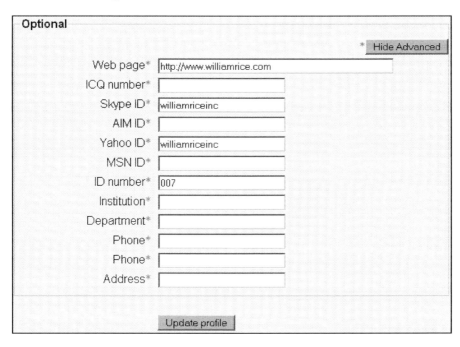

This **ID number** will match the student in Moodle to a record in the enrolment file. For example, the following line from the file enrols student 007 into the course with the ID of EM102:

```
add, student, 007, EM102
```

In the Moodle database, you will find the student's ID number in the table, **mdl_user**, in the field, **idnumber**:

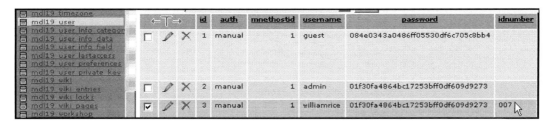

If you want to use a flat file to mass enrol a group of students, and your users don't have ID numbers, speak to your administrator about loading those numbers directly into the Moodle database. They might be able to use a database command to fill that field.

Course ID Required

If you use a flat file to enrol students in a course, the file will identify each course by its ID number. The example we used peviously was the following:

```
add, student, 007, EM102
```

This ID can consist of any alphanumeric characters, not just digits, and can be up to 100 characters in length. In the **Edit course Settings** page, you can see that **Course ID number** is an optional field:

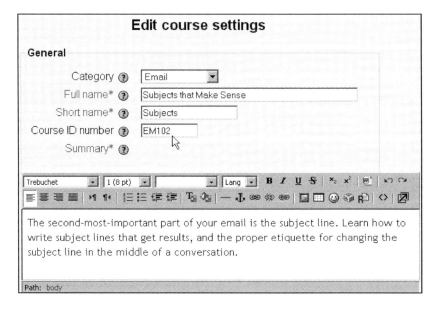

In the Moodle database, you will find the course ID number in the table, **mdl_course**, in the field, **idnumber**:

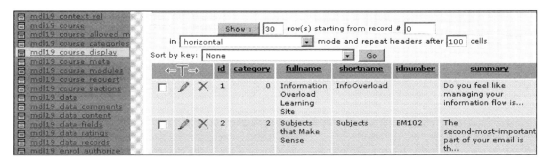

If you want to use a flat file to mass enrol a group of students, and your courses don't have ID numbers, you can add them in the Edit course Settings page for each course. If you need ID numbers for a lot of courses, your database administrator might be able to use a database command to fill that field.

Role

A user's role in a course determines what the user can do in that course. Later in the book, we'll discuss Moodle's built-in roles in detail—how to customize roles, and how to create new ones. For now, let's look at the built-in roles that Moodle gives you in a standard installation:

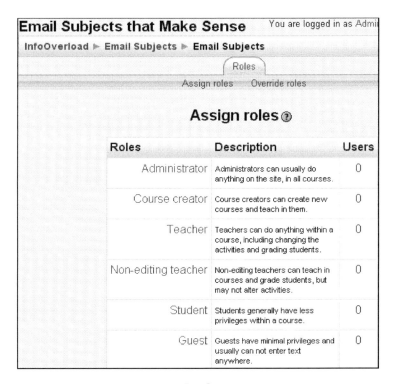

A user can have a role in the site, and a role in a course. The most permissive role wins.

When you use a flat file to enrol students in a course, the file specifies the role of each user in the course. Let's return to our example:

```
add, student, 007, WP102
```

This line from the file specifies that user ID number `007` will be added as a `student` to course ID number `WP102`.

Notice that the flat file uses 'student' with a lowercase 's', while the role is called 'Student' with a capital 'S'. They don't match exactly because the flat file uses the 'short name' of the role. To find out the short name of a role, go to **Site Administration | Users | Permissions | Define roles**, and select the role from the list. In the following screenshot, you can see that the **Short name** of the role **Administrator** is **admin**:

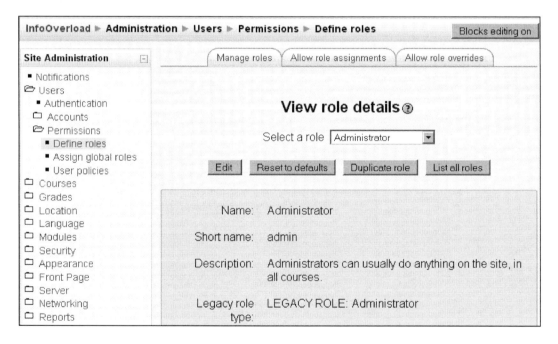

Summary

A flat file is an effective way to mass enrol a large group of students into one or more courses at once. Remember that this method requires you to have a student ID number and course ID number, which are optional. You'll need to populate those fields in your student records and course settings manually or automatically. If you're authenticating users against an external system that has ID numbers, such as your school's LDAP server, consider mapping the student ID number field to your server's ID numbers.

IMS Enterprise File

An IMS Enterprise File is a flat file (text file) that conforms to standards set by the IMS Global Learning Consortium. Many student information systems and human resource information systems can export an IMS-compliant file. For example, PeopleSoft and Oracle can export IMS files. These standards enable human resources systems and learning management systems to exchange data. Just like many word processors can read and write `.rtf` files, many human resources and learning systems can read and create IMS files.

If your organization uses an HR system that can produce IMS files, you can use this method to enrol students. You can also use this method to create new courses. This would be especially useful for a school that wanted to offer teachers the option of an online work space for every course. Each semester, the school could export an IMS file from their enrolment system, read it into Moodle, and use it to create an online course for every class that your school offers. Or, let's return to an example used in the flat file section couple of pages back. Suppose that all the nurses in your hospital need to be trained in patient privacy laws. We can assume that these nurses have records in the hospital's human resource system. The human resource system may also be used to track the courses and certifications that the nurses need. You could export the nurses' information from the HR system, including the courses and certifications that they need. When you import the IMS file into Moodle, it will create the necessary courses and enrol the nurses in them.

You can find the IMS Enterprise Best Practice and Implementation Guide at `http://www.imsglobal.org/enterprise/enbest03.html`. Here is an extract from that document:

> *Corporations, schools, government agencies, and software vendors have a major investment in their systems for Training Administration, Human Resource Management, Student Administration, Financial Management, Library Management and many other functions. They also have existing infrastructure and systems for managing access to electronic resources. To be effective and efficient, Instructional Management systems need to operate as an integrated part of this Enterprise system environment.*

> *The objective of the IMS Enterprise specification documents is to define a standardized set of structures that can be used to exchange data between different systems.*

LDAP

Remember that authentication happens when a user logs into your site, and enrolment happens when a user is made a student in a specific course. LDAP can be used for both authentication and/or enrolment. If you use LDAP for one, you do not need to use it for the other.

LDAP, External Database, and IMS Enterprise file are all able to create new courses as they enrol students. All the other methods can only enrol students in existing courses.

External Database

You can use an external database to control student enrolment. In this case, Moodle looks in the designated database and determines if the student is enrolled. As of version **1.9**, Moodle will not write back to the external database. All changes in the external database are made by another program.

In addition to using the external database, you can also allow Moodle's normal enrolment routine. Showing (un-hiding) this setting under **Administration | Courses | Enrolments** enables Moodle to use an external database for enrolment. If you enable internal enrolment in addition to enrolment to the external database, Moodle checks both the external and the internal databases when a student tries to enter a course.

In the **External Database** screen, you designate the field in Moodle that corresponds to the course name field in the external database:

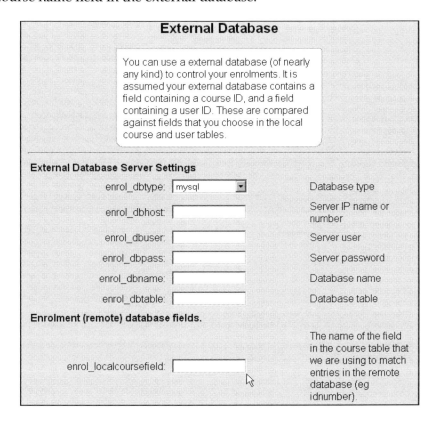

In the following example, you can see the **Edit course settings** for the **Email Subjects** course. I've given this course an **ID number** of **EM102**. This **Course ID number** will correspond to the same ID number in the external database. To match the field **ID number** from course settings against the external database, I need to enter the field name for ID number in **enrol_localcoursefield**.

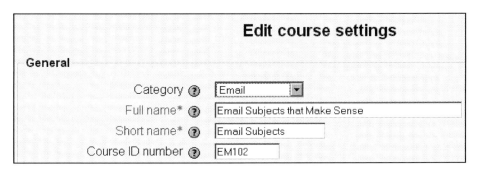

The temptation is to type ID number into **enrol_localcoursefield**, as it is the **ID number** that you see in the **Edit course settings** screen. Surely, that is the field name, right? Well, no! Take look at the Moodle database, in the `mdl_course` table, and you'll find that the real name of this field is `idnumber`:

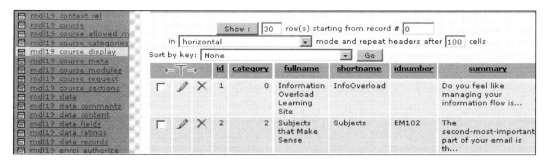

Similarly, we would look up the field name for the student's ID number, and enter that into **enrol_localuserfield** (the field name is **idnumber**).

Authenticating Moodle against an external database can make integrating Moodle into your institution much easier. For example, if you are teaching personnel to use a new human resources system, having Moodle authenticate against that system can give your users a single sign-on for both. However, once you implement the authentication, the fewer the usernames and passwords your users need to remember, the better.

PayPal

The PayPal option enables you to set up paid access to the site, or to individual courses. When you select this option, you enter a value into the field, **enrol_cost**. This becomes the fee for joining the site. If you enter zero into **enrol_cost**, students can access the site for free. If you enter a non-zero amount, students must pay to access the site.

Selecting this option also puts an **enrol_cost** field into each of the **Edit course settings** pages. Again, entering zero into **enrol_cost** for a course enables students to access it for free. Entering a non-zero amount requires students to pay to access the course.

The **PayPal** payment screen displays a notice that **This course requires a payment for entry.**:

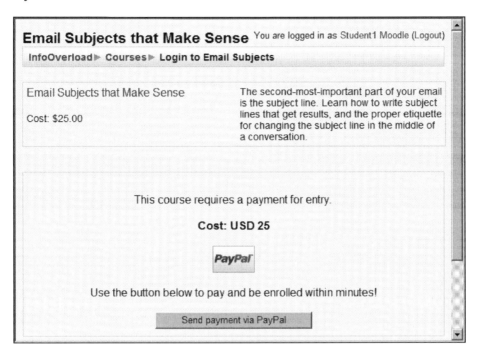

Note that this screen displays a very basic message. You can modify this screen by modifying the source file at `enrol/paypal/enrol.php`.

Authorize.net

The Authorize.net payment plug-in works similar to the PayPal method. Just as you need to create an account with PayPal to use their method, you need to create an account with Authorize.net to use this plug-in. And, you can also set the cost for the site and/or for each course. From your student's point of view, the main difference between PayPal and Authorize.net is the ease of payment, and the types of payments they accept. With both PayPal and Authorize.net, a customer can enter the account they have created with the payment provider. For example, the students can enter their PayPal email address and password, and payment is processed right away. If the students do not have an account with PayPal or Authorize.net, he or she can use a credit card instead.

As PayPal is more popular, more potential students are likely to have a PayPal account rather than an Authorize.net account. This makes payment easier and faster for most students. However, Authorize.net accepts a greater variety of credit cards.

You can use both payment methods, but you must be aware of the potential confusion that can cause against the greater audience you can serve. One possible solution is to make PayPal the preferred option (over Authorize.net). Then, modify the PayPal payment page with a message which lists the cards that PayPal accepts and the cards that Authorize.net accepts. Add instructions and a link that sends the student to the Authorize.net payment page for the cards that PayPal doesn't accept. This gives the many PayPal account holders an easy, quick payment method, while making it easier for those who use the card types that PayPal doesn't accept.

Moodle Networking

The official Moodle documentation describes Moodle Networking as:

> *The network feature allows a Moodle administrator to establish a link with another Moodle, and to share some resources with the users of that Moodle.*

> *The initial release of Moodle Network is bundled with a new Authentication Plug-in, which makes single-sign-on between Moodles possible. A user with the username Jody logs in to her Moodle server as normal, and clicks on a link that takes her to a page on another Moodle server. Normally, she would only have the privileges of a guest on the remote Moodle, but behind the scenes, single-sign-on has established a fully authenticated session for Jody on the remote site.*

If you need to authenticate users across Moodle sites that are owned by different people, then Moodle Networking is an obvious choice. However, if all the sites are owned by the same person or institution, you need to weigh the advantages and disadvantages of using Moodle Networking against some kind of central login. For example, suppose that several departments in your university install their own Moodle sites. If they want to authenticate students on all their sites, they could use Moodle Networking to share student login information. This would make sense if the university's IT department could not, or would not let them authenticate students against the university's LDAP server or student database. But if all the departments could authenticate against a central database maintained by the university, it would probably be easier for them to do so.

Language

The default Moodle installation includes many Language packs. A language pack is a set of translations for the Moodle interface. Language packs translate the Moodle interface, and not the course content. Here's the Front Page of a site when the user selects Spanish from the language menu:

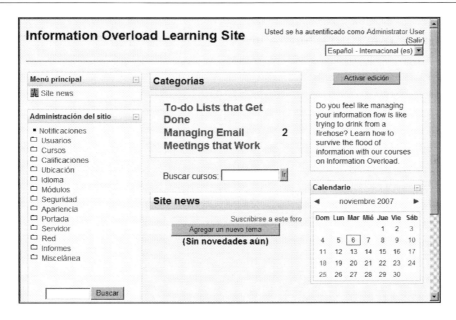

Note that every aspect of the interface is being presented in Spanish: menu names, menu items, section names, buttons, and system messages. Now, let's take a look at the same Front Page when the user selects Romanian from the language menu:

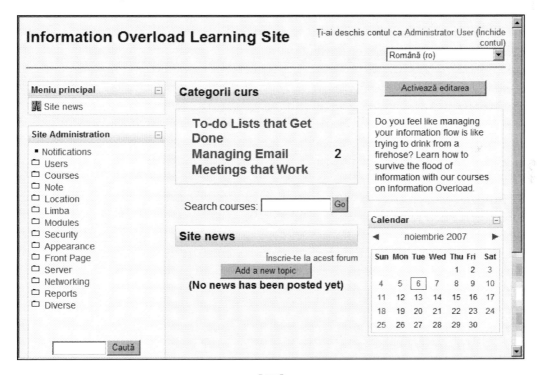

Note that much of the interface has not been translated. For example, the **Site Administration** menu and section name for **Site news** are still in English. When a part of Moodle's interface is not translated into the selected language, Moodle uses the English version.

Language Files

When you install an additional language, Moodle places the language pack in its data directory under the subdirectory /lang. It creates a subdirectory for each language files. The following screenshot shows the results of installing the International Spanish and Romanian languages:

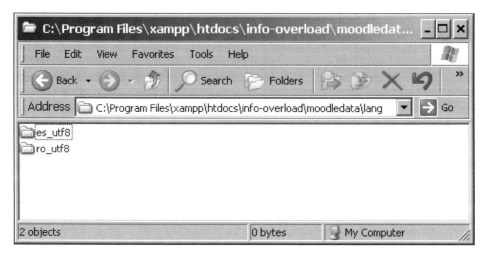

For example, the subdirectory, /lang/en_us, holds files for the U.S. English translation, and /lang/es_es holds the files for traditional Spanish (Espanol / Espana).

The name of the subdirectory is the 'language code'. Knowing this code will come in handy later. In the previous example, es_utf8 tells us that the language code for International Spanish is es.

Inside a language pack's directory, we see a list of files that contain the translations:

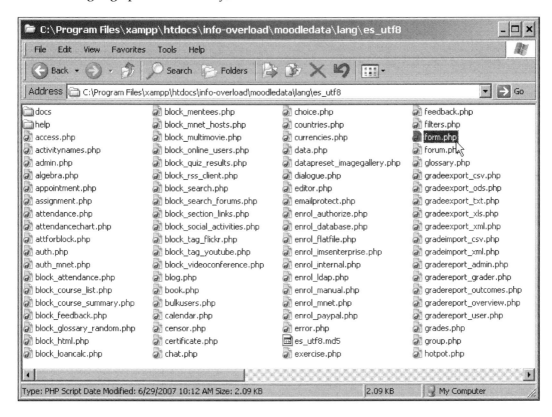

For example, the `/lang/es_utf8/forum.php` file holds text used on the forum pages. This includes the text that is displayed to the course creator while creating the forum, and the text that is displayed to the students when they use the forum. Here are the first few lines from the English version of that file:

```
$string['addanewdiscussion'] = 'Add a new discussion topic';
$string['addanewtopic'] = 'Add a new topic';
$string['advancedsearch'] = 'Advanced search';
```

And here are the same first three lines from the Spanish version of that file:

```
$string['addanewdiscussion'] = 'Colocar un nuevo tema de discusión
aquí';
$string['addanewtopic'] = 'Agregar un nuevo tema';
$string['advancedsearch'] = 'Búsqueda avanzada';
```

The biggest task in localizing Moodle consists of translating these language files into the appropriate languages. Some translations are surprisingly complete. For example, most of the interface has been translated to **Irish Gaelic**, even though this language is used by only about 350,000 people everyday. The Romanian interface remains mostly untranslated although Romania has a population of over 23 million. This means that if a Moodle user chooses the Romanian language (**ro**), most of the interface will still default to **English**.

Language Settings

You access the **Language settings** page from the **Site Administration** menu.

Default Language and Display Language Menu

The **Default language** setting specifies the language that users will see when they first encounter your site. If you also select **Display language menu**, users can change the language. Selecting this displays a language menu on your Front Page.

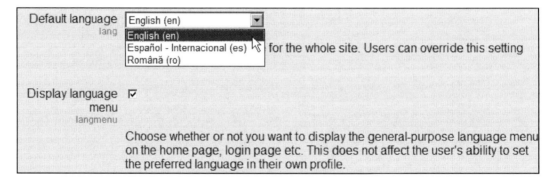

Languages on Language Menu and Cache Language Menu

The setting **Languages on language menu** enables you to specify the languages that users can pick from the language menu. There are directions for you to enter the 'language codes'. These codes are the names of the directories which hold the Language packs. In the subsection on *Language Files* on the previous page, you saw that the directory **es_utf8** holds the language files for International Spanish. If you wanted to enter that language in the list, it would look like this:

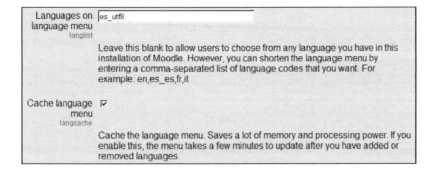

Leaving this field blank will enable your students to pick from all available languages. Entering the names of languages in this field limits the list to only those entered.

Sitewide Locale

Enter a language code into this field, and the system displays dates in the format appropriate to that language.

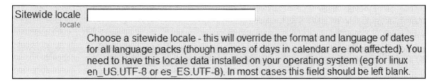

Excel Encoding

Most of the reports that Moodle generates can be downloaded as Excel files. User logs and grades are two examples. This setting lets you choose the encoding for those Excel files.

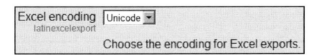

Your choices are **Unicode** and **Latin**. The default is **Unicode**, because this character set includes many more characters other than **Latin**. In many cases, Latin encoding doesn't offer enough characters to completely represent a non-English language.

Offering Courses in Multiple Languages

The settings on the **Language settings** page are also applicable for translating the Moodle interface. However, they are not applicable for translating course content.

If you want to offer course content in multiple languages, you have several choices. First, you could put all the different languages into each course. That is, each document would appear in a course in several languages. For example, if you offered a botany course in English and Spanish, you might have a document defining the different types of plants in both English and Spanish, side by side in the same course–**Types of Plants** or **Tipos de Plantaras**. While taking the course, students would select the documents in their language. Course names would appear in only one language.

Second, you could create separate courses for each language, and offer them on the same site. Course names would appear in each language. In this case, students would select the course in English or Spanish– **Basic Botany** or **Botánica Básica**.

Third, you could create a separate Moodle site for each language, for example, `http://moodle.williamrice.com/english` and `http://moodle.williamrice.com/spanish`. At the Home Page of your site, students would select their language and would be directed to the correct Moodle installation. In this case, the entire Moodle site would appear in the students' language: the site name, the menus, the course names, and the course content. These are things you should consider before installing Moodle.

Finally, and most elegantly, you could use the filter described later in this chapter to display course content in the language selected by your user.

Installing Additional Languages

To install additional languages, you must be connected to the Internet. Then, from the **Site Administration** menu, select **Language | Language packs**. The page displays a list of all available Language packs:

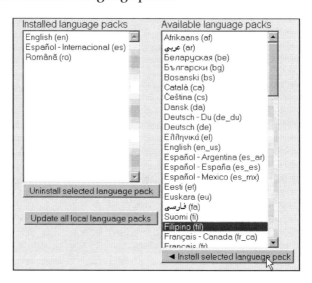

This list is taken from Moodle's `/install/lang` directory. In that directory, you will find a folder for each language pack that can be installed.

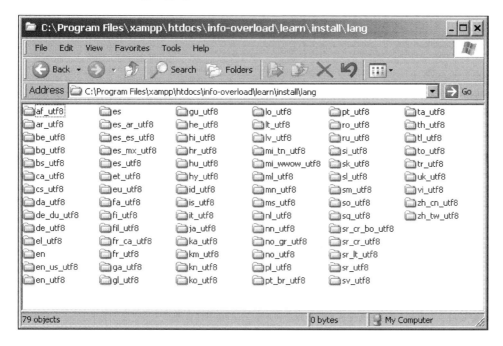

The folder contains a file called `install.php`. That file retrieves the most recent version of the language pack from the Web and installs it. This is why Moodle must be connected to the Web to use this feature. If Moodle is not connected, you will need to download the language pack and copy it into the `/lang` directory yourself.

If you don't see the language you want on the list of **Available language packs**, either it's not available in the official Moodle site, or your list of available languages is out of date. Click to update this list. If the language doesn't appear, it's not available from official sources.

Security Settings

You will find the security settings under **Site administration | Security**. This section will not cover every option under that menu. Instead, it will focus on the options that are not self-explanatory, and how they affect your users' experience.

Open to Google

This setting lets the Google indexing robot into courses that allow guest access. If you want to know more about the **Googlebot**, visit `http://www.google.com/bot.html`.

It seems that everyone with a website wants his or her site to be ranked high in Google's search results. However, you should consider whether you really want Google to add each of your guest-enabled courses to its search engine. There are several disadvantages:

1   If your course content changes frequently, Google might index out-of-date information for your courses.

2   Your students and teachers might not want their names and materials indexed and available to the public.

3   If Google indexes all your guest-enabled courses, you have less control over the information that appears about your site in Google. Everything on the pages that the Googlebot searches is used for indexing your site. There might be items on those pages that don't accurately represent your site. For example, a negative forum posting or an off-topic discussion could become associated with your site. Also, if the focus or structure of your Moodle site changes, it may take a while before the Google references to all those pages are corrected.

If you want strict control over the information that appears in Google about your site, then set **Open to Google** to **No**. Put only the information that you want to appear in Google on the Front Page of your site, and do not allow teachers or students to modify anything on the Front Page. This way, Google will index only your Front Page.

You should also request anyone who links to your site to link only to the Front Page (for example, 'Please link only to `http//www.moodle.williamrice.com`, not directly to a course page.') Google and other search engines use links to your site to calculate your ranking. If all those links point to the same page, you can better control your site's public image. By disabling **Open to Google**, and requesting that people link only to the Front Page, you are trading away some of your search engine presence in exchange for greater control of your site's public image.

For the ultimate in control of what information about your site is indexed, consider this plan: Disable **Open to Google** and enable **Force users to login** to keep search engine robots out of Moodle completely. Under **Users | Authentication**, set **Guest login button** to **Hide** to eliminate the possibility that any other search engine's robots crawl your guest courses. Now, you've locked out all but registered users.

Put Moodle into a subdirectory of your site's Link to Moodle from the index page at the root of your site. In my case, I would put Moodle into `moodle.williamrice.com/moodle/` and link to it from `moodle.williamrice.com/index.htm`. Then, use `index.htm` as an introduction to your site. Ensure that `index.htm` contains exactly the kind of information that you want the public to know about your site, and optimize it for the best search engine placement.

Login Settings

Under **Security | Site policies**, you will find three settings that affect the login to your site:

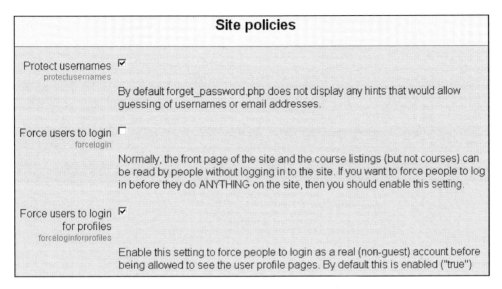

Protect Usernames

If you forget your password, Moodle can display a page that enables you to retrieve it. If you enter your username or email address, Moodle will send an email with your login information:

When Moodle sends this email, it confirms the sending, but does not display the email address to which the message was sent:

The email address is hidden to protect the user's privacy. Many countries have laws that forbid the disclosure of personal information. If someone could guess the usernames (which is often the case in large institutions), they could enter them into the lost password page and harvest email addresses for abuse.

Force Users to Login

As stated in the directions, setting this to **Yes** causes the Front Page to become hidden until a visitor logs in to Moodle. When visitors first hit your Moodle site, they see the Moodle login page.

Setting this to **Yes** means that you cannot use Moodle's Front Page as an information and sales tool. You can customize the text on the login page, but you won't be able to add all the features available on the Front Page.

Setting this to **No** enables you to use a non-Moodle page as your introduction to the site. If you want your Front Page to be something that cannot be created in Moodle, this is a good option. For example, I could make `moodle.williamrice.com/index.htm` into a flash presentation about my site. Visitors then click on an **Enter** link and are taken to the Moodle login page at `moodle.williamrice.com/moodle/index.php`. Note that this required me to put Moodle into its own subdirectory. If you want a non-Moodle introduction page that leads to a Moodle login page, put Moodle into its own subdirectory or subdomain.

Force Users to Login for Profiles

What the directions don't state is that setting this to **No** enables anonymous visitors to read not only the teachers' profiles, but also the profiles of students enrolled in courses that have guest access. This may be a privacy issue.

The effect of enabling **Force users to login for profiles** is that anonymous visitors cannot read the profiles of the teachers in a course that accepts guest access. They must register as a student before being able to read student and user profiles. This may be a drawback if your teachers' profiles are a selling point for the course.

Consider enabling this to force people to register before reading the profiles of students or teachers. Then, if your teachers' profiles are a selling point, you can add a section to the Front Page for 'About Our Teachers'.

Use HTTPS for Logins

This setting is found under **Security | HTTP security**. If you enable this setting, but your server doesn't have HTTPS enabled for your site, you will be locked out of your site. Moodle will require you to use HTTPS when you log in, but you won't be able to comply. If that happens, then you must go into the Moodle database and change this setting to No.

The following screenshot shows an administrator using the web-based product, **phpMyAdmin**, to edit this setting in Moodle's database. Note that the setting for logging in via HTTPS is in the table, mdl_config. The administrator is clicking on the edit icon. If this cell contains 0, HTTPS login is not required. If it contains 1, HTTPS login is required. If you're locked out because of HTTPS login, change the contents of this cell to 0. Then try logging in again.

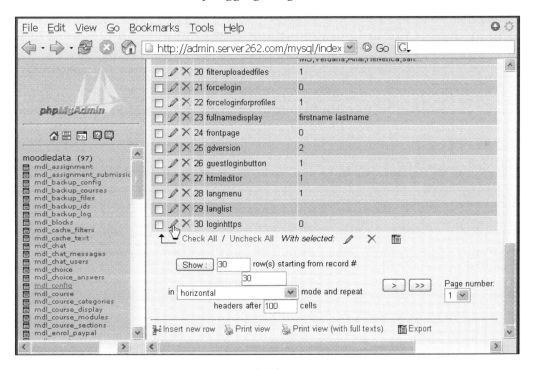

Maximum Pploaded File Size

Also under **Security | Site policies,** you will find a setting to limit the size of files that users and course creators can upload:

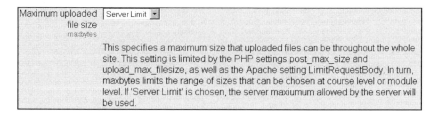

This setting affects students, teachers, and course creators. If you're creating a course that has a large file, such as a video, and Moodle forbids you from uploading the file, this setting might be the cause.

As stated in the directions on the page, there are three other settings that limit the size of a file that can be uploaded on your server. The first two are PHP settings, and the third is an Apache setting. To see the PHP settings on your server, go to **Site Administration | Server | PHP info**. Scroll down until you see `post_max_size` and `upload_max_filesize`.

The Apache setting, `LimitRequestBody`, also sets a limit on the size of uploaded files. The following is an extract grom the official Apache 2 documentation:

> *This directive specifies the number of bytes from 0 (meaning unlimited) to 2147483647 (2GB) that are allowed in a request body.*

> *The* `LimitRequestBody` *directive allows the user to set a limit on the size allowed for an HTTP request message body within the context in which the directive is given (server, per-directory, per-file or per-location). If the client request exceeds that limit, the server will return an error response instead of servicing the request. The size of a normal request message body will vary greatly depending on the nature of the resource, and the methods allowed on that resource. CGI scripts typically use the message body for retrieving form information. Implementations of the* PUT *method will require a value at least as large as any representation that the server wishes to accept for that resource.*

Changing the Limit on the Uploaded File Size in PHP

If you have your own server, you can change the values for `post_max_size` and `upload_max_filesize` in the file, `php.ini`. You will usually find this file in `/apache/bin`.

If you are using someone else's server (such as a hosting service), you probably can't change anything in php.ini. Try creating a file called .htaccess that contains these lines:

```
php_value post_max_size 128M
php_value upload_max_filesize 128M
```

Replace 128M with any value you need. If the server times out while uploading large files, you may add the following lines to .htaccess:

```
php_value max_input_time 600
php_value max_execution_time 600
```

The variables, max_execution_time and max_input_time, set the maximum time allowed by a page to upload and process the files to be uploaded. If you want to upload several megabytes of data, you may want to increase this setting. The execution time is specified in milliseconds (thousandths of a second). You can check your host's settings for these under **Site Administration | Server | PHP info**.

Then, place .htaccess into the directory with the PHP scripts that you want to run. For example, the script for uploading files is in the directory, /files.

Your hosting service can disable .htaccess, which would make this solution impossible. You would need to ask your hosting service to change these values for you.

Changing the Limit on Uploaded File Size in Apache

Just as you may be able to use .htaccess to override PHP settings, you may also be able to use it to override Apache settings. For example, placing this line in .htaccess changes the limit on uploaded files to 10 megabytes:

```
LimitRequestBody 10240000
```

Note that the limit is specified in bytes, and not megabytes. Setting it to zero will make the setting unlimited. The highest number you can specify is 2147483647, or two gigabytes.

Filters

Moodle's filters read text and media that users put on the site. The filters can then do three things with that material: **link**, **interpret**, and/or **restrict**.

First, a filter can automatically link words and phrases to items in your site. For example, suppose that you create a glossary that contains the phrase, 'self-determination'. If you activate the **Glossary Auto-linking** filter, whenever the phrase (self-determination) appears on your site, it will be highlighted and will link to its glossary entry. When a reader clicks on the phrase, the reader is taken to the glossary entry.

Second, a filter can interpret what you have uploaded. For example, you could upload a document that is written in the markup language called TeX (think HTML on steroids). The **TeX Notation** filter would interpret this document, and enable Moodle to display it correctly. There's also an **Algebra Notation** filter that interprets a special markup language for writing math formulas.

Third, a filter can restrict the kind of content that a user can place on the site. For example, the **Word Censorship** filter can filter out a list of 'bad words' that you don't want to appear on your site. Every time that text is uploaded or entered, it is checked against the list of forbidden words.

You'll find the **Filters** settings under **Site Administration | Modules | Filters**. Read the following descriptions for detailed information about what each filter can do for your site.

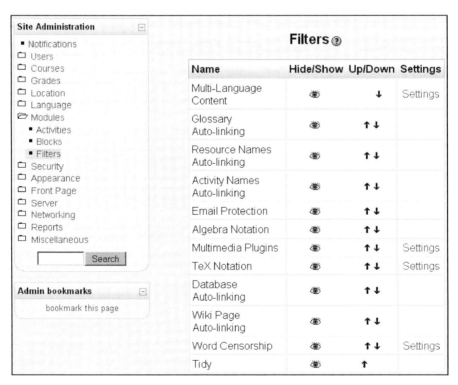

Auto-Linking Filters

The Auto-linking filters search the text on your site, and automatically link to the item mentioned in the text. For example, Glossary Auto-linking looks for terms that are in any glossary, and on finding them, links them to the glossary entry. The term is highlighted, and when a user clicks it, he or she is taken to the glossary.

Resource Names Auto-linking searches course text for the names of course resources. When it finds the name of a resource, it links the name to the resource. This means that whenever a student sees the name of a document, web page, or other course resource, the student can just click on the name and be taken to the resource. **Activity Names Auto-linking** works the same way for course activities. **Wiki Page Auto-linking** creates a link to a wiki page whenever the page is mentioned on the site. The database module enables the teacher and/or students to build, display, and search a database about any topic. **Database Auto-linking** creates a link to an entry in the database whenever the name of that entry appears in text.

Math Filters

Algebra Notation and TeX Notation search the text for special characters used to describe mathematical formulas. For example, if you enter `@@cosh(x,2)@@`, the Algebra Notation filter will display it as:

$$\cosh^2(\ )$$

If you enter `$$\Bigsum_{i=\1}^{n-\1}$$`, the TeX Notation filter will display it as:

$$n-1$$

$$i=1$$

Algebra Notation and TeX Notation are standard markup languages. The `http://www.moodle.org` site contains more information about Algebra Notation. For more information about **TeX**, see the **TeX Users Group** at `tug.org`. TeX is more mature and complete as compared to Algebra Notation. If you plan on writing more complex equations, I suggest making the TeX Notation filter active, and leaving the Algebra Notation filter inactive.

Email Protection Filter

Activating this filter makes email addresses on the site unreadable to search engines, while keeping them 'human-readable'. If you set **Open to Google** to **No**, or require users to log in, then you probably don't need to worry about search engines picking up your students' email addresses automatically. If your site is open to search engines and anonymous users, then you might want to use this filter to protect the users' email addresses.

Multimedia Plug-Ins

If you leave this filter inactive, then multimedia content will usually play in a separate window. For example, without this filter, when a user clicks on a video, that video might open and play in a separate **Windows Media Player** or **RealPlayer** window. By activating this filter, you embed multimedia so that it plays on the page in which it was linked.

Multi-Language Content

Earlier, you might have used the setting **Display language menu** to give your users a list of languages for the site. When a user selects one of these languages, only the Moodle interface is translated. The course content remains in whatever language you created it. If you want your site to be truly **multi-lingual**, you can also create course content in several languages. Activating the **Multi-Language Content** filter will then cause the course material to be displayed in the selected language.

To create course content in multiple languages, you must enclose text written in each language in a <span> tag, like this:

```
<span lang="en">Basic Botany</span>
<span lang="es">Botánica Básica</span>
```

This requires that you write course material in HTML. This can be done for headings, course descriptions, course material, and any other HTML document that Moodle displays.

Word Censorship

When this filter is activated, any word on the offensive list is blacked out. You can enter a list of banned words under the **Settings** for this filter. If you don't enter your own list, Moodle will use a default list that is found in the language pack.

Tidy

This filter checks HTML that is written or uploaded to Moodle, and attempts to 'tidy' it by making it compliant with the XHTML standard. If your audience is using a wide variety of browsers (or browser versions), or a screen reader for the blind, making your pages compliant with this standard could make them easier to render.

Configuring the Front Page

Your site's Front Page welcomes the world to your learning site. Moodle treats your Front Page as a special course. This means that you can do everything on the Front Page that you can do in a normal course, plus a few additional settings.

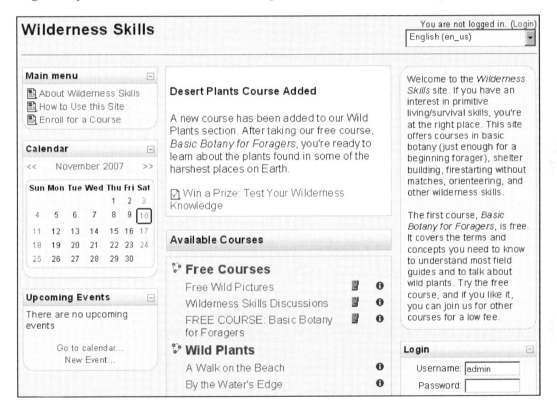

How to Use this Section

Early in the process of building your site, you can make some decisions about how your Front Page will look and function. This section deals with those settings that make sense to select when you're first building your site. Some configuration settings on the Front Page won't make sense until you've created some courses, and seen how Moodle works. You will find those settings covered in the chapter on *Welcoming Your Students*.

If you have already created courses for your site, consider working your way through this section, and then working through the chapter, *Welcoming Your Students*. These two will give you a fairly complete process for configuring the Front Page of your site.

Front Page Settings Page

The settings for the Front Page of your site are found under **Site Administration | Front Page | Front Page settings**:

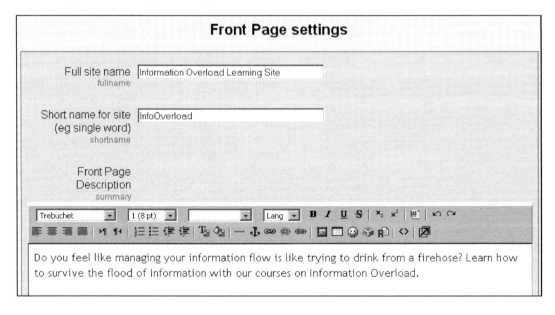

Full Site Name

The **Full site name** appears at the top of the Front Page in the browser's title bar, and also on the page tab while browsing with tabs:

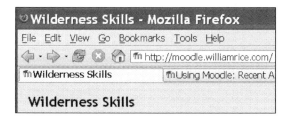

The **Full site name** also appears in the metadata for the Front Page. Here are the first few lines of HTML code from my Front Page. The line containing the **Full site name** is in bold:

```
<html dir="ltr">
<head>
<meta http-equiv="content-type" content="text/html; charset=iso-8859-1" />
<style type="text/css">@import url(http://moodle.williamrice.com/lib/editor/htmlarea.css);</style>
<meta name="description" content="
Welcome to the Wilderness Skills site. If you have an interest in
primitive living/survival skills, you're at the right place. This site
offers courses in basic botany (just enough for a beginning forager),
shelter building, firestarting without matches, orienteering, and
other wilderness skills.The first course, Basic Botany for Foragers,
is free. It covers the terms and concepts you need to know to
understand most field guides and to talk about wild plants. Try the
free course, and if you like it, you can join us for other courses for
a low fee.">
<title>Wilderness Skills</title>
<meta name="keywords" content="moodle, Wilderness Skills " />
```

Short Name for Site

Once a user enters your Moodle site, a navigation line is displayed at the top of each page. This shows the user where he or she is in the site. The first item in this navigation line, or breadcrumbs, is the **Short name for site**:

Front Page Description

This description appears in the left or right column of your site's Front Page. If you require visitors to register and log in before seeing the Front Page, remember that visitors will see this description after they have logged in. In that case, the Front Page description can't be used to sell your site. Instead, it can instruct students on how to get started with your site. For example, "Take the Introduction course to learn how to use this site…"

If your Front Page is visible to all visitors, then you can use this description to sell your site, tempt visitors to take a sample course, tell them what's inside, and so on.

Also, this description appears in the metadata of the first page. For example, I used my browser's **Show Source Code** function to show the HTML code for the site's Front Page. I made the description bold, so it's easier for you to spot it:

```
<html dir="ltr">
<head>
<meta http-equiv="content-type" content="text/html; charset=iso-8859-
1" />
<style type="text/css">@import url(http://moodle.williamrice.com/lib/
editor/htmlarea.css);</style>
<meta name="description" content="
Welcome to the Wilderness Skills site. If you have an interest in
primitive living/survival skills, you're at the right place. This site
offers courses in basic botany (just enough for a beginning forager),
shelter building, firestarting without matches, orienteering, and
other wilderness skills.The first course, Basic Botany for Foragers,
is free. It covers the terms and concepts you need to know to
understand most field guides and to talk about wild plants. Try the
free course, and if you like it, you can join us for other courses for
a low fee.">
<title>Wilderness Skills</title>
<meta name="keywords" content="moodle, Wilderness Skills " />
```

The metadata of a page is used by search engines to help place it in the correct search results. So even if you decide to hide the box that displays the Front Page description, enter the description into the Front Page settings. It will make your site more findable on search engines.

Front Page Items

Two settings determine whether the center column of the Front Page shows news items, a list of courses, and/or a list of course categories. These settings are **Front Page** and **Front Page items when logged in**:

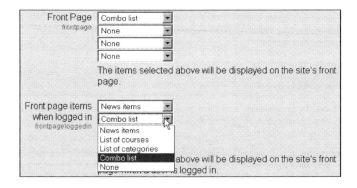

Note that the Front Page settings apply to visitors who are not logged in. In the previous example, I want to entice visitors with a list of the courses that I offer. However, as site news would probably not be of interest to anonymous visitors, I will show site news only to logged in users. Each choice has its unique advantages.

Using a Topic Section on the Front Page

Remember that the Front Page description always appears in the left or right column of the Front Page. It does not appear in the center column. If you want your site description (for example, **Welcome to the**....) top and center, you'll need to include a topic section, which always appears in the center of your Front Page:

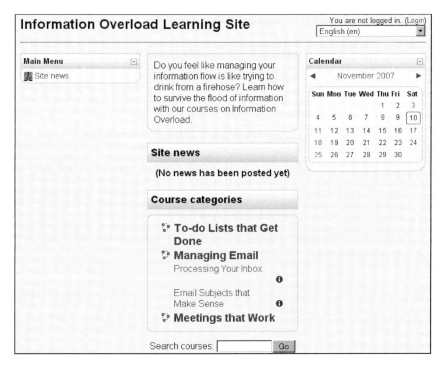

You could make your site description the first topic. In this example, I turned the **Front Page Description** off. I'm using the first topic to introduce my site instead. That puts my site description top and center, where I think it's most noticeable.

Show News items

This setting is useful if the content of your site changes frequently, and you want to keep visitors informed. If one of the primary purposes of your Front Page is serving repeat customers, showing news items on the Front Page is a good idea.

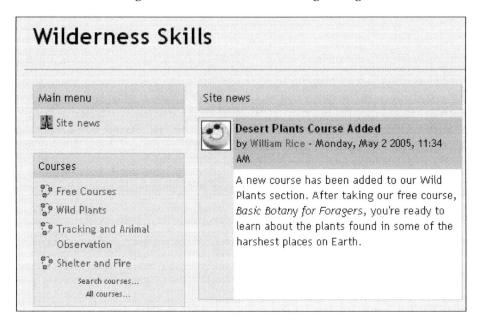

Note that instead of using the setting **List of courses** to display a list of course in the middle of the Front Page, I'm using a block to display my course categories on the left side of the page. I'm doing this because I want to keep both site news and course categories 'above the fold', in the top part of the page, so that my visitors don't need to scroll to see them.

Show a List of Courses

In the following example, note that the Front Page is displaying both site news and a combo list. The combo list consists of course categories plus courses:

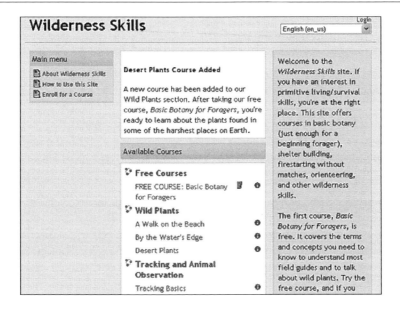

Also note that I've added a **Main menu** in the left column, with links to detailed information about the site, how to use it, and the enrolment/payment page. The welcome message in the right column and the links to detailed information about the site in the left column serve my new visitors. The announcements **Desert Plants Course Added** and **Available Courses** in the center serve my existing customers. The challenge is to include material on the Front Page that will serve both new and existing customers, without making it too busy and crowded.

Notice the ❶ icon next to each course. Clicking this gives the visitor a description of the course (later in the section on creating courses, you'll see how to enter a course description). If you want to encourage visitors to do this, you could insert another label between the announcements, **Desert Plants Course Added** and the **Available Courses** section, which says something like, 'For a short description of each course, click on the ❶ next to it.'

The drawback to using **Show a list of courses** is that the course list can get very long. You must decide how much tolerance your visitors will have for scrolling and browsing through a long list of courses.

Backup

You'll find the backup settings under **Site Administration | Courses | Backups**. Most of these settings enable you to choose the type of data that gets backed up. You also choose the days of the week on which the backup will automatically run. The backup is activated by the cron job routine.

The backups are stored in compressed or ZIP format. Under **Site Administration | Server | System paths** page, you indicate whether your hosting service has a zip program, or whether Moodle should use its own, built-in zip program. If you activate automatic backups, and Moodle must use its built-in zip program during the backups, you might see backup failures caused by lack of memory. If you plan on using the backup feature for more than a handful of courses, ensure that your hosting service offers a zip program on their servers. Running out of memory, while backing up large courses or large sites, is one of the most common causes for a Moodle crash.

Set Up the Cron Job

Some of Moodle's functions happen at regular, timed schedules. The most visible example is the mailing out of notices to the subscribers of a forum stating that a new message has been posted. A script called `cron.php` periodically checks to see if new messages have been posted to any forum. If so, the script causes the notice to be emailed to the members of that forum.

The script `cron.php` must be triggered at regular intervals. You can set this interval. The mechanism that triggers the script is called a **cron job**. Directions for setting up the cron job are in the `http://moodle.org/` installation guide.

Some web-hosting services allow you to set up cron jobs. If you're buying hosting services, look for a host that allows you to set a cron job to run every hour, or even every few minutes. Some hosting services allow you to run a cron job only once a day. This means that Moodle will perform those functions that depend on `cron.php` only once a day.

If you've been given space on your school's or company's web server, speak to the system administrator about setting up the cron job. Moodle's `cron.php` uses very little memory and few system resources. Most servers could run it every 15 minutes without affecting the server's performance.

If you cannot set up the cron job on your host, then your only other option is to set up the cron job on a Windows machine that you control. The cron job will reach out over the Internet to your Moodle site, and activate the script, `cron.php`. Again, directions for this are available in the `http://moodle.org/` installation guide. However, if you choose this option, you must always keep that Windows PC running, and it must also be connected to the Internet at all times. If the Windows PC goes down or offline, the Moodle functions that requires periodic triggering will also go down.

The following is a screenshot illustrating the installation of the **MoodleCron** application, where I specify the location of the `cron.php` script. In this example, you can see the line **Location: /www/moodle/admin**, which on my server corresponds to `www.moodle.williamrice.com/admin`. Moodle's `/admin` directory, holds `cron.php`.

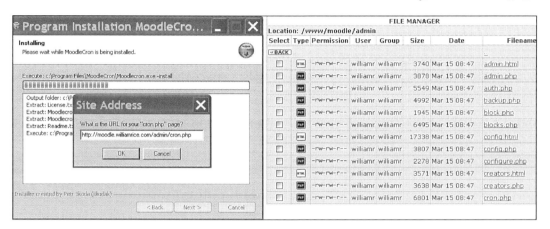

Summary

This chapter tells you how to make changes to your site's configuration. I've covered the settings that, in my experience, you are most likely to change. Many of these settings affect the behavior of the entire site. You don't need to get these choices perfect, the first time, because you can return to these settings and edit them at will. As you proceed with building your site, you will probably want to experiment with some of them.

4
Creating Categories and Courses

This chapter's focus is on helping you create different categories and courses. While someone else may have installed Moodle and made these choices for you, you can always go back and change them.

The following sections will help you create and organize course categories. It will also tell you how to put a course into several categories.

Using Course Categories and the User Experience

Every Moodle course belongs to one course category. When a student selects a course, they must first select a category. In the next example, the student selected the **Tracking and Animal Observation** category from the Front Page, and is selecting a course from that category:

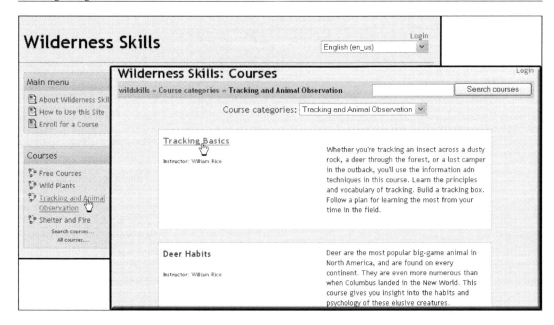

Notice that even though the student is looking at the **Tracking and Animal Observation** category, a drop-down list of **Course categories** enables the student to see the other categories. Typical of Moodle, this enables the student to jump to another part of the site without having to return to the Front Page.

Categories are a site-wide way to organize your courses. You can also create subcategories. The categories or subcategories become an online course catalog. Organize them in the same intuitive way you would a printed course catalog.

Creating Course Categories

You create course categories under **Site Administration | Courses | Add/edit courses**. After logging in as someone with the permission to create courses and categories, the fastest way to reach this screen is by selecting **All courses** from the Courses block:

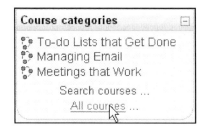

If you have sufficient privileges in the system, you can use either method to reach this page. In this page, you create new categories and courses. You also arrange the order in which the categories are displayed:

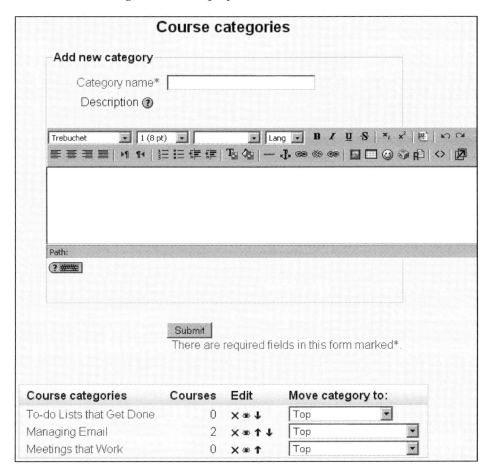

Organizing Course Categories

To move a course category up or down in the list, click ⬆ or ⬇ in the **Edit** column. To hide a course category, while you're working on it, click 👁. The eye will then close, indicating the category is hidden from users. To delete a category, select ✖.

You can use subcategories in Moodle. In the following page, you can see that I'm adding **Inbox Zero** as a subcategory of **Managing Email**. After I do that, perhaps I will move the course **Processing Your Inbox** to that sub-category, which I can do on this same page:

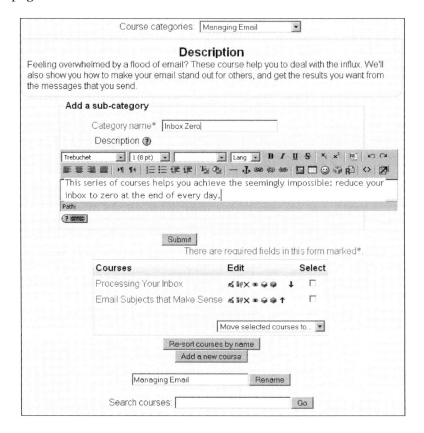

Putting a Course into Several Categories

One of the Moodle's limitations is that you can put a course into only one category. In some situations, you might want to put the same course into several categories. You have several options:

- You can forgo the use of categories, and use direct links to the courses. In Chapter 4, you'll see how to add labels and links to the Front Page. You can use labels as your category names, and put the links below the labels.

- You can create the course in one category, and then create an identically-named course in the second category. However, you will put only one thing into the second course: a JavaScript that automatically forwards the user to the real course.

You can either search the Web for a free JavaScript, or pick this one from
`http://javascriptkit.com/` that you can add to the course as a label:

```
<form name="redirect">
<center>
<font face="Arial"><b>You will be redirected to the script in<br><br>
<form>
<input type="text" size="3" name="redirect2">
</form>
seconds</b></font>
</center>
<script>
<!--
/*
Count down then redirect script
By JavaScript Kit (http://javascriptkit.com)
Over 400+ free scripts here!
*/
//change below target URL to your own
var targetURL="http://javascriptkit.com"
//change the second to start counting down from
var countdownfrom=10

var currentsecond=document.redirect.redirect2.value=countdownfrom+1
function countredirect(){
if (currentsecond!=1){
currentsecond-=1
document.redirect.redirect2.value=currentsecond
}
else{
window.location=targetURL
return
}
setTimeout("countredirect()",1000)
}
countredirect()
//-->
</script>
```

Creating Courses

Don't worry if you mistakenly put a course into the wrong category. In the next section, the *Course Settings Page*, the site administrator can change the category.

1. Select **Site Administration | Courses | Add/Edit courses**.

2. Select the category that currently holds the course.

3. Scroll to the bottom of the page, where the courses are listed.

4. Click the checkbox next to the course whose category you want to change.

5. From the drop-down list, select the new category for the course:

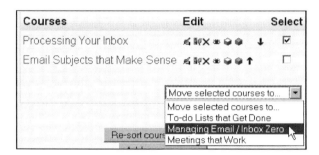

6. After you select the (sub) category from the drop-down list, the course is immediately moved.

The Course Settings Page

When you create a course, you must fill out fields on the Course Settings page. Many of these fields are self-explanatory. Some of them, especially **Format** and **Group mode**, have a profound effect on the user experience. You can always return to this page and change the course settings. The course, and its structure, will be updated with the new settings as soon as you save them.

The page itself does a good job of explaining the purpose of each setting. However, the directions do not tell you the implications of the choices you make on this page. I've added some commentary here to help you determine how your choices will affect the operation of your site, and given information to help you decide upon the right choices for your needs.

Category

If you've selected a course category and then created the course, you'll see the category displayed in this field. You can use the drop-down list to change the category at any time. The list shows both visible and hidden categories.

As your site grows, and you add categories, you may want to reorganize your site. However, if a student logs in while you are in the middle of creating categories and moving courses, he or she might be confused. It would be best if you could make the reorganization as quickly as possible—ideally, instantaneously.

You can speed the reorganization time by hiding your categories as you create them. This lets you take your time while thinking about which categories to use. Then, move the courses into the categories. Each course will disappear until you finally reveal the new categories.

Full Name and Short Name

The full name of the course appears at the top of the page while viewing the course, and also in course listings. The short name appears in the breadcrumb, or trail, at the top of the page. In this example, the full name is **Basic Botany for Foragers** and the short name is **Wild Plants 1**:

> **FREE COURSE: Basic Botany for Foragers**
> wildskills » Wild Plants 1

The full name also appears in the page's title and metadata, which influences its search engine rankings. Here's the HTML code from the example above:

```
<title>Course: FREE COURSE: Basic Botany for Foragers</title>
<meta name="keywords" content="moodle, Course: FREE COURSE: Basic
Botany for Foragers " />
```

Notice the full course name in the `<title>` and `<meta>` tags. Many search engines give a lot of weight to the title and keywords tags. Choose your course title with this in mind.

Course ID Number

Chapter 2 talks about using an external database for enrolment information. The ID number that you enter into this field must match the ID number of the course in the external database. If you're not using an external database for enrolment information, you can leave this field blank.

Summary

The **Summary** is displayed when a reader clicks on the info icon, and when the course appears in a list. In the following screenshot, the course is listed on the Front Page of the site. The visitor clicked on the info icon, and a pop-up window displays the course summary:

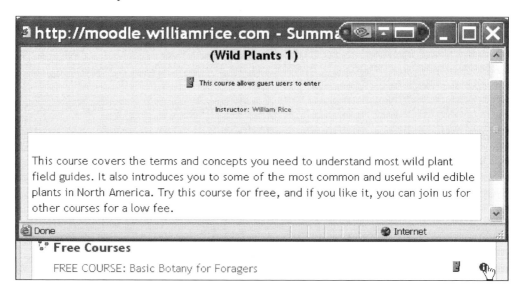

If you allow visitors to see your Front Page without logging in, then they will probably read your course summaries before enrolling. Consider the **Summary** to be a course's resume. Your course summaries need to be informative and work as a sales tool. They should offer enough information to help your visitors decide if they want to enrol, and should describe the courses in their best light.

Format

You can select three formats for a course:

- Topics
- Weekly (this is the default format for a new course)
- Social

The following subsections explain how each format affects the user experience:

Topics Format

The **Topics** format is the most intuitive format to use for a course. As it displays each part of the course as a numbered topic, this format encourages most students to proceed through the course sequentially. However, it does not enforce this sequence, so students are free to jump ahead and behind in the course.

Topic outline

Welcome

Have you ever picked up a wild plants field guide, read a plant's description, and felt confused by all those specialized botanical terms? It's as if they expect you to have a degree in botany before reading the book. Or have you ever tried to memorize a few wild edible plants just by reading their descriptions over and over, but gave up trying to memorize them by brute force?

If so, this course is for you.

Welcome to *Basic Botany for Foragers*. This course introduces you to foraging. Foraging is identifying, gathering, and using wild plants for food, medicine, and tools.

Before continuing, it is very important that you read and understand the following warning: **Eat only those plants you can positively identify and that you know are safe to eat. Identify and collect wild plants only under the guidance of an experienced forager.** This course is an excellent preparation for learning to identify plants under the guidance of an expert, but is not a substitute. You should learn under someone qualified and experienced in the collection of wild plants in your area. Common sense dictates that if you have any doubt as to a plant's safety, don't eat it.

To learn more about this course, select *Course Goals and Outline* below. To meet your fellow foragers, join the *Course Discussion*. To jump into the course, just select a lesson.

Course Goals and Outline
Course Discussion

1 Types of Plants

Identifying the basic types of plants: woody, herbaceous, and succulents.

2 Life Cycles of Plants

Like all living things, plants have a life cycle. This lesson covers the different types of life cycles found in the plant world.

3 Leaves

Leaves are one of the most important identifying features of a plant. This section covers many of the terms used in field guides and botany texts.

4 Flowers

Along with leaves, flowers are the most important identifying feature. This section covers flower parts and terminology used to describe

Every course has a **Topic 0**. In this example, **Topic 0** includes the **Welcome** message, **Course Goals and Outline,** and the **Course Discussion** board. I put this introductory information under **Topic 0** so that **Topics 1** through **7** could be reserved for lessons. This further reinforces the sequential feel of the course.

Weekly Format

The **Weekly** format appears almost identical to the Topics format, except that it displays dates for each topic. As of now, Moodle does not automatically enforce these dates. That is, Moodle does not turn weekly sections on and off on the appropriate dates. The site administrator or teacher must do that. Alternatively, you can just allow students to access the weeks in any order.

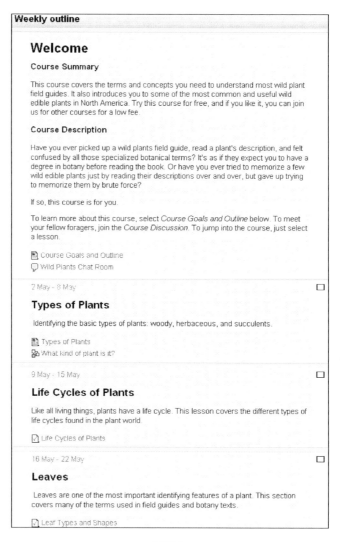

In the example shown here, we've selected the Weekly format, and then hidden each of the future weeks (we'll cover hiding and revealing course weeks/topics later). The only week showing is the current one. We also chose to allow hidden weeks to appear in a collapsed form, instead of making them disappear completely. Students can access this week, and see how many weeks remain in the course. In this arrangement, the site administrator or teacher will need to reveal or "unhide" the weekly topic.

We could also have hidden the future weeks completely, and then put a list of the weeks in the **Welcome** message. It would look like the following example. The result is the same either way—the current and past weeks are available, and students can immediately see how many weeks remain.

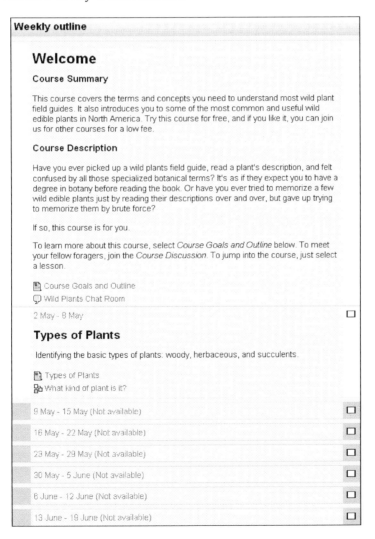

Social Format

The **Social** course format turns the entire course into one discussion forum. Discussion topics are displayed on the course's Home Page, as you see in the following screenshot. Replies to a topic are added and read by clicking on **Discuss this topic**.

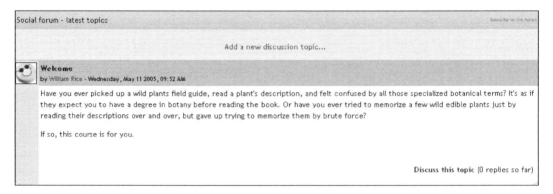

One of the settings available for forums enables you to prevent students from creating new topics, so that they can only post replies to existing topics (later, we will cover the settings that are available in a forum). By default, only the administrator or teacher can create new topics, which appear on the course's Home Page. Students then discuss these topics by adding replies to them. This enables you to control the discussion better, by preventing the creation of many topics and checking the course's Home Page from becoming too big. Later, when we discuss how to edit roles, you will see how you can edit the students roles, so that students can also create new topics.

The Social format is very different from a traditional, sequential course. It lacks the organization and ability to add activities and resources, which you will find in the Topic and Weekly formats. However, because the Social format turns the entire course into a discussion forum; it offers you the chance to put a discussion forum right into the course listings. In this example, we created a course called **Discussion**, selected the Social course format, and put it into the **Free Courses** category. Now, it appears in the course listing on the Front Page:

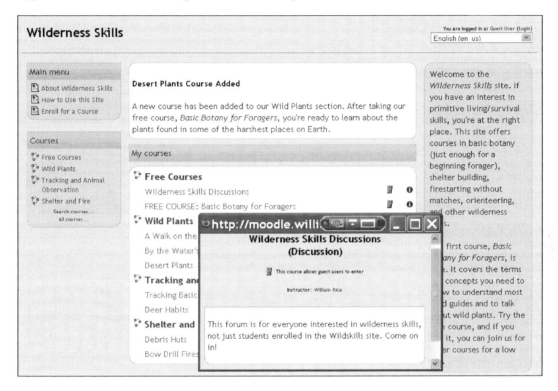

Notice the block listing course categories in the left column. If you choose to display this block, students can always quickly get to the list of courses. As **Wilderness Skills Discussions** is a course, students can always get to the site-wide forum quickly and conveniently.

Instead of using a Social course for the site-wide forum, we could have just added a discussion forum to the site's Front Page, like this:

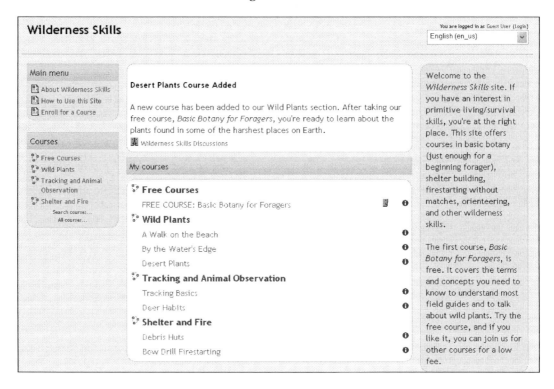

Did you notice **Wilderness Skills Discussions** just beneath the news item, near the top? It's not as prominent as it was when the site-wide forum was a course. Also, as it doesn't appear in the **Free Courses** category, it's not immediately apparent that the forum is free and open to all. Finally, if a student is in a course and wants to get to this forum, the student must navigate back to the Front Page, which is less convenient than clicking on the ever-present **Courses** in the left column. For this site, I thought that making **Wilderness Skills Discussions** into a **Social** course and putting it into the **Free Courses** category is the better option.

Remember that the Front Page is a real course, like any other in your site. Students need to be enrolled in it to participate in any activities on the Front Page, including a forum.

Number of Weeks/Topics

You can change the number of weeks or topics in a course on-the-fly. If you increase the number, then blank weeks/topics are added. If you decrease the number, then weeks/topics are deleted. Or, so it seems.

One of Moodle's quirks is that when you delete some sections in a course and the sections that are deleted contain any material, they're not really deleted. They're just not displayed, even for the teacher. If you increase the number of sections so that those sections are added back to the course, they reappear with their content intact.

Notice that this is different from hiding weeks/topics from students. When you hide sections from students, the teacher can still see those sections. When a section disappears because the number of weeks/topics in the course was reduced, it is hidden from everyone, even the teacher. The only way to bring it back is to increase the number of weeks/topics.

Course Start Date

For a Weekly course, this field sets the starting date shown. It has no effect on the display of Topic or Social courses. Students can enter a course as soon as you display it; the course start date does not shut off or hide a course until the start date. Logs for course activity also begin on this date.

Hidden Sections

The setting, **Number of weeks/topics,** determines how many weeks or topics your course has. Each week or topic is a section. You can hide and reveal any section at will, except for **Topic 0,** which is always displayed. To hide and reveal a section, turn course editing on and click on the open or closed eye icon next to the section. The following example shows a course creator hiding and revealing section **1** of our sample course:

If you select **Hidden sections** as shown in collapsed form under **Hidden Sections,** then the titles or dates of sections that you have hidden will appear grayed out. The user cannot enter that section of the course, but does see that it is there. This is most useful, if you plan to make sections of a course available in sequence, instead of making them available all at once. If you select **Hidden sections** to be completely invisible, then the hidden sections are invisible to students. Course creators and teachers can still see those sections and access the resources and activities in them.

If you choose to make hidden sections completely invisible to students, then there is no real disadvantage to having more sections than you're using. You can keep a section that you're working on hidden, and then reveal it when you're finished. If you want to modify an existing section, you can create a hidden duplicate of the section, work on it, and with a few clicks in a few seconds, hide the old section and reveal the new one.

You can move resources between sections in a course. This makes the hidden section a convenient place to hold resources that you might want to use later, or the ones that you want to archive. For example, if you find a site on the Web that you might want to use in your course later, but you're not sure, you can create a link to the site in a hidden section. If you eventually decide you want to use the site, you can just move that link from the hidden section to one of the sections in use.

News Items to Show

For Weekly and Topics course formats, a News forum automatically appears on the course's Home Page.

As we are looking at the Front Page of the site, the new forum is labeled **Site news**. If we were looking at one of the courses instead, it would be labeled **Latest news**.

The News forum is like any other forum, except that it appears in the Latest news block. Like other forums, the course creator and editor can enable or disable the ability of students to create new topics, and to reply to existing topics.

The Latest news block automatically disappears if you have News items to show set to zero, or if there are no news items (no topics in the forum). Also, the Latest news block can be manually hidden, regardless of this setting, or the number of news items posted.

[The maximum number of news item that the block will show is 10.]

Show Grades and Show Activity Reports

These settings determine whether the grades and activities of each student can be seen by other students in the course. If your **Group mode** is set to **Separate groups**, then the reports are segregated by group. Regardless of this setting, teachers and administrators can always see the grade and activity reports.

For a course that allows guest access, setting this to **Yes** usually doesn't make much sense. Remember that every anonymous, unregistered user enters the course under the name **Guest**. So having a report that shows the grades and activities for Guest is usually not very useful. If you want to track how many people tried a sample course, and what parts of the course they sampled, allow the users to create a free account to use in the fully functioning sample course. Make this easier by not requesting for an email confirmation when the student registers, but by giving an instant approval instead. Now, you can track and study individual usage in the sample course. To keep the anonymous users out of the courses requiring registration or payment, use a Login Page for those courses.

Maximum Upload Size

This setting limits the size of a file that a student can upload into this course. There is also a site-wide limit set under **Site Administration** (see Chapter 3: *Configuring Your Site*). The smaller of the two settings, site-wide or course takes precedence here.

Is This a Metacourse?

A metacourse is a parent course that shares its enrolment with a list of child courses. For example, suppose my site offers several courses on managing email:

- Email Subjects that Make Sense
- Processing Your Email
- The Five-line Email

Perhaps I'd like a place where any student in any of these courses can socialize and share information. In that case, I would create a fourth course, using the Social course format: Email Avalanche Lounge.

The Lounge would be a place where anyone taking an email course can socialize. I would make the Lounge a metacourse, and designate each of the other courses as a child course.

Whenever someone enrols in one of the child courses, they will automatically be enrolled in the Lounge. However, enrolling in a child course does not enrol a student into the other child courses; it only enrols the student into that course and the parent metacourse. If I'm charging a separate tuition for each child course, this is exactly what I want.

However, suppose I'm charging as one tuition for all three courses? In that case, I would like to be able to enrol a student in all the courses all at once. I can do this by enrolling the student into the parent metacourse. In this example, if I enrol a student into the Lounge, then, he or she is automatically enrolled into each child course.

After you make course a metacourse, a link for **Child courses** is added to the **Administration** block on the meta course's Home Page:

Selecting this link takes you to the Assign Courses page where you can make other courses children of the metacourse:

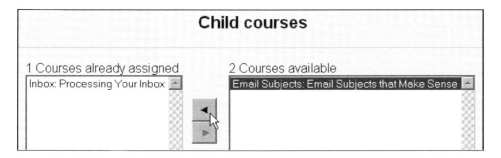

Enrolment Plug-Ins

In Chapter 3 (*Configuring Your Site*), you saw that there are a few interactive enrolment plug-ins available. These are Internal, PayPal, and Authorize.net. This setting enables you to choose the default interactive enrolment plug-in for this course. This setting affects only interactive enrolment plug-ins.

Default Role

When someone is enrolled in the course, this setting determines the role that the person is given in the course. That person's role can however be changed after enrolment.

Course Enrolable

If you are using an interactive enrolment plug-in, setting this to **Yes** enables students to enrol themselves in the course. This setting affects only interactive enrolment plug-ins. For a non-interactive plug-in (like LDAP or Manual enrolment), this setting has no effect.

Enrolment Duration

This field specifies the maximum amount of times a user can be enrolled in the course. After the time is up, the student is automatically unenrolled.

 The maximum time of enrolment is one year.

If you leave this set to **Unlimited**, you must manually unenrol students from this course. When you learn about using **Discussions** (or **Forums**) in your courses, you'll learn that one of the uses for a forum is to send mass emails to everyone enrolled in a course. You can do this by selecting a setting that forces everyone enrolled in a course to subscribe to the forum, and then posting the message to the forum. The message will be broadcast to everyone in the course. Please remember that if you leave all students enrolled permanently, students who are no longer participating in the course will still get these announcements.

Enrolment Expiry Notification

Under this setting, **Notify** determines if the teacher is sent a notice that a student's enrolment is about to expire. **Notify students** determines if the students are also notified. The **Threshold** determines how far ahead of expiration, the notice (s) are sent.

Groups

Group mode applies to activities in this course. Each course can have no or several groups. When set to **No**, all students in the course are considered to be in one big group. When set to **Separate**, all the students in the same group can see each other's work. However, students in different groups, even if they are in the same course, cannot see work from another group. That is, the work done by different groups is kept separate. When set to **Visible**, students are divided into groups, but can still see work from other groups. That is, the work done by one group's students is visible to the other group's students.

You can change this setting for individual activities. For example, suppose you want to run groups through a course separately. However, you may have one project where you may want all students, in all groups, to be able to see each other's work. You can choose **Separate** here, and in that project, override the setting with **Visible**. Now, the groups can see each other's work.

Running Separate Groups Through a Course, Versus Having Separate Courses

Using 'Separate groups' enables you to reuse a course for many groups, while giving the impression to each group that the course is theirs alone. However, this doesn't work well for a Weekly format course, where the weeks are dated. If you start each group on a different date, the weekly dates will become incorrect.

If you're running a Topics format course, you can easily reuse the course by separating your students into groups and running each group individually. Later, you'll see how to assign teachers to a course. You can also assign a teacher to a group, so that each teacher can see only his or her students.

If you run several groups through a course, and those groups are at different points in the course, note that the teacher cannot regulate the flow of students through the course by turning topics off and on. That is, you cannot reveal Topic 1 until the group has finished it, and then reveal Topic 2 until the group has worked through it, and then Topic 3 and so on. If you try this while running several groups who were at different points in the course, you'd be turning off topics that some groups need.

If you really must enforce the order of topics by revealing them one at a time, create a copy of the course for each group. Later, we'll cover duplicating courses.

Force Group Mode

Normally, the course's **Group mode** can be overridden for each activity. When the course creator adds an activity, the teacher can choose a different Group mode from the default set for the course. However, when **Force** is set to **Yes**, all activities are forced to have the same Group mode as the course.

Availability

While you're working on a course, you may want to set this to **This course is not available to students**. This will completely hide your course from the students' view. Teachers and administrators can still see the course, so that you can collaborate on the course content with them.

Enrolment Key

If you use an **Enrolment key**, each student must enter the key the first time that student enters the course. After that, the student can access the course without the key.

If you change the key, students who have already accessed the course under the old key can continue to do so. However, new students will need to enter the new key the first time they enter the course.

You usually supply the Enrolment key using something other than Moodle. For example, if you're charging for courses, you can put the Enrolment key on the payment confirmation page, or in a confirmation email sent to the payer. If you're using Moodle to supplement a live classroom, you can put the Enrolment key on the syllabus. If you're using Moodle within a corporation, you can put the Enrolment key on your intranet where only employees can get it, or even have it physically delivered to their mailboxes.

The Enrolment key enables a student to enter the course even if you have a payment plug-in applied to the course. If you have a mix of paying and non-paying students, you can make paying students use one of the payment plug-ins (Paypal or Authorize.net), and give an Enrolment key to your non-paying students.

Guest Access

Under **Site Administration | Users | Authentication | Guest Login** button, you chose whether to allow guests into your site. If you chose to allow guests, the Front Page shows a **Login as a guest** button:

If you allow guests on your site, you can use the **Guest access** setting to allow guests into a course. This is useful for free courses, or when you want to allow people to look around a course before enrolling. Guests cannot post or submit content to a course. They can only read the course content.

Should You Allow Guest Access?

If the real value of a course is in the interaction, then you have little to lose by allowing guests to look around the course. If the real value is in the content that they read, then allowing guests might be giving too much away. Consider offering a free course instead.

Using Enrolment Key and Guest Access to Market Your Site

One of the best advertisements your site can have is a fully functioning sample course. However, if the only access to a sample course is **Guest access**, then potential students cannot post or submit content. They don't experience an interactive course. Instead of using Guest access for the sample course, consider the following strategy:

Close your site to guest access. Explain on the Front Page, and on the Login Page (you'll learn how to customize that later) that users must create a free account to experience the fully functioning sample course. If you want to make this easier, don't ask for email confirmation when the student registers, but instead give him or her instant approval.

Do not request an Enrolment key for your sample course. However, do ask for an Enrolment key for paid courses. Now that the students in the sample course have user IDs, they can post to forums, take quizzes, enter journal entries, and upload content. Hopefully, experiencing this interaction will get them hooked on your courses. When they pay for a course, you supply them with an Enrolment key.

Cost

This field appears only if, under **Site Administration**, you selected **PayPal** or **Authorize.net** for one of the methods of enrolment. Selecting one of those puts the **Cost** field in the **Course Settings** window.

You can enter a cost here for the specific course. If you enter any amount other than zero, when a student attempts to enrol in this course, the student is taken to a payment page. After the student pays, he or she is enrolled in the course and forwarded to the course's Home Page.

Force Language

Selecting **Do not force** enables a student to select any language on the pull-down list of languages. Remember that the languages on the pull-down list are limited by the setting you choose under **Site Administration | Language | Language Settings | Languages** on the menu. And you must have the Language pack installed for any language that you want to use.

Also remember that only Moodle's standard menus and messages are automatically translated when a student selects a different language. Course material is not translated unless the course creator entered material in another language and used the Multi-language Content filter.

Roles (Words for Teacher and Student)

Moodle inserts your term for teacher or student into its standard messages. For 'Teacher', you can substitute any term such as 'Instructor', 'Leader', and 'Facilitator'. For 'Student', you could use terms such as 'Participant' or 'Member'.

Manually Enrolling Teachers and Students

The easiest way to add teachers and students to a course is to use **Assign roles** under the **Administration** block:

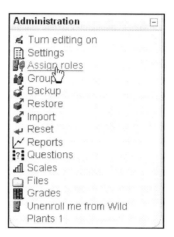

By default, a site administrator or course creator only assigns teachers. Teachers, in turn, enrol students.

1. Selecting this link takes you to the **Assign roles** page:

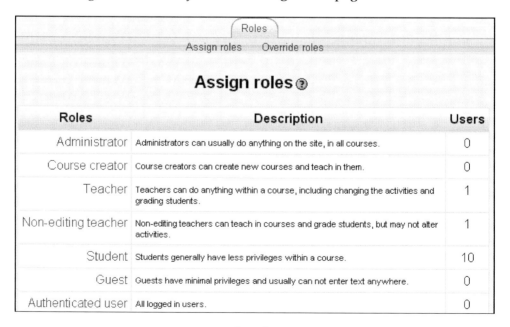

Roles	Description	Users
Administrator	Administrators can usually do anything on the site, in all courses.	0
Course creator	Course creators can create new courses and teach in them.	0
Teacher	Teachers can do anything within a course, including changing the activities and grading students.	1
Non-editing teacher	Non-editing teachers can teach in courses and grade students, but may not alter activities.	1
Student	Students generally have less privileges within a course.	10
Guest	Guests have minimal privileges and usually can not enter text anywhere.	0
Authenticated user	All logged in users.	0

2. Select the role to which you want to assign the user, and you will be taken to the **Assign roles** page:

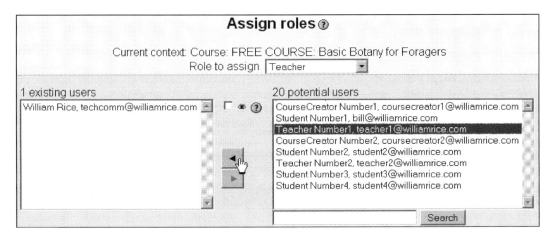

This screen lists all the users in the system. Any authenticated user can be given any role in the course.

Note the drop-down list next to **Role to assign**, at the top of the page. You don't need to leave this page to assign different roles in the course.

1. In the right side column, select the user(s) to whom you want to assign a role. If the user isn't listed, you can use the **Search** box to find the user. To select multiple users, use *Ctrl*+click.

2. Click the left-facing arrow to assign the selected user(s).

Blocks

A block displays information in a small area in one of the side columns. For example, a block can display a **Calendar**, the latest news, or the names of students enrolled in a course. Think of a block as a small applet. A block appears in the left or right column on the site's Front Page or a course's Home Page. A block does not appear when a course's resource or activity is displayed.

While configuring the site, you can choose to display, hide, and position blocks on the site's Front Page. While configuring a course, you can also show, hide, or position blocks on the course's Home Page. The procedure is the same whether working on the site's Front Page or a course's Home Page. We put this section on "*Blocks*" in the chapter on building courses, but it would have also been appropriate in the chapter on *Installing and Configuring Moodle*. We put it here because you will use this feature most often in the context of a course, and the site's Front Page is essentially a course. Before showing how to hide, show and position blocks, let's talk about what each block does, and how you can use each block in your course.

The Standard Blocks

These blocks are available to you in a standard Moodle installation. You can also install additional blocks, available through `http://moodle.org/`.

Activities

The **Activities** block lists all of the types of activities available in the course:

If the type of activity is not used in the course, the link for that type is not presented. When a user clicks on the type of activity, all those kinds of activities for the course are listed. In this example, the user clicked on **Quizzes** in the **Activities** block, and a list of the quizzes in the course is presented. Notice that **Topic 1** has two quizzes, and **Topic 3** has one:

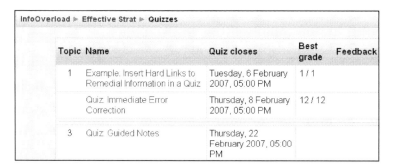

InfoOverload ▶ Effective Strat ▶ Quizzes

Topic	Name	Quiz closes	Best grade	Feedback
1	Example: Insert Hard Links to Remedial Information in a Quiz	Tuesday, 6 February 2007, 05:00 PM	1 / 1	
	Quiz: Immediate Error Correction	Thursday, 8 February 2007, 05:00 PM	12 / 12	
3	Quiz: Guided Notes	Thursday, 22 February 2007, 05:00 PM		

If this block is on the site's Front Page, clicking on a type of activity gives a list for the activities on the Front Page (not for the entire site!).

Administration

The full content of the **Administration** block appears only when someone with administration rights logs into the course. Usually, that's the teacher. For students, only the **Grades** option appears in the **Administration** block.

Turn Editing Off/On

When editing is turned on, you can edit the course material: add, change, remove, or rearrange material. You know that course editing is turned on when you see editing icons next to items on the course page. When editing is turned off, you can see but not change the course material.

If you have the Teacher role in a course, then you can grade assignments, read chat logs, view hidden topics, post to the site News forum, and edit the course material. If you have the Non-editing teacher role, you can do all the above except editing the course material. That is why this link appears only for Teacher and not Non-editing teacher.

Settings

Clicking this link takes you to the **Course Settings** page, which we covered in the section on *The Course Settings Page*. Remember, if your course settings aren't working for you, you can go back and change them. Moodle's courses are online, not written in stone!

Assign roles

A role is a collection of permissions. Each user is assigned one or more roles. For example, the role called **Student** permits a user to enter a course, participate in forums in that course, upload assignments, take quizzes, and other activities that the course creator added to the course. The role Student does not permit a user to grade other student's quizzes, create new activities in the course, or enrol and unenrol other students. However, the role **Teacher** does permit the user to do all those things in the course.

 Enrolling a student in a course is almost always the same thing as assigning that user the Student role in the course.

When you assign a role to a user, you must be aware of where you are in the system. That's because a role is local; it exists in a certain context. For example, if you're on the Front Page of your site, and you assign someone the role of **Teacher**, you have just made that user a Teacher for every single course in your site. The user has the role Teacher at that level or down, or as the Moodle documentation says, for the current context and all 'lower' contexts.

The **Assign roles** page looks the same whether you are accessing it from the site's Front Page, or from a course, or from a single activity inside a course:

Roles	
Assign roles	Override roles

Assign roles ⑦

Roles	Description	Users
Administrator	Administrators can usually do anything on the site, in all courses.	0
Course creator	Course creators can create new courses and teach in them.	0
Teacher	Teachers can do anything within a course, including changing the activities and grading students.	0
Non-editing teacher	Non-editing teachers can teach in courses and grade students, but may not alter activities.	0
Student	Students generally have less privileges within a course.	0
Guest	Guests have minimal privileges and usually can not enter text anywhere.	0

In this section, we are discussing about assigning roles to users in a course. So, if you make someone a Teacher in your course, that person has all the permissions of a Teacher, while on the course's Home Page, and inside all the activities and resources that you add to other course.

We are going to look at roles in more detail, in a separate section. Later, we'll discuss:

- What each role allows a user to do
- How to override permissions in a role
- How and why to create a custom role
- The effect of assigning different roles for different activities in your course

For now, we will look at how to assign a role. Moodle's built-in roles are suitable, as they are, for most situations. But understanding and customizing roles does merit further discussion. It is one of the keys to exactly creating the kind of learning experiences that you want.

To assign a role in your course:

1. From the **Administration** block, select **Assign roles**.
2. On the **Assign roles** page, select the role that you want to assign the user(s).

Assign roles ⓘ

Roles	Description	Users
Administrator	Administrators can usually do anything on the site, in all courses.	0
Course creator	Course creators can create new courses and teach in them.	0
Teacher	Teachers can do anything within a course, including changing the activities and grading students.	0
Non-editing teacher	Non-editing teachers can teach in courses and grade students, but may not alter activities.	0
Student	Students generally have less privileges within a course.	0
Guest	Guests have minimal privileges and usually can not enter text anywhere.	0

3. In the resulting window, double check a few settings before you assign the role. Look at the **Current context**. Are you in the right course? Also check the **Enrolment duration** and **Starting from** settings:

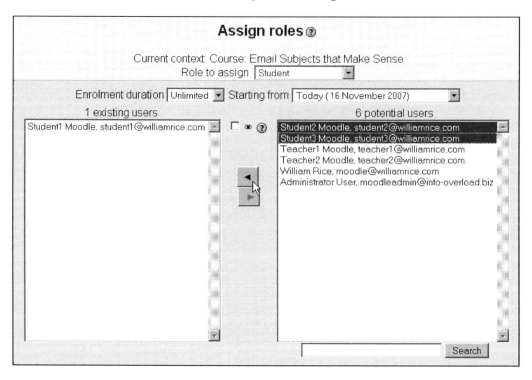

4. If the user you want to assign is not listed on the right, use the **Search** function to find the user. You should be able to search for and select all the users in the system.

5. Select the user (s) that you want to assign, and click the left-facing arrow to add them to the role.

Grades

Grades display grades for the students enrolled. Every activity and assignment that has grades enabled appears in the grading page. When viewing the site's Front Page, this link is not available. If you place a graded activity on the Front Page, like a quiz, and want to see the grades for that activity, you will need to select the activity, and then select another link to view grades for that activity.

Backup and Restore

Backup and **Restore** do exactly what their labels indicate—back up and restore the course. When you back up a Moodle course, the system creates a .zip file containing the parts of the course that you specify. This file is saved on the server, in the course's data directory. You can then download that ZIP file to your local computer and archive it, or upload it to another Moodle site and recreate the course.

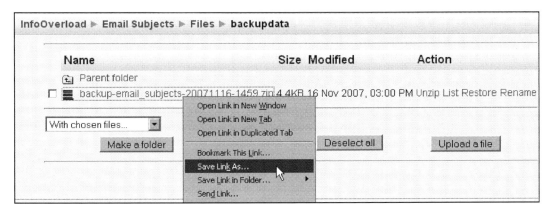

Import and Reset

Import enables the course creator to import the course material from any course that the teacher can access, on the same Moodle site. The teacher can select from the different types of materials: assignments, chats, forums, lessons, and so on. It does not import the enrolment or record of activity from the course.

[If you need to copy a course from another Moodle site, use **Backup** and **Restore**. If you need to copy a course from your own site, use Import.]

Reset enables you to empty a course of user data. It sets the course back to its state at the beginning of the class, before students were enrolled. Before you do this, consider using Backup to back up the course and all its user data. You can archive the backup file (the zip file). That way, you get a fresh course, and you can recover the user data if you need it. **Reports** displays a page that enables you to choose from course and site logs, where you select the information you want to see. Your choices are the same no matter which course you are in. You can display logs for the site, a selected course, a group, a student, a date, an activity, or any combination of these.

Questions brings you to the Edit Questions page, where you can edit, categorize, import, and export quiz questions. Note that this is the question bank for the entire site, not just the course that you are in. This contains all the questions that other teachers have published. Note that unpublished questions are private, and visible only in the course in which they were created.

You won't use this page to create **Quizzes**. We'll cover that in a later section devoted to quizzes. Instead, you use this page to manage the questions in your site. If you haven't created any quizzes in Moodle, this link might not make sense to you yet. Its relevance will be clear when you've read the section on quizzes later.

Scales brings you to the scales page, where you edit and create rating scales. Note that these are scales for the course, and for the entire site. Just as a question can be published to the site, so can a scale be published. If you haven't used any custom rating scales in Moodle, this link might not make sense to you yet. Its relevance will be clear when you've read the section on scales later.

Files enable teachers and course creators to upload files to the course area. These files can then be linked to and used in the course. Course files can be seen by anyone enrolled in the course. While viewing the site's Front Page, this link is labeled **Site Administration | Front page | Site files**. Site files can be seen by any site user.

Grades brings you to the course's gradebook. A later section will cover grades in more detail.

Blog Menu

By default, every Moodle user has a personal blog on the site. Selecting this block puts the blog menu into the course's sidebar:

We'll discuss blogs in more detail, in a later section. For now, this block provides a fast way for a student to get to the student's and other students' blogs. This menu also appears in the user profile page.

Blog Tags

This block displays a list of the blog tags used site-wide. The tags are listed in alphabetical order. The more the blog entries using a tag, the larger the tag:

Calendar

Workshops, assignments, quizzes, and events appear on the **Calendar**:

In the previous screenshot, you can see that the user is pointing to an event that begins on the **May 20**. A pop-up window shows the name of the event (it is obscuring the first two dates, which is common behavior for this block). This quiz was added to the Front Page, so it is a site-wide event.

When the course creator or administrator clicks on one of the four links at the bottom of the Calendar, it disables the display of that type of event. For example, if this Calendar is displayed on a course's Home Page, you might want to disable the display of global events and user events by clicking those links. This would result in the Calendar displaying only events for the course and the groups in the course.

Course/Site Description

The **Course Summary** block displays the course summary from the course's **Settings** page. This is the same course summary that is displayed when someone clicks the ❶ icon in the course listing, as shown in the following figure. You can see the pop-up window that displays the course summary, and the course listing behind the pop-up.

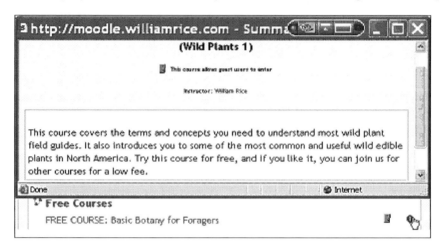

In this situation, the student has not yet entered the course, but is instead looking at the list of courses. To enter a course, a student only needs to click the course name. A student might enter a course without clicking the ❶ icon. In that case, the student proceeds to the course's Home Page, without reading a course summary first. Displaying the Course Summary block on the course's Home Page gives the student another chance to see the course summary before proceeding with the course. In our sample course, it looks like the following:

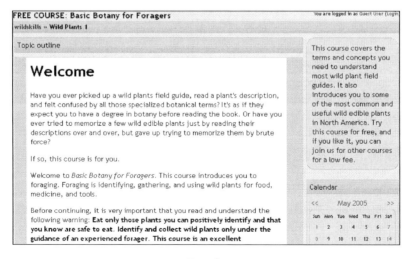

You could copy the course summary into Topic 0, so that it becomes the first item that the students see. Then, the Course Summary block becomes redundant, and you can use that space for something else, as I've done here:

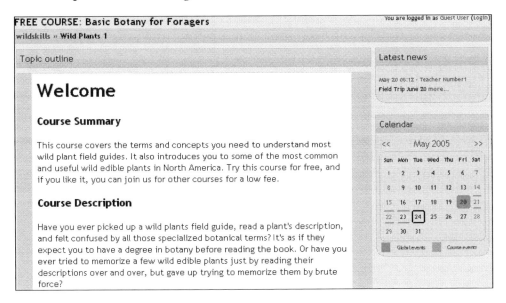

Courses Categories

The **Courses** block displays links to the course categories:

Clicking a link takes the student to the list of courses. This is useful if you want to enable students to move between courses quickly, or want to encourage visitors to explore the site. However, you must balance this flexibility against using the space that the block occupies. Browser space is always precious. If you expect students to enter the course and stay there, then you may want to forgo the display of this block. Instead, just display the list of courses on the Front Page of the site.

HTML

The HTML block creates a block in the sidebar that can hold any HTML (any Web content) that you can put on a web page. Most experienced Web users are accustomed to the content in sidebars being an addition to the main content of a page. For example, we put menus and interesting links in the sidebars in most blogging software. I suggest you keep up with that standard, and use the HTML block to hold the content, which is an interesting addition to the course, but not part of it. For example, you could put an annotated link to another site of interest:

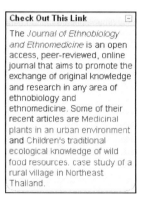

When you edit an HTML block, Moodle gives the same full-featured web page editor that you get while adding a web page to a course:

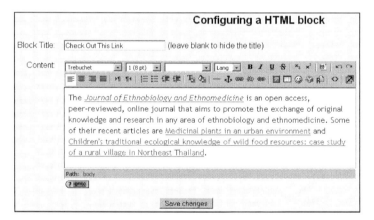

Think of an HTML block as a miniature web page that you can put into the sidebar of your course.

Latest News

When you create a new course, by default, it has a News forum. The **Latest News** block displays the most recent postings from this forum.

Even if the forum is renamed, this block displays the postings. The number of postings displayed in this block is determined by the field, News items to show, in the **Course Settings** page.

Recall that the Front Page of your site is just like another course. If the **Latest News** block is displayed on the site's Front Page, it displays the latest postings from the site-wide News forum, or **Site News**.

If you have set the News forum to email students with new postings, you can be reasonably sure that the students are getting the news, so you might not need to display this block. However, if the news items are of interest to visitors not enrolled in the course, or if the course allows guest access, you may probably want to display this block.

Login

The **Login** block is available only for the site's Front Page. After the user logs in, this block disappears. If a visitor is not logged in, Moodle displays small **Login** links in the upper-right corner and bottom-center of the page. However, the links are not very prominent. The Login block is much more prominent, and contains a message encouraging visitors to sign up for an account.

The main advantage of the Login block over the small Login link is its greater visibility. If you want to make the Login link in the upper-right corner larger, look in Moodle's `index.php` file for this line:

```
$loginstring = "<font size=2><a href=\"$wwwroot/login/index.php\">".
get_string("login")."</a></font>";
```

Change `<font size=2>` to a larger number. This increases the font size of the Login link.

If you want to edit the message displayed in the Login block, look for the string, `startsignup`, in the `moodle.php` file under the language folder, for the string, `startsignup`. In my example site, I'm using the `language en_us`, so I look in the file `/lang/en_us/moodle.php` for this line:

```
$string['startsignup'] = 'Start now by creating a new account!';
```

Main Menu

The **Main menu** block is available only on the site's Front Page. Anything that can be added to a course can be added to this block, as you can see from the pull-down menus labeled **Add a resource...** and **Add an activity....**

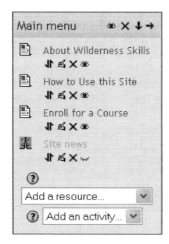

In my example site, I use the Main menu to convey information about the site and how to use the site. I want visitors to be able to get instructions for enrolling and using courses easily. Perhaps I should change the name of this block to **How to Use this Site**. I can do that by looking for the string, startsignup, in the moodle.php file under the language folder, for this line:

```
$string['mainmenu'] = 'Main menu';
```

Change Main menu to whatever you want displayed for the name of the menu.

Mentees

In Moodle, each role has specific permissions that determine what a person with the role can do in the system. For example, the role of Teacher has permissions that enable it to create courses, add material to courses, grade activities, and enrol students. The role Student has permissions that enable it to access a course and complete assignments.

A role is applied to a user in a specific context or place, in the system. For example, if you apply the role Teacher to a user in a course, that user is a Teacher only in that course. If you apply the role Teacher to a user at the Front Page of the site, that user is a Teacher in all courses on the site. We'll discuss roles and permissions in more detail later. For now, let's look at a single permission in a single context.

One of Moodle's permissions allows you to view other users' profiles. The roles Teacher and **Administrator** both have this permission. The following is a screenshot of the **Permissions** page for the Teacher role. You can see that **View user profiles** is one of the permissions given to this role:

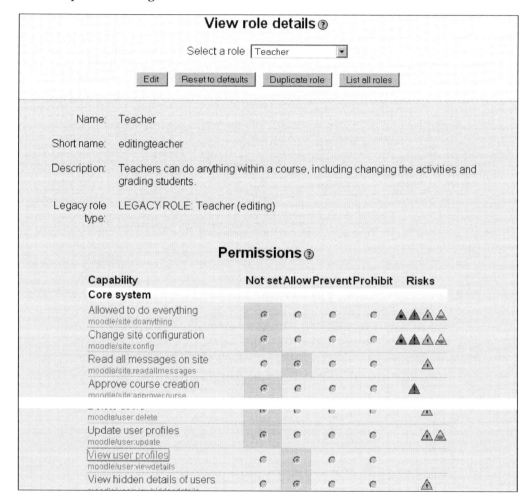

That is, if you're assigned the role Teacher for a course, you can see the user profiles of others who are in that course. If you're assigned the role Teacher from the site's Front Page, you can see the user profiles of every student on the site.

What does this have to do with the mentee block? In Moodle, a user becomes your mentee when you are assigned a role from the user's profile page that can see the user's profile. In the following screenshot, you can see that we are looking at the site-wide courses, and the profile page for **Student Number2**. We got to that page by selecting **Site Administration | Users | Accounts | Browse** list of users, and selecting **Student Number2**:

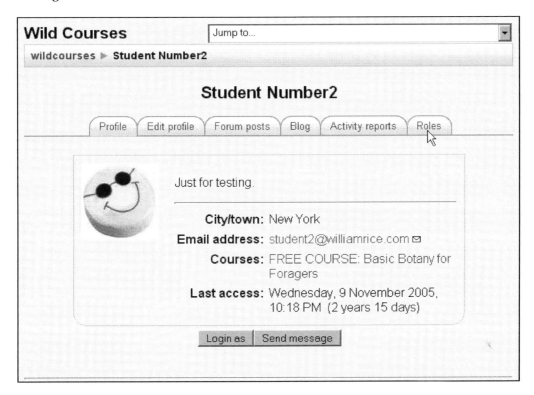

From within the user's profile page (that is, from the context of the user's profile page), We select the **Roles** tab, and then **Assign roles**:

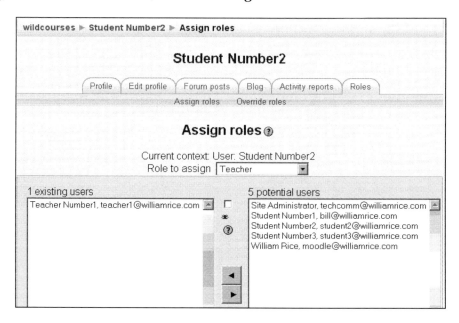

Notice that **Teacher Number1** has been assigned the role of **Teacher**, not from a course page, but from this user's profile page. Now when **Teacher Number1** logs in, the **Mentees block** displays the following:

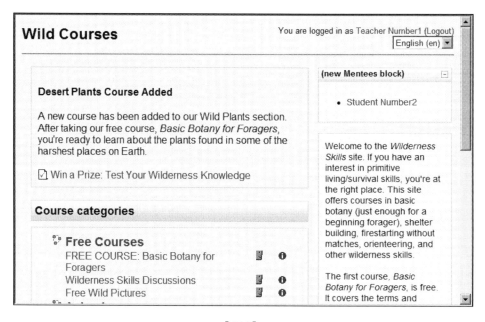

Selecting the mentee brings up that user's profile page. In the following screenshot, the mentor is looking at the activity logs for his mentee:

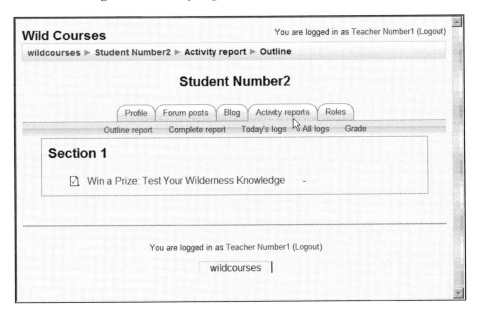

Note the **Student Number2** isn't this teacher's mentee because the student is enrolled in a course that the teacher is teaching. The student is the teacher's mentee because of the role assignment made from the student's profile page.

I had stated earlier that any role which gives you the right to view a user's profile page will make you a mentor, if you're assigned that role from the mentee's profile page. You can create a special Parent role, which has this right. Then you could assign this role to the parent of a child. That parent could see the child's forum postings, blog entries, and activities on the site. For a more detailed discussion, and instructions for doing this, visit `http://docs.moodle.org/en/Parent_role`.

Messages

The **Messages** block provides a shortcut to Moodle's **Messages** center. It displays the latest messages received. You can also access the Messages center from your personal profile. We'll cover the Messages in more detail in a later section, in the chapter on Social Course Material.

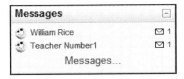

Network Server

This block displays other Moodle sites that share login information with the current site. It is relevant only if you are using Moodle Networking to authenticate users across sites.

Online Users

The **Online Users** block shows who is in the current course at the present time. If it is on the site's Front Page, it shows who is on the site. Every few minutes, the block is updated:

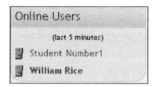

You set the number of minutes under **Site Administration | Blocks | Online Users | Settings**.

People

When the **People** block is added to the site's Front Page, it lists the users enrolled on the site.

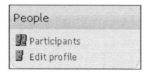

When it's added to a course, it lists the user enrolled in that specific course. If the site or course uses groups, it provides a link to those groups. It also provides a link to the user's profile page, if you're allowed to view it.

In the **Override roles** page, you use the **View participants** setting to determine if a role can see this list.

Quiz Results

The **Quiz Results** block is available only if there is a quiz in the course. It displays the highest and/or the lowest grades achieved on a quiz, within a course. You can anonymize the students' names in the block.

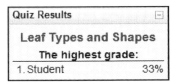

Random Glossary Entry

Moodle's **Random Glossary Entry** block pulls entries from a selected glossary, and displays them in a block. It can pull entries from any glossary that is available from that course. In the following screenshot, the glossary that the block is using is a class directory, where each student is an entry in the glossary:

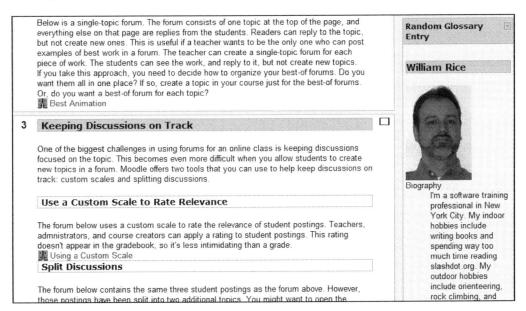

Even though the name is Random Glossary Entry block, you can control the order in which entries are pulled from the glossary, and how often the block displays a new entry. For example, in the following screenshot, the **Random Glossary Entry** block is set to display each entry in order, and to change each day:

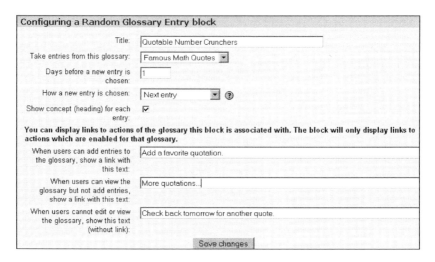

Here are some ideas for using the Random Glossary Entry block for something other than a glossary:

- Highlights from the work that past students in a class had submitted. If the class is working on a long-term project, create a glossary that contains the best work submitted by the previous classes who hadcompleted that project. Display the glossary while the current class is working on that project.

- Inspirational or informative quotes related to the field of study.

- If you're teaching in a corporate setting, consider putting rules and procedures into their own glossaries. You could create a separate glossary for each type of rule, or procedure (for example, a Human Resources Policies glossary, a Purchase Order glossary, and so on). Then, display random entries from these glossaries in the appropriate courses.

- Create a glossary with past exam questions and their answers. Students can use this as another resource to prepare for your exams.

- Funny anecdotes related to the field of study.

- Common mistakes and their corrections, for example, how to spot software bugs, or common foreign language grammar errors.

Recent Activity

When the **Recent activity** block is added to a course's Home Page, it lists all of the student and teacher activity in that course since the user's last login. The link for **Full report of recent activity** displays a page that enables you to run reports on course activity.

When added to the site's Front Page, it lists all of the student and teacher activity on the Front Page, but not in the individual courses, since the user's last login. If someone is logged in as a Guest user, this block displays activity since the last time that Guest logged in. If Guest users are constantly coming to your site, this block may be of limited use to them. One strategy is to omit this block from the site's Front Page, so that anonymous users don't see it, and add it only to courses that require users to authenticate.

Remote RSS Feeds

When the **Remote RSS Feeds** block is added to a course, the course creator chooses or creates RSS feeds to display in that block.

The next example shows an RSS feed from an adventure racing site. This feed is the result of the configuration shown in the following screenshot:

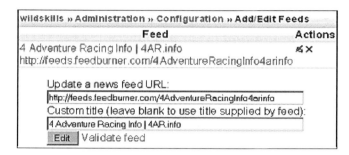

A feed can be added by the site administrator, and then selected by the course creator for use in an RSS block, or when the course creator adds the RSS block, he or she can add a feed at that time. The new feed then becomes available to all other course creators, for use in all other courses. This is similar to the way quiz questions work. All quiz questions, no matter who created them, are available to all course creators for use in their courses.

Search Forums

The **Search** block provides a search function for forums. It does not search other types of activities or resources. When this block is added to the site's Front Page, it searches only the forums on the Front Page.

When it's added to a course's Home Page, it searches only the forums in that course. In Chapter 8, the *Custom Strings* section discusses how to customize Moodle's display strings, including the name of this box. You might want to change the name to **Search forums** to avoid giving the impression that it searches all content.

This block is different from the Search courses field that automatically appears on the site's Front Page. The Search courses field searches course names and descriptions, not forums.

Section Links

The **Topics** block displays links to the numbered topics or weeks in a course. Clicking a link advances the page to that topic. This block does not display the names of the topics. If you want to display links to the topics that show their names, you'll need to create those links yourself. The following screenshot shows an example of this:

Welcome

Course Summary

This course covers the terms and concepts you need to understand most wild plant field guides. It also introduces you to some of the most common and useful wild edible plants in North America. Try this course for free, and if you like it, you can join us for other courses for a low fee.

Course Description

Have you ever picked up a wild plants field guide, read a plant's description, and felt confused by all those specialized botanical terms? It's as if they expect you to have a degree in botany before reading the book. Or have you ever tried to memorize a few wild edible plants just by reading their descriptions over and over, but gave up trying to memorize them by brute force?

If so, this course is for you.

Welcome to *Basic Botany for Foragers*. This course introduces you to foraging. Foraging is identifying, gathering, and using wild plants for food, medicine, and tools.

Before continuing, it is very important that you read and understand the following warning: **Eat only those plants you can positively identify and that you know are safe to eat. Identify and collect wild plants only under the guidance of an experienced forager. This course is an excellent preparation for learning to identify plants under the guidance of an expert, but is not a substitute. You should learn under someone qualified and experienced in the collection of wild plants in your area. Common sense dictates that if you have any doubt as to a plant's safety, don't eat it.**

To learn more about this course, select *Course Goals and Outline* below. To meet your fellow foragers, join the *Course Discussion*. To jump into the course, just select a lesson.

Jump to a Topic

Types of Plants

Life Cycles of Plants

Leaves

Flowers

Roots

Other Identifying Features

Habitats

Here's one way to create those links:

1. While viewing the Home Page of the course, you will see the web address of the course in the address bar of your browser. In my example, it was `http://moodle.williamrice.com/course/view.php?id=4`. Select and copy this address.

2. In Topic 0, add a label. Do this by clicking the **Add a resource** drop-down menu, and selecting **Insert a label**.

3. You should see a word processor-like window, where you enter the text of the label. In my example, I added a horizontal rule and then typed **Jump to a Topic**. You can add any text you want to introduce these links.

4. Type the name of the first topic, such as **Types of Plants**.

5. Select the name of the topic by dragging across it.

6. Click the 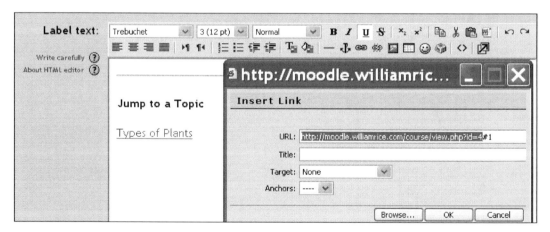 button to create the link. You should see a pop-up window where you enter the link.

7. In the **Insert Link** pop-up window, paste the link that you copied before. This is the link to the course's Home Page. Immediately after the link, type the hash sign (#) and the number of the topic or week. In the example that follows, I have highlighted the link to the course, which I had copied earlier. I then type **#1** to link to the first topic:

8. Repeat steps 4 through 7 for each topic.

9. When you're finished in the **Edit label** window, select the **Save changes** button to return to your course's Home Page. You will see the links in Topic 0.

Upcoming Events

The **Upcoming Events** block is an extension of the Calendar block. It gets event information from your calendar. By default, the Upcoming Events block displays 10 events; the maximum is 20. It looks ahead a default of 21 days; the maximum is 200. If the upcoming events are more than the maximum chosen for this bloc, the most distant events will not be shown.

Summary

Just as Moodle enables students to explore courses in a nonlinear fashion, it also allows you to build courses in a flexible, nonlinear method. After you fill out the Course settings page, the order in which you add material and features to your course is up to you. Don't get stuck if you don't know where to begin. For example, if you're unsure whether to use a Weekly or Topics format, just pick one and start adding material. If the course content begins to suggest a different type of course format, you can change the format later.

If your course is still under development when it's time to go live, use hidden sections to hide the unfinished portions. You can reveal them as you complete them.

While deciding which blocks to display, consider the comfort level of your students. If they're experienced Web surfers, they may be comfortable with a full complement of blocks displaying information about the course. Experienced web surfers are adept at ignoring information they don't need (when was the last time you paid attention to a banner ad on the Web?). If your students are new computer users, they may assume that the presence of a block means that it requires their attention or interaction. And remember that you can turn blocks off and on as needed.

In general, make your best guesses when you first create a course, and don't let uncertainties about any of those settings stop you. Continue with the next chapter, *Adding Static Course Material*. As you add static, interactive, and social materials in the forthcoming chapters, you can revisit the course structure and settings in this chapter and change them as needed.

Adding Static Course Material

5

Static course materials are resources that students read but don't interact with, such as web pages, graphics, and Adobe Acrobat documents. This chapter teaches you how to add those resources to a course, and how to make best use of them.

What Kinds of Static Course Material Can Be Added?

Static course material consists of resources that the student reads, but doesn't interact with. It is added from the **Add a resource...** drop-down menu. Using this menu, you can create:

- Text pages
- Web pages
- Links to anything on the Web
- A view into one of the course's directories
- A label that displays any text or image
- Multimedia files

Links to these resources appear where you add the resource. The one exception is the label, which doesn't display a link. Instead, it displays the actual text or image that you put into the label.

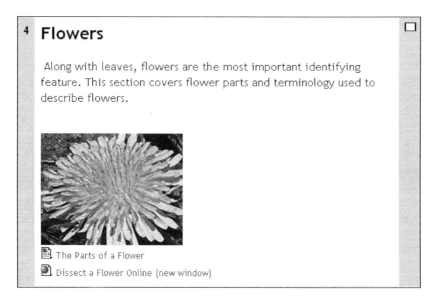

The example shown here is **Topic 4** of our sample course, **Flowers**. The descriptive text immediately below **Flowers** is the topic summary, which was entered when the topic was created.

Below that, you can see a picture of a *Dandelion* flower. This picture was added as a label. The label can contain any text or picture that you want. However, you probably want to keep your labels small so that they don't dominate the course's Home Page. A single picture, a decorative divider, or a heading are the most common uses for a label.

Below the picture you can see a link to a web page created in Moodle, **The Parts of a Flower.** The *page* icon indicates that this page is a part of your Moodle site. Below that you can see a link to a web page that is outside of the Moodle site, **Dissect a Flower Online**. The *world* icon indicates that this page is not a part of your Moodle site. I indicate that link opens a new window by adding **new window** to its name.

The Resource Summary

When you create a new resource, you give it a **Name** as shown. Unless it's a label, you also give it a **Summary**. The other fields in the new resource window may change, but the name is always present, and the summary is present for all except labels.

The name appears as the link to the resource. The summary appears only when the resource is shown in a list. To list the resources in a course, the student selects **Resources** from the **Activities** block.

This means that if you want students to be able to list the resources in a course, you must display the **Activities** block.

When the student selects **Resources**, the **Resources** window appears, listing the resources in that course. In the next example, notice that the **Topic** number, **Name**, and **Summary** are shown for each resource:

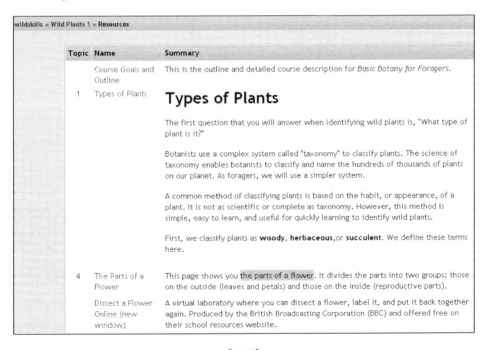

The items listed by the **Activities** block do not appear in context. If you are requiring students to proceed through a course in sequence, you may want to hide this block. If you want to encourage exploration in the course, it is a good block to display.

Files

Moodle enables anyone with course creator privileges to upload files to the site, or to an individual course. This is done with the **Files** link in the **Administration** block. The **Files** link appears only for users with course creator privileges, such as course creators and teachers. The ability to add files is hidden from Non-Editing teachers. And of course, students will never see the **Administration** block.

Note that uploading a file is different from uploading an assignment. When a course creator uploads a file, it is with the intention that the file will be used in the course. When a student uploads an assignment, it is with the intention that it will be graded by the teacher.

Why Upload Files?

When a file is added from a course's Home Page, links to the file can be easily created within that course. When a file is added from the site's Front Page, a course creator can easily create links to that file from anywhere on the Front Page. (Remember that the site's Front Page is really just another course.) This ease of creating links is one of the advantages to uploading files to Moodle, instead of linking to them on the Web.

Another advantage to using uploaded files is that Moodle enables you to easily rename and move the files. Notice the **Rename** links in the screenshot overleaf. Also, I can select any of these files, and from the **With chosen files** drop-down list, move them to any other course in Moodle.

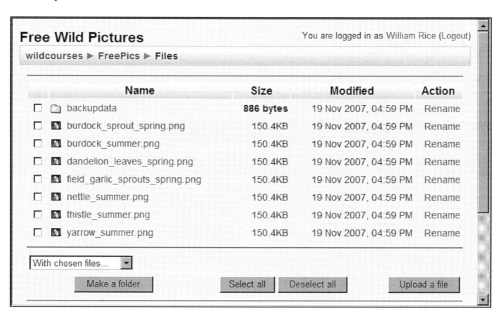

In the example, I've added files to the course called **FreePics**. The navigation links across the top of the page indicate that I started at the site's Front Page (**wildcourses**), selected the course **FreePics**, and then from the **Administration** block selected **Files**. I then uploaded seven image files.

File Types

You can upload any kind of file into Moodle. Remember that the file will be accessed by the user's web browser, so consider whether the user's web browser can open the file. Images, MP3 files, Flash files, Adobe Acrobat documents, and other file types commonly found on the Web are a safe bet for uploaded files.

You may want to upload a file that cannot be opened by a web browser. In that case, the file must be opened by an application on the user's computer. For example, if you're teaching a course on architecture, you might add AutoCAD drawings to your course. The students' browsers cannot open AutoCAD files. Instead, when the student clicks on the file, their computer will attempt to download and open the file with the correct application. In the following example, the student has selected a Microsoft Word file:

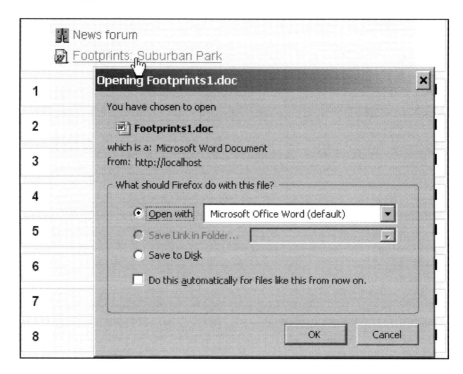

Linking to Uploaded Files

Linking to an uploaded file is easy. From anywhere in the course, select the **Add a resource...** drop-down menu, and then select **Link to a file or web site**:

The Editing Resource window appears as follows:

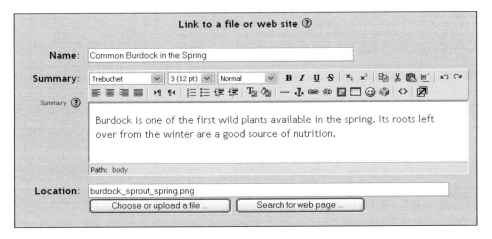

The following is what you need to do:

1. Enter a **Name** for the link. This is the text that will be displayed for the user.

2. The **Summary** will be displayed when this link appears in a list of resources.

3. If you were linking to a file on the Web, you would enter the URL (web address) into the **Location** field. To link to an uploaded file, select the **Choose or upload a file...** button.

4. The **Files** window appears. Next to the file you want to link to, select **Choose**:

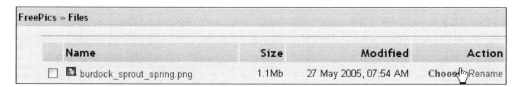

5. Click the **Save changes** button.

6. The file is displayed in its own window, as the students will see it. You are now seeing what students will see when they click on the link to the file.

To return to the course, select the course name from the navigation bar. Back at the course, you will see the link you created.

When to Use Uploaded Files

Upload files into Moodle when:

- You want a file to be used at several places in the course. Creating links to an uploaded file is easy, and if you change the file, it will be updated in all places in the course.

- You need to ensure that you have control over the file. Linking to a file on another web page outside of Moodle puts the author of that web page in control of the content. Bringing the file into Moodle ensures that the file will always be available to you.

- You're confident that your server can handle the load of serving the file to your users.

- You might want to use the file in another course. Moodle's file window enables you to copy and move files between courses.

- You are certain that you have the legal and moral right to use the file in your course.

Text Page

Under the **Add a resource...** drop-down menu, use **Compose a text page** to add a text page to any course, including the site's Front Page. A link then appears to the page that you have created. The page is stored in Moodle's database.

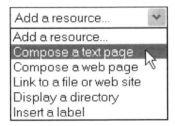

The name 'text page' implies an unformatted, text-only page. However, Moodle's text pages can take several formats. Each of these formats offers some advantages and disadvantages.

Choosing a Format for a Text Page

When you edit a text page, Moodle gives you a drop-down list where you select the format for that page:

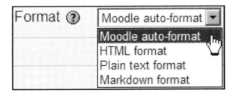

The online help explains what each format is, and how to use it. This section expands on that, and covers when to use each of the text page formats:

- Moodle auto-format

- HTML format

- Plain text format

- Markdown format

There are four types of formats you can use while creating a new text page. Each offers some advantages and disadvantages. They all offer a limited set of formatting commands. If you need more formatting options than what is offered by these four, add a web page instead of a text page.

Moodle Auto-Format—for Quick, Limited Formatting

The Moodle auto-format offers a simple way to add limited formatting to a text page. It automatically turns codes into *smilies*, such as turning :-) into 😊. It turns any word starting with www or http:// into a clickable link. It also enables you to add some HTML tags for text formatting, such as bold, underline, and font size.

You can see that its only real advantage over plain text is a few formatting commands. However, you will need to learn the HTML tags for these formats. If you're going to learn these HTML commands, you may as well add an HTML (web) page instead. Then later, when you learn more than these simple HTML commands, you can return to the web page and add to it.

HTML Format—for HTML Pages Composed Offline

If you were adding a web page to your course instead of a text page, you would see the Richtext HTML editor. This editor provides a word-processor interface, and enables you to edit web pages in a WYSIWYG (What You See Is What You Get) editor, while producing normal HTML code:

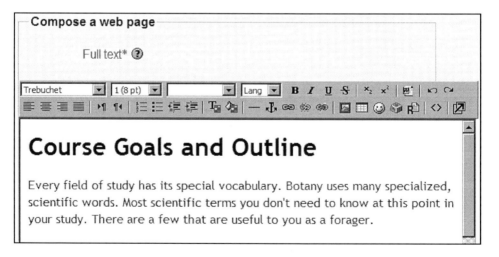

If you create a text page, and select HTML format, you don't get the Richtext HTML editor. Instead, you get a plain text interface, where you edit the HTML code:

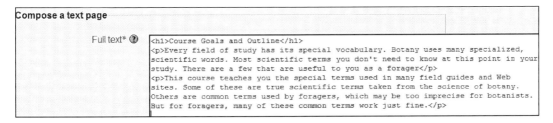

The question is: If you're going to create an HTML page, why not use the friendlier, WYSIWYG Richtext editor? If you've created the HTML code in another program, like Nvu, Dreamweaver, or FrontPage, you will probably switch to HTML view ('code view') to copy the code out of your HTML editor, and paste it into the Moodle page. This is a little easier and simpler using a text page in HTML format.

Plain Text Format—for Program Listings

This is true, unformatted, plain text. It displays your text exactly as you type it. A plain text page is especially useful for presenting a large block of computer code exactly as you write it. Computer code and HTML code are not translated at all.

For example, suppose you write the following passage in Moodle auto-format:

```
HTML supports three kinds of lists. The first kind is a bulleted list,
often called an unordered list. It uses the <ul> and <li> tags, for
instance:
<ul>
  <li>the first list item</li>
  <li>the second list item</li>
  <li>the third list item</li>
</ul>
```

In auto-format, Moodle will try to translate this code instead of displaying it exactly as you typed. The page will look like the following:

HTML supports three kinds of lists. The first kind is a bulletted list, often called an unordered list. It uses the

and
- tags, for instance:
    - the first list item
    - the second list item
    - the third list item

Last modified: Thursday, 29 November 2007, 10:33 PM

Obviously, this page displayed with errors. But if you specify that the page is plain text format, it displays the code properly:

```
HTML supports three kinds of lists. The first kind is a bulletted list,
often called an unordered list. It uses the <ul> and <li> tags, for
instance:
<ul>
  <li>the first list item</li>
  <li>the second list item</li>
  <li>the third list item</li>
</ul>
```

Last modified: Thursday, 29 November 2007, 10:41 PM

Markdown Format—Intuitive, Fast Formatting

If you don't already know wiki formatting commands, and you just want to quickly create formatted text pages, Markdown format offers a good alternative. Its set of commands is larger than the Moodle auto-format, but smaller than Wiki or HTML. It's also intuitive. Writing in Markdown format is meant to be fast and simple. For example, the following is a fourth-level heading followed by a list in Markdown format:

```
####Trees
* A single trunk, which might fork above ground.
* Trunk is 3 or more inches in diameter.
* Over 16 feet tall, under favorable growing conditions.
```

It gets displayed like this:

> **Trees**
>
> - A single trunk, which might fork above ground.
> - Trunk is 3 or more inches in diameter.
> - Over 16 feet tall, under favorable growing conditions.

If you're an experienced touch typist, and you prefer to do your formatting from the keyboard without reaching for the mouse (there are still some of us who remember WordPerfect's formatting codes with fondness), Markdown format is for you.

Window Settings

The bottom of the text editing page displays window settings. By default, the text page is displayed in the top frame of the Moodle window. You can use the window settings to make the page display in its own window, and to control the look and size of that window.

When to Open Pages in a New Window

If you open the page in its own window, and this is not the usual behavior for resources on your site, the student who opens this page might not realize that he or she has opened a new window. Adding **new window** to the end of the page's name can avoid this confusion. For example, I might name my page like this:

If your pages usually open in a new window, or if you resize the new window so that it does not obscure the original Moodle site beneath it, this isn't necessary. Just make sure that the behavior the users sees when opening a new text page is consistent across your site.

Web Page

You can compose web pages in Moodle, and also copy-and-paste HTML code from other web pages into Moodle. Web pages give you more options than any of the text document types covered in this chapter, including the ability to include Java and other active code on the page. To start creating a web page, from the **Add a resource...** drop-down menu, choose the option **Compose a web page**.

You do not need to learn HTML to create web pages in Moodle. When you compose a web page, Moodle gives you a WYSIWYG word processor on screen. This word processor gives you basic formatting icons in the toolbar. Pointing to any icon displays a pop-up telling you the name of the command:

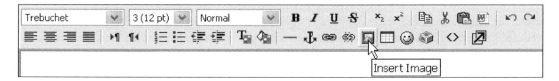

You can see from the icons on the toolbar that Moodle's built-in editor enables you to:

- Select the font face and size
- Tag paragraphs as Normal, Heading, Preformatted, and Address
- Create superscripts and subscripts
- Align paragraphs
- Increase/decrease paragraph spacing
- Create bulleted and numbered lists
- Indent and outdent paragraphs
- Insert horizontal lines
- Create anchors on the page
- Link to other web resources and anchors on this page
- Insert images
- Create tables
- Insert smilies
- Insert special characters

Advantages of Using HTML View When Editing Web Pages

This is quite a list of formatting commands. However, there are many more things that you can do in HTML that cannot be done through these icons. To do more, you must view and edit the raw HTML code. To access the HTML code, click the **View HTML** button <>. The following two screenshots show the same page in WYSIWYG and HTML view:

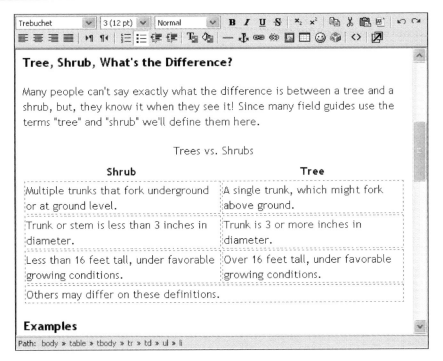

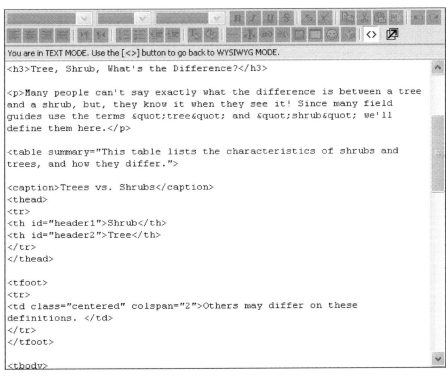

Notice that in the HTML code I've included features in the table that are not available in Moodle's (or most programs') WYSIWYG HTML editor. The table has a summary, caption, column IDs assigned to the headers, and footer. To add these more advanced HTML features, I had to go into HTML view.

Composing in an HTML Editor and Uploading to Moodle

For long or complex HTML pages, or just for your own comfort, you might want to compose your web page in an HTML editor like **DreamWeaver** or **FrontPage**. This is especially true if you want to take advantage of these editors' ability to insert JavaScript timing, and other advanced features into your web page. How then do you get that page into your Moodle course? You can copy-and-paste the HTML code from your web page editor into the Moodle page editing window. To do this you would:

- Select HTML view in your web page editor. For example, in DreamWeaver you would select **View | Code**, and in FrontPage you would select **View | Reveal Codes**.
- Select the HTML code in your web page, between the two body tags. That is, drag from just after the `<body>` tag near the top, to just before the `</body>` tag at the end. Copy the code with **Edit | Copy** or pressing *Ctrl+C*.
- Switch over to Moodle, and create the new web page.
- Show the HTML code by clicking the `<>` icon.
- Paste the code by pressing *Ctrl+V*.

A second method is to publish your web page to someplace outside of Moodle, and create a link to it from your course.

Learn More about HTML

To learn more about HTML code, you can start with the organization responsible for defining the standards. The World Wide Web Consortium maintains the complete standards for HTML online, at `http://www.w3.org/TR/html4`. It maintains a basic tutorial at `http://www.w3.org/MarkUp/Guide/`. Everything covered in this basic guide can be done using the WYSIWYG tools in Moodle. The advanced HTML guide at `http://www.w3.org/MarkUp/Guide/Advanced.html` covers some features that you would need to go into HTML view to add. For example:

- Flowing text around images
- Defining clickable regions within images
- Using roll-overs

Link

On the Moodle site, you can show other content from anywhere on the Web by using a link. You can also link to files that you've uploaded into your course. By default, this content appears in a frame within your course. You can also choose to display it in a new window.

When using content from outside sites, you need to consider the legality and reliability of using the link. Is it legal to display the material within a window on your Moodle site? Will the material still be there when your course is running? In this example, I've linked to an online resource from the BBC, which is a fairly reliable source:

Remember that the bottom of the window displays Window Settings, so you can choose to display this resource in its own window. You can also set the size of the window. You may want to make it appear in a smaller window so that it does not completely obscure the window with your Moodle site. This will make it clearer to the student that he or she has opened a new window.

When to Use a Link Versus a Web Page

In the previous screenshot, you see the link **Summary** entered by the course creator. The student will not see this summary when clicking on the link. Instead, the student is taken directly to the location of the link. The student will only see the summary after selecting **Resources** from the **Activities** block. Then, all of the web pages, text pages, and links in the course will be listed with their summaries. The link will be listed like this:

Dissect a Flower Online (new window)	A virtual laboratory where you can dissect a flower, label it, and put it back together again. Produced by the British Broadcasting Corporation (BBC) and offered free on their school resources website.

If you want the student to always see a description of the link before proceeding to the resource, create a web page and put the link on the page. For example, I added a web page using the **Add a resource...** drop-down menu and selecting **Compose a web page**. I filled out the edit web page window like the following:

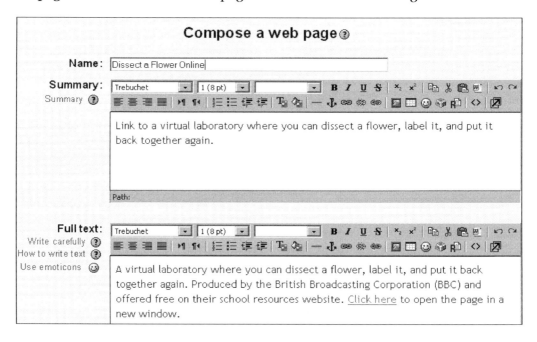

The result on the course's Home Page is a link to this web page:

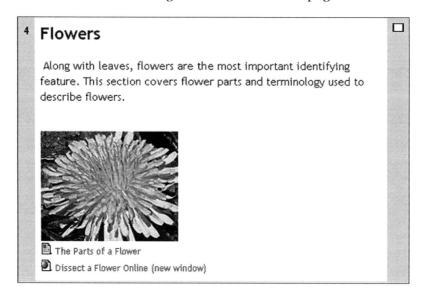

The resulting web page looks like the following:

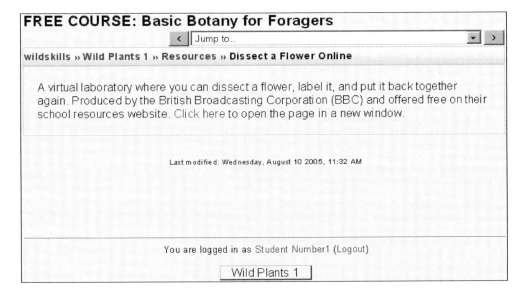

Directory

Adding a directory to a course is another way to display the files that you have uploaded to a course. Under the subsection **Files**, you saw that in the same window where you upload files to a course you can create folders:

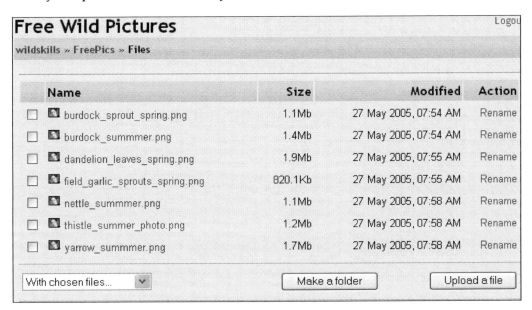

When you add a directory to a course, you're adding a link to the main files area or to one of the folders that you created. The directory resource creates a link on the course's Home Page, with a folder icon, like this:

When a student clicks the directory, the contents are displayed:

Why Use a Directory?

The other way to give students access to uploaded files is by creating a link to each individual file. For creating a link to several files, adding a directory is easier and simpler. If students need to download several files for a course, you can upload the files, put those files into a folder, and then create a directory to give them access to all the files. Also, a directory provides a level of organization for the files you supply to the student.

Label

Topic and weekly courses are organized into sections. Labels can help you organize material within a section, giving you another level of organization. A label can have any amount of text, images, or other content that you can put on a web page. It is essentially an HTML document. However, just because a label can handle any HTML content, you don't want to go overboard and create entire web pages in a label. A label's main purpose is to add organization to a course's Home Page. In the next screenshot, you can see that the **Wild Plants** course uses labels to organize course resources. The horizontal lines and **Jump to a Topic**, **Group Activities**, and **Before You Start the Course: Do These Activities** headlines are labels:

In our example, the course creators used text labels to organize the course content. A label can also hold a graphic. Adding a graphic to the beginning of each topic is a good way to add visual interest to a course. Also, a label can consist of a large amount of text. You can introduce activities with a paragraph-long label. In the preceding screenshot, perhaps a sentence explaining each activity would help the student understand the course flow. That can be added with a label. Make creative use of labels for organization, interest, and information.

Adding Multimedia (Audio and Video)

You can add audio and video to your course in two ways. One is to embed the multimedia in a web page. That is, you create a web page as normal; and just as you would place a graphic on that page, you place an audio or video file instead. Embedding a file means placing it inline, much like how an image is placed on a page. Just as you can introduce a graphic with some text on the page, you can introduce the multimedia file with some text on the page where the file is embedded.

The embedded file can be the one that you have uploaded to Moodle. That is, it can be a site file or course file. Or, the embedded file can be on another website. For example, it could be a video from YouTube. Either way, the file plays on the page in which it is embedded. Here's an example of an embedded movie being played on a Moodle web page:

The other way is to link to the multimedia file. Instead of putting the file on a web page, you are linking to it directly. Your web browser will decide what kind of player to use to play the file. The file can be on your Moodle site, or another website. Either way, the file exists elsewhere and you are giving the user a link to it. When the user clicks that link, the user's browser launches the correct plug-in for playing that kind of file, as in the following screenshot:

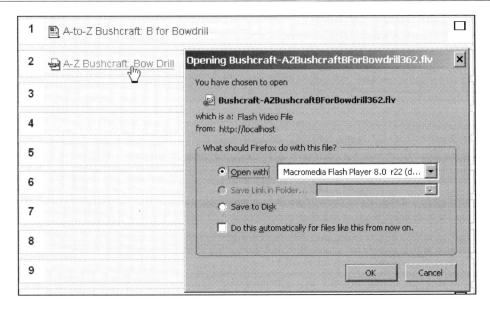

Notice that the first link on this page is for a web page. You can determine this because of the web page icon — 📄. The second link on this page is a direct link to the multimedia. The icon for that link tells us the target is a video file — 🎞️.

In the pop-up window, notice that the location of the file is `http://localhost`. That is, the file is on the same server as Moodle. It has been uploaded to the Moodle site, and is now a 'site file'. You can link to files that have been uploaded to your Moodle site, or to files that exist on other sites.

In the sections that follow, we'll cover how to embed and how to link multimedia files.

Embedding Multimedia

To embed multimedia in a web page, you must edit the page's HTML code. To access the HTML code for a web page, click the **View HTML** button ◇:

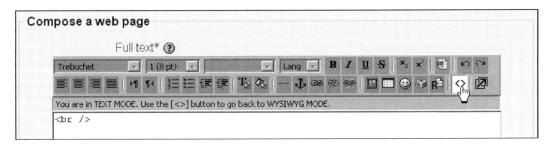

After you are in the HTML view mode, switch over to the site containing the multimedia. Copy the embed code from the video site. In the following example, clicking an icon in the lower-right corner brings up a pop-up widow containing the code to embed. I am copying the code from that window:

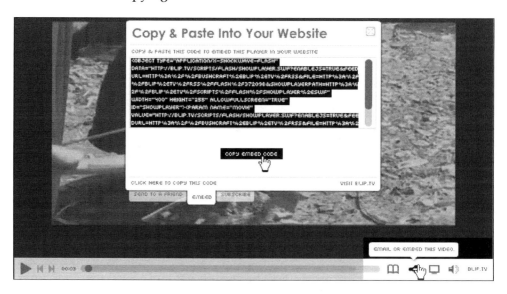

Then, paste the embed code into the web page:

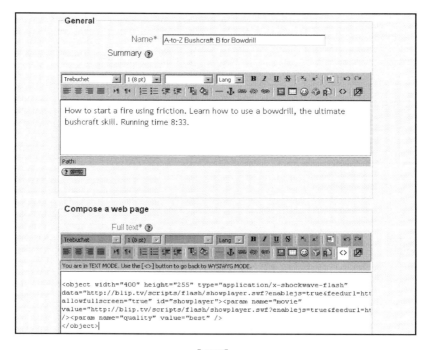

The result is the page shown at the beginning of this section.

Allowing Non-Trusted Users to Embed Items

Notice that the code starts and ends with the `<object>` tag. In Moodle, the default settings allow only trusted users to embed items with the `<object>` or `<embed>` tags. A trusted user is a site **Administrator**, **Course creator**, or **Teacher**. Other users are not permitted to embed objects with these tags. For example, if you require a student to upload a web page as part of an assignment, and that web page contains an `<object>` or `<embed>` tag, the tag will be removed. You can control this setting on the **Site administration | Security | Site policies** page. The setting **Allow EMBED and OBJECT tags** gives permission to non-trusted users to use these tags:

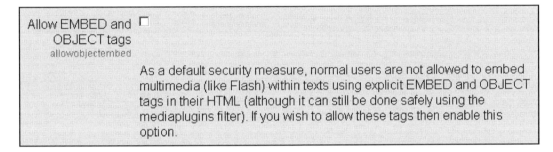

Note that a site administrator, course creator, or teacher can always use these tags. This setting affects only other users.

Uploading and Linking to Multimedia Files

In one of the screenshots at the beginning of this section, you saw a link to a multimedia file. That file was uploaded to the course. Uploading and linking to files is covered in the *Files* section near the beginning of this chapter. However, multimedia can present a special challenge because of the size of the files. In Chapter 2, (*Configuring Your Site*), the section *Maximum Uploaded File Size* deals with this issue. You can change the maximum file size that you can upload. However, changing this requires that you have access to the `.ini` files (the configuration files) for PHP and Apache on your server. If you don't have access to these files, you can't increase the size of uploaded files beyond what your hosting service permits. Instead, you will need to use a work-around.

Workaround for Uploading Large Files

In Moodle, every course has an ID number. When you select a course, the text of the link tells you that course's ID number. In the following example, you can see that the pointer is hovering over the link to the **Bow Drill Firestarting** course. The status bar at the bottom of the window tells us that this course's ID number is **4**:

Also recall that when you upload files to a course, those files are placed in the Moodle data directory, in the course's subdirectory. In our example, files uploaded to the **Bow Drill Firestarting** course are stored in `/moodledata/4`:

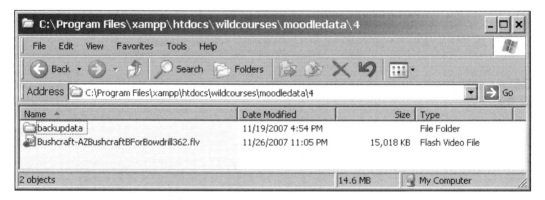

When you upload a file into the course using **Administration | Files**, that file is placed into the course's data directory:

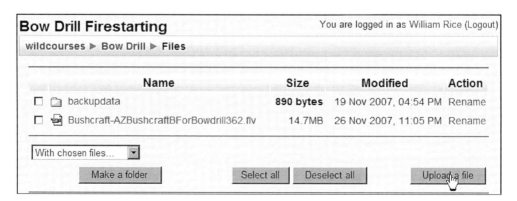

Also, if you upload a file into a course's data directory outside of Moodle, that file will show up as a course file. That is, instead of uploading the file through Moodle, use your FTP program or something similar to upload it right into the data directory. In the following screenshot, you can see that I have copied a new audio file to the course's data directory:

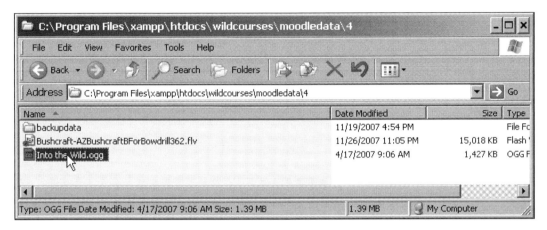

When I refresh the Course Files page, the new file is listed:

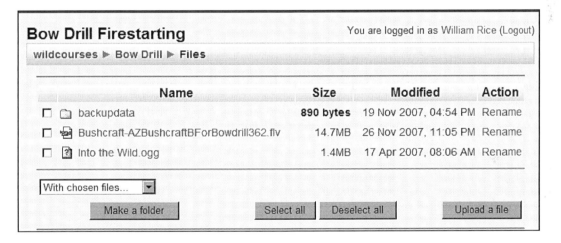

This workaround also works for site files. As the Front Page of your site is course ID number 1, uploading (or FTPing) a file to /moodledata/1 will add that file to the list of site files. This can be very useful when you must use large media files, but your hosting service will not enable you to raise the limit for uploads in PHP or Apache.

Summary

These five static course materials (text pages, web pages, links, directory views, and labels) form the core of most online courses. Most student/teacher interaction will be about something the student has read or viewed. Adding static material first gives you a chance to think about how the material will be discussed and used. In later chapters, you'll see how to add more interactive material.

6
Adding Interactive Course Material

Interactive course activities enable students to interact with the instructor, the learning system, or each other. Note that Moodle doesn't categorize activities into 'Interactive' and 'Static', as we do in this book. In Moodle, all activities are added from the **Add an activity...** menu after turning the editing on. We use the terms 'Interactive' and 'Static' as a convenient way to categorize the activities that Moodle offers.

The following table gives you a brief description of each kind of activity. The sections that follow the table describe how and when to use these activities.

Activity	Description
Assignment	An assignment is an activity completed offline, outside of Moodle. When the student completes the assignment, he or she either uploads a file for the instructor's review, or reports to the instructor in some other way. Regardless of whether the assignment requires uploading a file, the student receives a grade for the assignment.
Choice	A choice is essentially a single, multiple-choice question that the instructor asks the class. The result can either be displayed to the class, or kept between the individual student and the instructor. Choices are a good way to get feedback from the students about the class. You can plant these choices in your course ahead of time, and keep them hidden until you need the students' feedback. You can also add them as needed.
Journal	You can create an online journal, which will be unique for each student. A journal can be seen only by the student who writes it, and the instructor. Remember that a journal is attached to the course in which it appears. If you want to move a student's journal to another course, you'll need to make creative usage of the backup and restore functions.

Activity	Description
Lesson 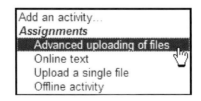	A lesson is a series of web pages displayed in a given order, where the next page displayed may depend upon the student's answer to a question. Usually, the 'jump question' is used to test a student's understanding of the material. Get it right, and you proceed to the next item. Get it wrong, and you either stay on the page or jump to a remedial page. But the jump question could also ask a student what he or she is interested in learning next, or some other exploratory question.
	A lesson gives Moodle some of the branching capability found in commercial computer-based training (CBT) products. You could make a course consisting of just a summary, one large lesson, and a quiz.
Quiz	Questions that you create while making a quiz in one course can be reused in other courses. We'll cover creating question categories, creating questions, and choosing meaningful question names.
SCORM/AICC	SCORM (**Sharable Content Object Reference Model**) is a collection of specifications that enable interoperability, accessibility, and reusability of web-based learning content. If a piece of learning material meets the SCORM standard, it can be inserted into any learning management system that supports SCORM (which is most of the major ones). Moodle's SCORM module allows you to upload any standard SCORM package into your course.
Survey	Moodle comes with prewritten surveys, designed by educational experts to help instructors learn about their students. If the stock survey questions are not appropriate for your usage, you have two choices: repurpose a quiz into a survey, or edit the survey's PHP code to change the questions. This section covers using the stock surveys, and those two options for custom surveys.

Wikis and workshops are covered in the next chapter.

Assignments

After logging in as a teacher, and turning on editing, you can add an assignment from the **Add an activity...** menu.

Types of Assignments

You can select from four types of assignments. Each of them is explained here:

Upload a Single File

Use this assignment type when you want the student to submit a single file online. The following screenshot shows what the student sees before he or she submits the file:

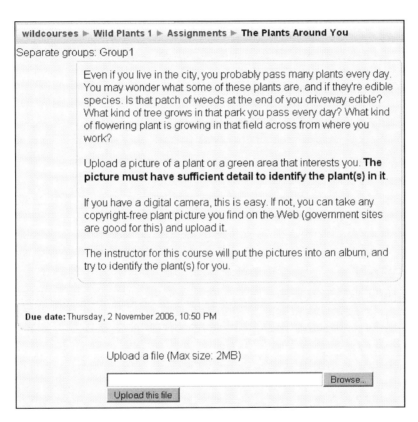

And this is what the student sees after submitting (uploading) the file; the submission is graded by the teacher:

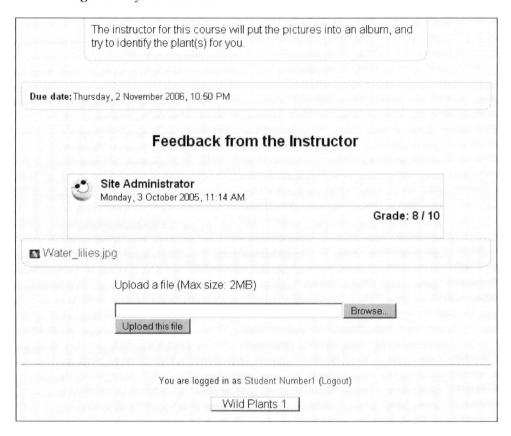

Advanced Uploading of Files

Just as with the *Upload a Single File* assignment, this type of assignment allows each student to upload a file in any format. However, the student can upload multiple versions, or drafts of the file. Until the student uploads the final version of the file, the submission is marked as a draft.

The teacher determines how many versions can be uploaded when he or she creates the assignment. The student can either upload that many versions, or indicate that a file is the final version.

Students can also enter notes with the submitted file. In the following screenshot, you can see that a student has uploaded a file, added a note, and that the submission is still a draft. Note that:

- The student can replace the existing file by uploading another one. That will count as another draft.

- The **Edit** button enables the student to edit the note.

- The **Send for marking** button enables the student to call this the final submission, even if he or she hasn't submitted the maximum number of drafts allowed.

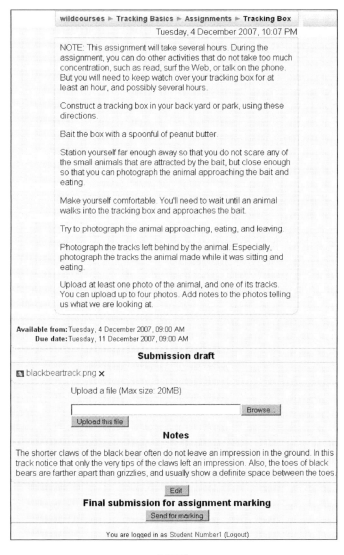

Online Text

Select this assignment type when you want the student to create a page online. While it's called 'Online text' assignment, note that the student can include anything on the page that you can include in a web page, such as graphics and links. That's because the student creates the page using Moodle's built-in web page editor. If you include this assignment type, consider giving your students directions on how to use the online editor for inserting graphics, links, multimedia, and tables. Most of the functions of the online editor are self-explanatory, especially for a generation of bloggers. But these functions may give your students some problems if you don't explain them.

While grading the assignment, the teacher can edit the student's online text page. When the student clicks on the assignment to see his/her grade, the student also sees the original and edited versions of their page. In the following screenshot, note the student's one-word submission, and the teacher's witty response:

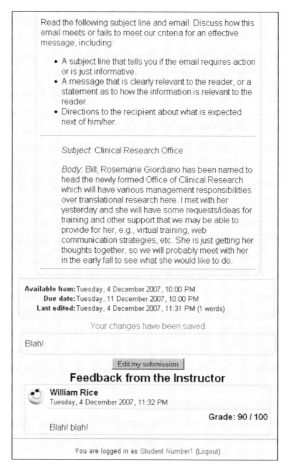

If the teacher allows resubmission of the assignment, then this back and forth feedback and grading can continue until the teacher decides upon the final grade for the assignment.

If you are familiar with the older, **pre-1.7** version of Moodle, you may remember an activity type called **journal**. The online text assignment is meant to replace the journal. However, as of **version 1.9**, the journal module is still included with the standard distribution. It is deactivated, but you can turn on the journal module under **Site administration | Modules**. Why would you do this—because, the journal still does some things that an online text assignment does not. For example, the student's journal entry is private, and can be viewed only by the student and teacher. In an assignment, the group mode causes the student's entry to be accessible by at least the other members of the student's group, if not the whole class. And, in a journal, the student's multiple entries are compiled in a single view. In an assignment, the student can make only one entry per assignment.

Offline Activity

Select this when you want the student to do something outside of Moodle. Note that 'outside of Moodle' doesn't have to mean 'offline'. The assignment could be something elsewhere on the Web, as in the following example. Or it could be completely offline, such as taking a photograph or visiting a museum.

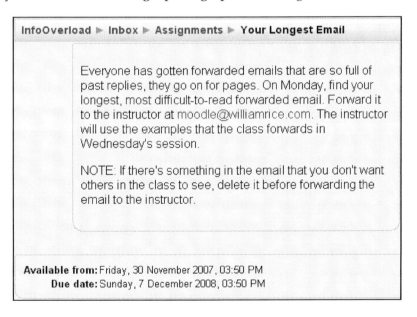

While the work is performed outside Moodle, the teacher still records the grade in Moodle.

Creating an Assignment

Adding an assignment automatically brings up the Editing Assignment window:

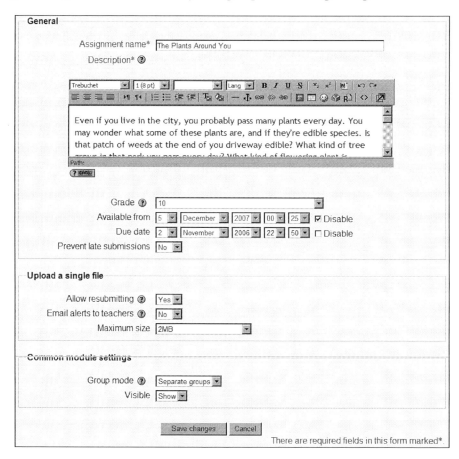

The **Assignment name** field is displayed on the course page. When a student clicks on the name, the **Description** field is displayed. The description should give complete instructions for completing and submitting the assignment.

Assignments that are due soon will appear in the **Upcoming Events** block (covered in Chapter 3). If you do not set a due date, by default, it will be set to today (the day you created the assignment). This will make the assignment show up in the Upcoming Events block, as if it's overdue. Make sure you set an appropriate due date for the assignment.

Printer-Friendly Directions

As assignments are completed offline, you may want the directions to be printer-friendly, so that students can take the directions with them. Make sure that any graphics you've embedded into the Description field are less than the width of the printed page. Or, you can upload the directions as an **Adobe Acrobat** (`.pdf`) file, and use the Description field to instruct students to print the directions and take the directions with them.

Make It Clear That Assignments Are Mandatory

On the course's Home Page, an assignment link appears with its own icon, like this: . It is not immediately apparent to a new student that this icon means 'Do this assignment'. You might want to use a label to indicate that the assignment is something the student should do. In this example, a label instructs the student to complete the assignment and a multiple-choice survey question:

You can also label the individual activities with an imperative, such as 'Read about the plants around you', or 'Answer a survey question about your experience with edible plants'.

Assignments are always added to the **Upcoming Events** block. If you have an assignment, consider adding the Upcoming Events block even if you have no other events planned for the course (such as a field trip, discussion, chat, and so on). This will serve as an additional reminder for the students.

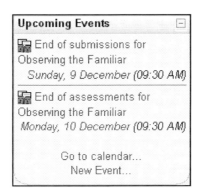

Also, if you display the **Recent Activity** block, content that was recently added or edited will appear in that block. If you add or edit an assignment while the course is underway, the Recent Activity block will serve as an additional reminder to complete the assignment.

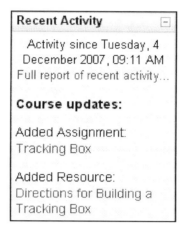

Lesson

A lesson is the most complex, and most powerful, type of activity. Essentially, a lesson is a series of web pages that presents information and questions.

A Moodle lesson can be a powerful combination of instruction and assessment. Lessons offer the flexibility of a web page, the interactivity of a quiz, and branching capabilities.

What Is a Lesson?

A lesson consists of a series of web pages. Usually, a lesson page contains some instructional material, and a jump question about the material the student just viewed. The jump question is used to test a student's understanding of the material. Get it right, and you proceed to the next item. Get it wrong, and you're either taken back to the instructional page, or you jump to a remedial page. But the jump question could also easily ask a student what he is interested in learning next, or who her favorite candidate is. Or it could also be labeled **Continue** to take the student to the next page.

The following is a screenshot of a lesson page. Its purpose is instructional. It appears like any other normal web page. Indeed, you can put anything on a lesson page that you can put on any other Moodle web page.

Relationship Between Distance and Perspective

In some photographs, space can appear compressed, so that objects appear closer together than they really are. In another photograph of the same scene, space can appear expanded so that objects appear farther apart than they are.

Distance from Camera Determines Perspective

Distortions in perspective are actually caused by the distance of the subject from the camera. The farther a scene is from the camera, the closer the objects in that scene appear. The closer a scene is to the camera, the farther apart objects in that scene appear. Distance compresses the space in a picture, and closeness expands the space.

In the photo below, look at the distance between the columns. The columns closer to the camera appear to be further apart, while those farther from the camera appear closer together.

Photo by Smiles for the world / Alex Lapuerta

Focal Length Does Not Determine Perspective

Many people think these distortions in perspective are caused the focal length of the lens being used. For example, they think that a long lens--a telephoto lens--compresses space, and a short lens--a wide angle lens--expands space. This isn't true.

A telephoto lens enables you to shoot a scene that is farther from the camera. Because the scene is far from the camera, it perspective is compressed. But it is the distance from the camera, not the telephoto lens, that is causing the compression.

A wide angle lens enables you to shoot a scene that is closer to the camera. Because the scene is close to the camera, it perspective is opened. But it is the closeness to the camera, not the wide angle lens, that is causing the opening of the space.

Click the Continue button below to go to the next page in this lesson.

Continue

At the bottom of the lesson page is the **Continue** button. In this lesson, when the student clicks this button, he or she is taken to the following question page:

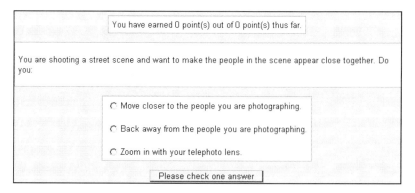

Each answer displays different feedback, just like a quiz:

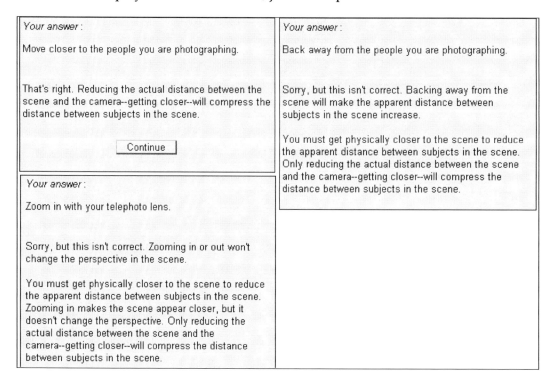

If the student answers correctly, he or she is taken to the next instructional page. An incorrect answer takes the student to a remedial page. The following is an example of a remedial page:

Remedial: Compressing Perspective

In the photo below, the space between each of the marchers in the front row is the same:

Photo by Celeste Hutchins.

Look at the two men closest to you. You can see that the space between them is over four feet. If one of them reached out his arm, he could not touch the other:

This is the simplest sequence for a lesson in Moodle. You can also add a few more advanced features. We'll discuss these later, after looking at the basic features.

Lesson Settings

When you first create a lesson, you are presented with a window where you choose the settings for the entire lesson. Before you can add even a single page to a lesson, you must select the lesson settings. If you're not sure about any of these settings, just take your best guess. You can always return to this page and change the settings. Remember, one of the advantages of Moodle is the ease with which you can experiment with, and change your course material. Get accustomed to taking a bolder, more experimental approach to using Moodle and you will enjoy it a lot more.

This window is broken into six areas:

- General
- Grade options
- Flow control
- Lesson formatting
- Access control
- Other

In this section, I'll go through the Editing Lesson page from top to bottom. I'll discuss most of the settings, and focus on the ones that are most useful for creating the effect of a deck of flash cards. By the end of this section, you will understand how most of the settings on the Editing Lesson page affect the student's experience.

General Settings

The following are the settings:

Name

This is the name of the lesson, which students will see on the course's Home Page.

Time Limit

This is the time limit for the entire lesson, and not for each individual page. Enabling this displays a timer, with a countdown. The timer uses JavaScript; so to use this feature, your students must have JavaScript installed and enabled in their browsers.

When the time limit is reached, the student is not ejected from the lesson. The student remains in the lesson. However, any question that the student answers after the time limit is reached does not count towards the student's grade.

Maximum Number of Answers/Branches

At the bottom of each question page in a lesson, you can place a quiz question. **Maximum number of answers/branches** determines the maximum number of answers that each question can have. If each answer sends the student to a different page, then the number of answers is also the number of branches possible. For true/false questions, set this to **2**. After creating question pages, you can increase or decrease this setting without affecting the questions that you have already created.

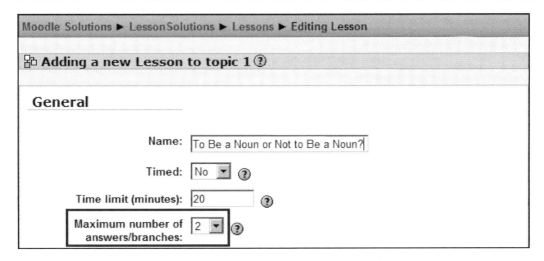

Grade Options

If a lesson is being used only for practice, most of the grade options are irrelevant.

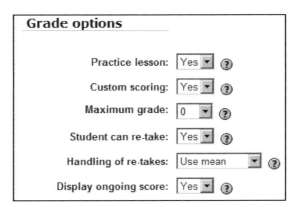

Practice Lesson

If you set **Practice lesson** to **Yes**, this lesson will not show up in the Gradebook.

Custom Scoring

Normally, a correct answer in a question is worth the entire point value for the question, and each wrong answer is worth zero. Enabling custom scoring allows you to set a point value for each individual answer in a question. Use this if some answers are 'more right' or 'more wrong' than others. You can also use this to set the point value for a question. If a question is more important, use custom scoring to give it more points.

Maximum Grade

If you set **Maximum grade** to **0**, the lesson does not appear in any of the Grades pages. The student's score in this lesson will not affect the student's final grade for the course.

Student Can Re-take

This setting determines if the student can repeat the lesson.

Handling of Re-takes

This setting is relevant only if the student is allowed to repeat the lesson (the setting above is set to **Yes**). When the students are allowed to re-take the lesson, the grades shown in the Grades page are either the average of the re-takes or the student's best grade.

Display Ongoing Score

When this is set to **Yes**, each page of the lesson displays the student's score and the number of possible points so far. Note that this displays the number of points that the student could have earned for the pages that he or she has viewed so far.

If a lesson is not linear (that is, if it branches), then the path that each student takes through the lesson can change. This means that each student can have the chance to earn a different number of points. So in a branching lesson, the 'total number of points possible for the entire lesson' is not meaningful because the lesson can be different for different students. For example, you might create a lesson with many branches and pages. Then, require the student to earn at least 200 points on that lesson. This would encourage the student to explore the lesson, and try different branches until he or she has earned the required points.

Flow Control

Some of the options under **Flow control** make the lesson behave more like a flash card deck. Other settings on this page become irrelevant when a lesson is used for flash cards.

Flow control

Allow student review:	No
Display review button:	No
Maximum number of attempts:	1
Action after correct answer:	Show an unanswered Page
Display default feedback:	Yes
Minimum number of questions:	0
Number of pages (cards) to show:	10

Allow student review enables a student to go backwards in a lesson, and retry questions that he or she got wrong. This differs from just using the Back button on the browser, in that the setting enables the student to retry questions while using the Back button does not.

Look at the setting for **Action after correct answer**. Note that in this case, it is set to **Show an unanswered Page**. This means that after a student answers a question correctly, Moodle will display a page that the student either hasn't seen or has answered incorrectly. The **Show an unanswered Page** setting is usually used during a flash card lesson to give the student second chances at answering questions correctly. During a practice lesson, you will usually use **Allow student review** to enable students to go back to questions they got wrong.

Display review button displays a button after the student answers a question incorrectly. The button allows the student to re-attempt the question. If your questions have only two answers (true/false, yes/no), then allowing the student to retry a question immediately after getting it wrong doesn't make much sense. It would be more productive to jump to a page explaining why the answer is wrong, and use the **Show an unanswered Page** setting to give the student another chance at the question at a later time.

Maximum number of attempts determines how many times a student can attempt any question. It applies to all questions in the lesson.

Minimum number of questions sets the lower limit for the number of questions used to calculate a student's grade on the lesson. It is relevant only when the lesson is going to be graded.

Number of pages (cards) to show determines how many pages are shown. If the lesson contains more than this number, the lesson ends after reaching the number set here. If the lesson contains fewer than this number, the lesson ends after every card has been shown. If you set this to **0**, the lesson ends when all cards have been shown.

Lesson Formatting

The settings under **Lesson formatting** are used to turn the lesson into a slide show, which appears in a pop-up window. The **Slide Show** setting creates the slide show window. **Slide show width**, **height**, and **background color** set the format of the slide show. The **background color** setting uses the Web's 6-letter code for colors. This code is officially called the 'Hex RGB'. For a chart of these color codes, try a web search on the terms 'hex rgb chart', or see a partial chart at `http://www.w3.org/TR/2001/WD-css3-color-20010305#x11-color`.

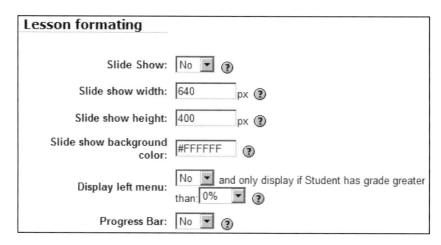

Display left menu displays a navigation bar on the left side of the slide show window. The navigation bar enables the student to navigate to any slide. Without that navigation bar, the student must proceed through the slide show in the order that Moodle displays the lesson pages, and must complete the lesson to exit (or the student can force the window to close). Sometimes, you want a student to complete the entire lesson in order, before allowing him or her to move freely around the lesson. The setting **only display if Student has grade greater than** accomplishes this. Only if the student achieved the specified grade will he or she see the navigation menu. You can use this setting to ensure that the student goes completely through the lesson the first time, before allowing the student to freely move around the lesson. The **Progress Bar** setting displays a progress bar at the bottom of the lesson.

Access Control

However, recall that in the beginning of the chapter, we learned that lessons are the only activity that can be made dependent on completing another activity. That is, you can require that the student completes a specific lesson in your course before allowing him or her access to the current lesson. Now, look at the **Dependent on** setting in the following screenshot:

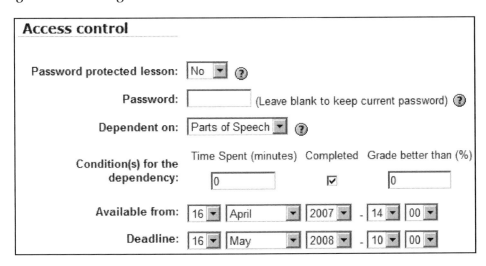

Pop-Up to File or Web Page

The following is what this page looks like:

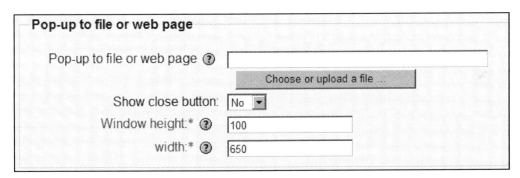

When the student launches the lesson, you can make a new web page or file launch with the lesson. This page or file will launch in a separate window. This enables you to use the page or file as the focal point for your lesson. For example, you could launch an animation of a beating heart in a pop-up window, and use the lesson to point out parts of the heart, and quiz the student on what each part does during the heartbeat.

Moodle will display the following file types in their own viewer:

MP3	Plain Text
Media Player	GIF
Quicktime	JPEG
Realmedia	PNG
HTML	

File types for which Moodle does not have a built-in viewer get a download link instead.

Even if your file type is supported by one of Moodle's viewers, you might want to embed the file in a web page instead. Putting the file on a web page enables you to write an explanation at the top of the page, say, 'You will refer to this graphic during the lesson. Reposition this window and the lesson window, so that you can see both at the same time, or easily switch between the two.'

If you combine this with the **Slide Show** setting (the screenshot on the last page), you'll have the Moodle slide show displayed in one window, and the file specified here displayed in another.

Other Lesson Settings

The **Other** settings area has some settings that can make the lesson more interesting for the student.

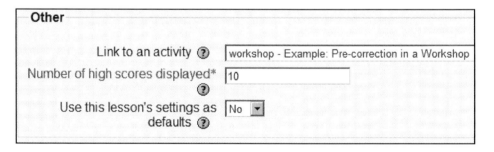

Notice in this screenshot, **Link to an activity** is set to **workshop - Example: Pre-correction in a Workshop**. This setting places a link on the last page of the lesson to the activity or resource specified. The drop-down list for **Link to an activity** contains all of the resources and activities in the current course. The user must click the link to be taken to the location, so this setting doesn't force the user to proceed to a specific place after the lesson.

Number of high scores displayed lets the high scoring students choose a name to post their scores under. This setting doesn't do anything if you make the lesson a **Practice lesson.**

When you are creating a lesson, you see all of the pages in the lesson in their logical order. The logical order is the order in which a student would see them, if the student answered every question correctly and proceeded straight through the lesson. At any time, you can preview the lesson from the student's point of view. This section will cover previewing a lesson.

A lesson can be graded or ungraded. It also can allow students to retake the lesson. While Moodle allows you to grade a lesson, remember that a lesson's primary purpose is to teach, not test. Don't use a lesson to do the work of a quiz or assignment. The lesson's score is there to give you a feedback on the effectiveness of each page, and to enable the students to judge their progress.

Adding the First Question Page

Immediately after you save your lesson settings, Moodle presents you with the following page:

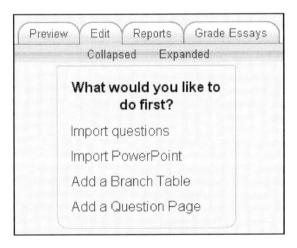

At this point, it is time to create the first question page or import question pages from another system. Let's take a look at each of your options.

Importing Questions

If you choose to **Import questions**, you can import questions created by Moodle and other online learning systems. Some of the formats that you can import are:

GIFT and Moodle XML	These are Moodle's proprietary formats. GIFT is text only, and XML can include graphics and special characters.
Aiken	This format is for multiple choice questions.
Missing Word	This format is for missing word multiple choice questions.
Blackboard	If you're converting from Blackboard to Moodle, you can export questions from Blackboard and import them into Moodle.
WebCT	This format supports multiple choice questions, and short answers questions from WebCT.
Course Test Manager	If you're converting from Course Test Manager to Moodle, you can export questions from Course Test Manager, and import them into Moodle.
Embedded Answers (Cloze)	This format is a multiple question, multiple-choice question with embedded answers.

Each question that you import will create a lesson page.

Importing PowerPoint

If you've created a complex PowerPoint presentation—with animations, special text effects, branching, and other advanced features—don't expect to import those advanced features into a Moodle lesson. Basic text and graphics will import from PowerPoint into Moodle, but advanced features are lost.

Also, before you import your PowerPoint slideshow, you must export it as a series of web pages. This ability is built into PowerPoint. So it is not difficult, and does not require additional software. But you should be aware that Moodle does not read PowerPoint files directly. Instead, it reads the web pages that PowerPoint exports.

Add a Branch Table

A branch page consists of a page of links to the other pages in your lesson. At this point, immediately after you've finished the lesson settings page, your lesson doesn't have any pages. So adding a branch table at this point doesn't make much sense. Let's deal with branch tables later, after we've added some question pages to the lesson.

Add a Question Page

This option enables you to add a question page to your lesson, using Moodle's built-in editor. The process for creating a question page is covered in the next section, *Creating the Question Pages*.

Creating the Question Pages

After you fill out and save the **Settings** page, it is time to create the first question page. Even though it's called a 'question page', the page can contain more than just one question. It's a web page, so you can add any content to it. Usually, it contains information and a question to test the student's understanding. You can choose different types of questions:

- Multiple choice
- True/false
- Short answer
- Numeric
- Matching
- Essay

You can also create feedback for each answer to the question, similar to creating feedback for the answers in a quiz question. And, you can make the lesson jump to a new page, based upon the answer the student selects.

In the following example, you can see the question page contains some text, a graphic, and three answers to the question. Note that for each answer, there is a **Response** that the student sees immediately after submitting the answer. And, there is also a **Jump** for each answer. For the two incorrect answers, the **Jump** displays the same page. That allows the student to try again. For the correct answer, the **Jump** displays the next page in the lesson.

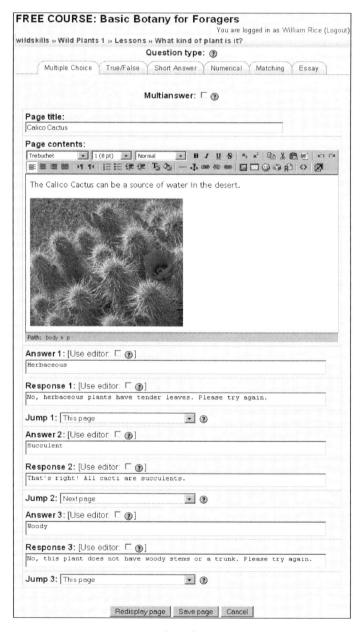

Page Title

The **Page title** will display at the top of the page when it is shown in the lesson.

Page Contents

As was said before, a lesson page is really a web page. It can contain anything that you can put on any other Moodle web page. Usually, it will contain information, and then a question to test the student's understanding.

Answers

The answers will be displayed at the bottom of the lesson page, after the **Page contents**. The student selects and answers in response to the question posed in the **Page contents**.

Responses

For each **Answer** that the student selects, its **Response** is shown before the student is taken to a new page.

Jumps

Each **Answer** that a student selects results in a **Jump** to a page.

This Page

If **Jump** is **This page**, the student stays on the same page. The student can then try to answer the question again.

Next or Previous Page

If **Jump** is **Next page** or **Previous page**, the student is taken to the next or previous page. After you rearrange the pages in a lesson, this jump might give you different results. Just be aware that this is a relative jump.

Specific Pages

You can also select a specific page to jump to. The pull-down list displays all the titles of the lesson page. If you select a specific page to jump to, the jump will remain the same, even if you rearrange the pages in your lesson..

Unseen Question within a Branch

Recall that a `Branch Table` is a Table of Contents, listing the pages in a lesson. When you insert a `Branch Table` into a lesson, you can also insert an `End of Branch` later in the lesson. The pages between the `Branch Table` and `End of Branch` become a branch. For example, a lesson with two branches might look like this:

```
Branch Table 1
    Question Page
    Question Page
    Question Page
End of Branch1
Branch Table 2
    Question Page
    Question Page
    Question Page
End of Branch 2
```

For a **Jump**, if you select **Unseen question with a branch**, the student will be taken to a question page that he or she has not yet seen in this session. That question page will be in the same branch as the current page.

Random Question within a Branch

For a **Jump**, if you select **Random question within a branch**, the student will be taken to a random question page in the same branch as the current page.

In the Lesson Settings page, if **Maximum number of attempts** is set to something greater than **1**, the student might see a page that he or she has seen before. But a page will be repeated only if **Maximum number of attempts** is greater than **1**. If it's set to **1**, a random question page that the student has not seen before will be displayed, which has the same effect as choosing **Unseen question within a branch**.

To restate this, when the lesson setting **Maximum number of attempts** is set to **1**, then **Random question within a branch** acts exactly like an **Unseen question within a branch**. When **Maximum number of attempts** is set to greater than **1**, then **Random question within a branch** displays a truly random question page.

One strategy for using this setting is to forgo the use of **Unseen question within a branch**. Whenever you want to use **Unseen question within a branch**, instead use **Random question within a branch** and set the **Maximum number of attempts** to **1**. Then you have the option of converting all of your lessons to random jumps just be setting **Maximum number of attempts** to **2** or greater.

Random Branch Table

Recall that a Branch begins with a Branch Table, has one or more question pages, and then ends with an End of Branch page. You can nest branches within branches.

If **Jump** is **Random branch table**, the student is taken to a random Branch Table between the current Branch Table and the End of Lesson or the next End of Branch.

Create Pages and Then Assign Jumps

When filling out a question page, **Answer 1** is automatically assumed to be the correct answer, so **Jump 1** automatically reads **Next page**. This is because in most cases, you want a correct response to result in the next page in the lesson being displayed. However, you can select any existing page in the lesson for the jump. Note that when you are filling out the first question page, there are no other pages to jump to, so all the jumps on the first page will direct to **This page**. After creating more pages, you can go back and change the jumps.

It is usually most efficient to create all of your question pages first, and then go back and assign the jumps.

The jumps that you create will determine the order in which the pages are presented to the student. For any answer, you can select a jump to the last page of the lesson. The last page displays an End of Lesson message and, if you choose, the grade for the lesson. It also displays a link that takes the student back to the course's Home Page.

The Flow of Pages

The most obvious usage of question pages and jumps is to enforce a straight-through lesson structure. A correct answer results in a positive response such as 'That's correct!', and then jumps to the next page. An incorrect answer results in a negative response or a correction. An incorrect answer can then redisplay the page, so the student can try again, as in the previous example, **Jump 1: This page**. Or, an incorrect answer can jump to a remedial page.

The order of pages the student would follow if he or she has answered every question correctly is called the **logical order**. This is how the teacher sees the lesson while editing it and displaying all of the pages in the same window.

Question Pages without Questions

You are not required to add a question to a **Question** page. If you omit the question, Moodle displays a **Continue** link that takes the student to the next page. This is useful on remedial pages, where you want to ensure that the student returns to the main lesson flow. It is also useful if you want to create a click-through demo, or other series of informational pages.

It is also useful if you want to enforce the reading of material in a certain order. Recall that on a course's Home Page, course material can be read in any order. However, using a lesson, you can enforce a given order for the reading of course material. If you want to enforce a particular order for the entire course, you can make the course one big lesson. This is as close as Moodle comes to a commercial learning management system's ability to enforce an order of material on a course.

Editing the Lesson

After you've created several lesson pages, you might want to see and edit the flow of the lesson. You can do this under the **Edit** tab.

Collapsed and Expanded

The **Edit** tab is where you edit the contents of your lesson. From here, you can add, delete, rearrange, or edit individual lesson pages.

Under the **Edit** tab, when you select **Collapsed**, you see a list of the pages in your lesson like the one shown in the following screenshot:

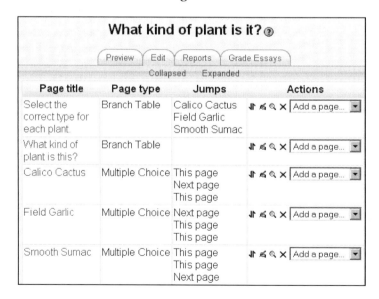

The pages display in their logical order, which would be the shortest path through the lesson if a student got all of the questions correct. Note that the contents of the pages do not display. The purpose of this screen is not to edit individual questions, but to help you see the flow of the lesson.

Rearranging Pages

To rearrange the pages, click the up/down arrow ⬍ to go to the page you want. Note that it is the jumps that determine the order in which Moodle presents the pages. If a question is set to jump to the next page, rearranging the pages can change the jumps. A question can also be set to jump to a specific, named page. In that case, the order in which the pages appear doesn't determine the landing point for the jump. So, rearranging the pages here won't affect that jump.

Editing Pages

From the **Edit** tab, to edit a page, click the edit icon: ▦. Clicking this takes you to the editing page of that page. The previous section gave detailed instructions for editing a lesson page.

Adding Pages

The **Add a page here** drop-down list enables you to insert a new page into the lesson. You can choose from several different kinds of pages.

A question page is the normal, lesson page.

As stated before, a Branch Table is a page that contains links to other pages in your lesson. Those pages will be between the Branch Table and the End of branch. We'll discuss more on branches in the next section.

A **Cluster** is a group of question pages, where one is chosen at random. You do not proceed through a Cluster like you do a branch. Instead, you hit one random page within a Cluster, and then you're out of the Cluster or back to the beginning.

Branch Tables

You can add a branch page, which enables students to jump to pages in your lesson. A branch page consists of a page of links to the other pages in your lesson. This page of links can act as a table of contents. For example, suppose you're developing a lesson on William Wallace. The traditional way of teaching about a person's life is to organize the information in a timeline. That would be easily accomplished with a straight-through lesson like the one just described.

But suppose you wanted to teach about the different areas of a person's life, and they do not all fit well on a timeline.

For example, Wallace's historical achievements would fit well on a timeline. But a timeline might not be the best way to teach about Wallace's personal beliefs and religion. Wallace's family might fit well on a timeline. But background information about the culture and society in which he lived might not. A straight-through lesson might not be the best way to present Wallace's life. Instead, you might use a branch table.

In this Branch Table, each branch could be an aspect of Wallace's life: historical achievements, personal beliefs, family, the world in which he lived, and so on. At the beginning of the lesson, the student would choose a branch to explore. At the end of each branch, the student would choose between going back to the branch table (beginning of the lesson), or exiting the lesson.

You can mark the end of a branch with an End of Branch page. This page returns the student back to the preceding Branch Table. You can edit this return jump, but most leave it as is. If you do not mark the end of a branch with an End of Branch page, you will proceed out of the branch and to the next question.

Quizzes

Moodle offers a flexible quiz builder. Each question is a full-featured web page that can include any valid HTML code. This means a question can include text, images, sound files, movie files, and anything else you can put on a web page.

In most instructor-led courses, a quiz or test is a major event. Handing out the quizzes, stopping class to take them, and grading them can take a lot of the teacher's time. In Moodle, creating, taking, and grading quizzes is much faster. This means that you can use quizzes liberally throughout your courses. For example, you can:

- Use a short quiz after each reading assignment to ensure the students completed the reading. Shuffle the questions and answers to prevent sharing among the students, and make the quiz available only for the week or month in which the students are supposed to complete the reading.

- Use a quiz as a practice test. Allow several attempts, and/or use the adaptive mode to allow students to attempt a question until they get it right. Then the quiz becomes both practice and learning material.

- Use a quiz as a survey. Ask the students to rate their understanding, satisfaction with the course or instructor, the pace of the course, and so on. The score at the end of the quiz is not their grade, but the grade they give to the course.

Quiz Settings

When you first create a quiz, you see the **Settings** page. This page is divided into nine areas. Let's look at the settings under each area, top to bottom.

General

The **General** page looks like the following:

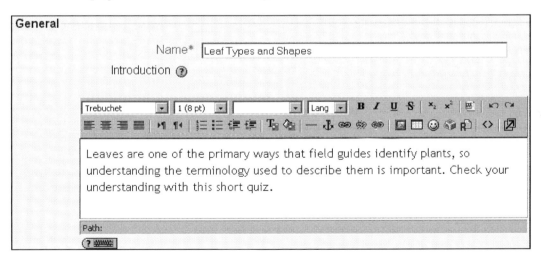

The **Name** of the quiz is displayed on the course's Home Page. The **Introduction** is displayed when a student selects the quiz, as shown in the following screenshot:

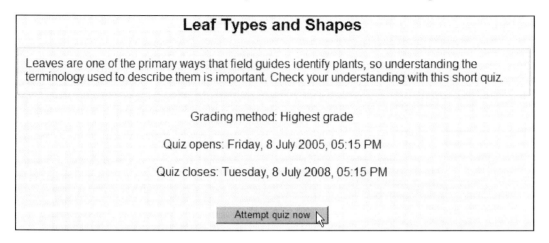

The **Introduction** should explain why the student is taking the quiz. It should also tell the student about any unusual features of the quiz, for example, whether it uses an animation that requires the Flash plug-in, or it uses a pop-up window. Remember that once the student clicks the **Attempt quiz now** button, he or she is into the quiz. So, give the student everything he or she needs to understand why and how to take the quiz before clicking that button.

Timing

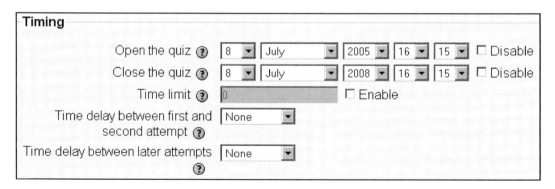

The **Open** and **Close** dates determine when the quiz is available. Selecting the **Disable** check box for **Open the quiz** means that the quiz will be permanently open, instead of becoming available on a given date. Selecting the **Disable** check box for **Close the quiz** means that once the quiz is open, it will stay open permanently, instead of becoming unavailable on a given date.

Note that even if the quiz is closed, it is still shown on the course's Home Page and students might still try to select it. When they do select a closed quiz, the students see a message saying it is closed. If you want to hide a quiz, you will see the setting **Visible** further down on this page; change this setting to **Hide**.

By default, a quiz does not have a **Time limit**. If you want to set a time limit, use this setting. When time runs out, the quiz is automatically submitted with the answers that have been filled out. A time limit can help to prevent the use of reference materials while taking the quiz. For example, if you want students to answer the questions from memory, but all the answers are in the course textbook, setting a timer might discourage students from taking the time to look up the answer to each question.

Further down the page, you can choose settings that enable the student to attempt the quiz multiple times. If, and only if, you enable multiple attempts, the **Time delay** settings here will take effect.

Display

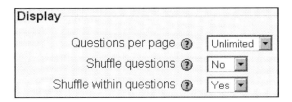

By default, all questions in a quiz display on the same page. **Questions per page** breaks the quiz up into smaller pages. Moodle inserts the page breaks for you. On the **Editing Quiz** page, you can move these page breaks. If you want to break up your quiz into pages that each hold the same number of questions, then this setting will work for you. If you want to break up your quiz into pages that hold different numbers of questions, then use this setting anyway, and edit the page breaks that Moodle creates for you.

Shuffle questions and **Shuffle answers** change the order of the questions and answers, each time the quiz is displayed. This discourages the sharing of quiz answers among students.

Attempts

The following is what an **Attempts** page looks like:

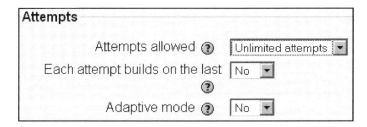

Attempts allowed allows the student to keep trying the quiz. **Each attempt builds on the last** retains the answers from one attempt to another. Taken together, these two settings can be used to create a quiz that the student can keep trying until he or she gets it right. This transforms the quiz from a test into a learning tool.

The **Adaptive mode** allows multiple attempts for each question. This is different from **Attempts allowed**, which allows multiple attempts at the whole quiz. When you make a quiz adaptive, each question offers you the option to:

- Display a message if the student answered incorrectly, and redisplay the question.
- Display a message if the student answered incorrectly, and then display a different question.

Grades

The following is the **Grades** page:

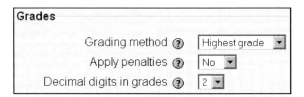

If you allow several attempts, the **Grading method** determines which grade is recorded in the course's gradebook: the **Highest**, **Average**, **First**, or **Last grade**.

Apply penalties only applies when a quiz is adaptive. For each question the student answers wrongly, points are subtracted from the student's score. You can choose the penalty for each question when you create that question.

Decimal digits in grades applies to the student's grade.

Students May Review

The following is what this page looks like:

Students may review					
Immediately after the attempt	☑ Responses	☑ Scores	☑ Feedback	☑ Answers	☑ General feedback
Later, while the quiz is still open	☐ Responses	☐ Scores	☐ Feedback	☐ Answers	☐ General feedback
After the quiz is closed	☐ Responses	☐ Scores	☐ Feedback	☐ Answers	☐ General feedback

Students may review controls if and when a student reviews his/her attempts at the quiz. If you allow the student to review the quiz **Immediately after** submitting his/her answers, but not **Later** or **After the quiz is closed**, then the student can review the quiz only once, immediately after submission. When the student navigates away from that review page, he or she will no longer be able to review the quiz.

In this matrix, **Responses** means the student's answers to the questions. **Scores** is the point value for each question. **Feedback** is the individual feedback for each question. **Answers** is the correct answer(s) for each question. **General feedback** is the feedback for the entire quiz.

Security

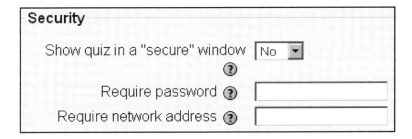

Show quiz in a "secure" window launches the quiz in a new browser window. It uses JavaScript to disable copying, saving, and printing. This security is not foolproof.

If you enter anything into **Require password**, the student must enter that password to access the quiz.

With **Require network address**, you can restrict access to the quiz to particular IP addresses. For example:

- 146.203.59.235 permits a single computer to access the quiz. If this computer is acting as a proxy, the other computers 'behind' it can also access the quiz.
- 146.203 will permit any IP address starting with those numbers. If those numbers belong to your company, then you effectively limit access to the quiz to your company's campus.
- 146.203.59.235/20 permits a subnet to access the quiz.

Techniques for Greater Security

You should understand that the only way to make a test secure, is to give the test on page, separate the students far enough apart so that they can't see each other's papers, place a proctor in the room to observe the students, and use different questions for each group that takes the test. There is no way to make a web-based test completely cheat proof. If you must give a web-based test that is absolutely resistant to cheating, consider these strategies:

- Create a very large number of questions, but have the quiz show only a small set of them. This makes sharing of questions less useful.
- Shuffle the questions and answers. This also makes sharing of questions more difficult.
- Apply a time limit. This makes using reference material more difficult.
- Open the quiz for only a few hours. Have your students schedule the time to take the quiz. Make yourself available during this time to help with technical issues.
- Place one question on each page of the quiz. This discourages students from taking screenshots of the entire quiz.

Common Module Settings

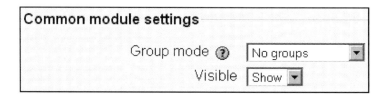

Group mode works the same as it does for any other resource. However, as each student takes the quiz himself or herself, the only real use for the group setting in a quiz is to display the high score for a group in the Quiz Results block.

Visible shows and hides the quiz from students, but as always, a teacher or the course creator can still see the quiz.

Overall Feedback

Moodle enables you to create several different kinds of feedback for a quiz. You can create feedback for:

- The **entire quiz**, which changes with the student's score. This is called **Overall Feedback**, and uses a feature called **Grade Boundary**.

- A **question**, no matter what the student's score is on that question. All students receive the same feedback. This is called **General Feedback**. Each individual question can have its own **General Feedback**. The exact type of feedback that you can create for a question varies with the type of question.

The following screenshot shows **Overall Feedback** with **Grade Boundaries**. Students who score **90−100**% on the quiz receive the first **Feedback−You're a geography wizard!**... Students who score **80−89.99**% receive the second **Feedback−Very good!**... Students who score **70−79.99**% receive the third **Feedback−Not bad.**... Below that, you can see the feedback for students who scored between **0** and **69.99**%.

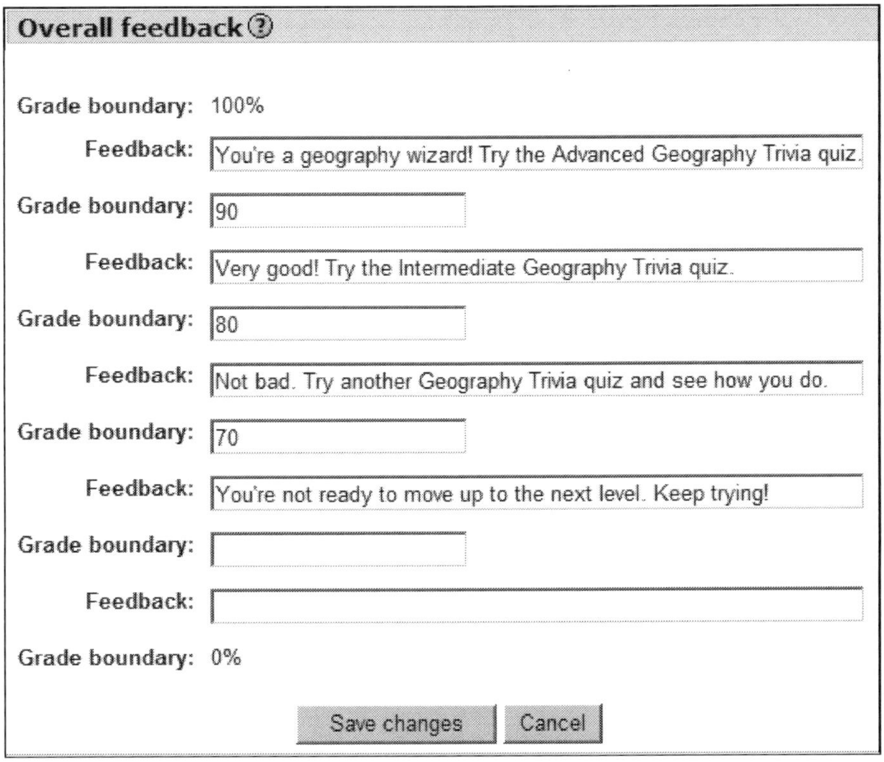

Overall feedback ⑦

Grade boundary: 100%

Feedback: You're a geography wizard! Try the Advanced Geography Trivia quiz.

Grade boundary: 90

Feedback: Very good! Try the Intermediate Geography Trivia quiz.

Grade boundary: 80

Feedback: Not bad. Try another Geography Trivia quiz and see how you do.

Grade boundary: 70

Feedback: You're not ready to move up to the next level. Keep trying!

Grade boundary:

Feedback:

Grade boundary: 0%

Save changes   Cancel

Editing a Quiz

Immediately after saving the **Settings** page, you are taken to the Editing Quiz page. This page is divided into five tabs. Each tab enables you to edit a different aspect of the quiz.

This tab...	Enables you to...
Quiz	• Add questions to the quiz.
	• Remove questions from the quiz.
	• Arrange the questions in order.
	• Create page breaks between questions.
	• Assign a point value to each question.
	• Assign a maximum point value to the quiz.
	• Click into the editing page for each question.
Questions	• Create a new question. Note that you must then add the new question to the quiz under the Quiz tab (see above). Also note that every question must belong to a category.
	• Delete a question, not just from the quiz but from your site's question bank.
	• Move a question from one category to another category.
	• Click into the editing page for each question.
	• Click into the editing page for each category.
Categories	• Arrange the list of categories in order.
	• Nest a category under another category (they become parent and subcategories).
	• Publish a category, so that questions in that category can be used by other courses on the site.
	• Delete a category (you must choose a new category to move the questions in the deleted category).
Import	• Import questions from other learning systems.
	• Import questions that were exported from Moodle.
Export	• Export questions from Moodle, and save them in a variety of formats that Moodle and other learning systems can understand.

Create and Edit Question Categories

Every question belongs to a category. You manage question categories under the **Categories** tab. There will always be a **Default** category. But before you create new questions, you might want to check to ensure that you have an appropriate category in which to put them.

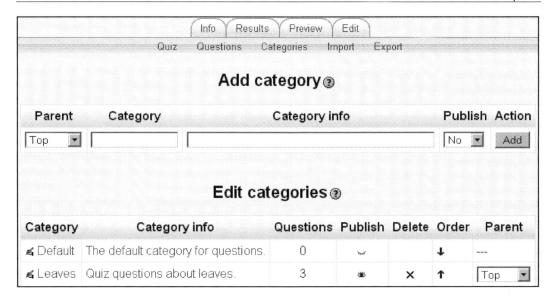

The categories which you can manage are listed on this page.

To Add a New Category

1. To add a new category, first select its **Parent**. If you select **Top**, the category will be a top-level category. Or, you can select any other category to which you have access, and then the new category will be a child of the selected category.

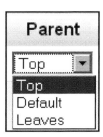

2. In the **Category** field, enter the name for the new category.

3. In the **Category Info** field, enter a description of the new category.

4. The **Publish** field determines whether other courses can use the questions in this category.

5. Click the **Add** button.

To Edit a Category

1. Next to the category, click the ✍ icon. The **Edit categories** page is displayed.
2. You can edit the **Parent**, **Category** name, **Category Info**, and **Publish** setting.
3. When you are finished, click the **Update** button. Your changes are saved and you are returned to the **Categories** page.

Managing the Proliferation of Questions and Categories

As the site administrator, you might want to monitor the creation of new question categories to ensure that they are logically named, don't have a lot of overlap, and are appropriate for the purpose of your site. As these question and their categories are shared among course creators, they can be a powerful tool for collaboration. Consider using the site-wide **Teachers forum** to notify your teachers, and course creators of new questions and categories.

Create and Manage Questions

You create and manage questions under the **Questions** tab. The collection of questions in your site is called the **Question bank**. As a teacher or the course creator, you have access to some or all the questions in the question bank.

When you create questions, you add them to your site's question bank. When you create a quiz, you choose questions from the question bank for the quiz. Both these functions can be done on the same Editing Quiz page. Pay attention to which part of the page you are using—the one for creating new questions or the one for drawing question from the question bank.

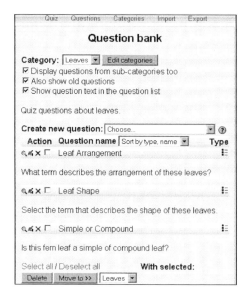

Display Questions from the Bank

You can display questions from one category at a time. To select that category, use the **Category** drop-down list.

If a question is deleted when it is still being used by a quiz, then it is not removed from the question bank. Instead, the question is hidden. The setting **Also show old questions** enables you to see questions that were deleted from the category. These deleted, or hidden, or old questions appear in the list with a blue box next to them.

To keep your question bank clean, and to prevent teachers from using deleted questions, you can move all the deleted questions into a category called **Deleted questions**. Create the category **Deleted questions** and then use **Also show old questions** to show the deleted questions. Select them, and move them into **Deleted questions**.

Move Questions between Categories

To move a question into a category, you must have access to the target category. This means that the target category must be published, so that the teachers in all the courses can see it.

Select the question(s) to move, select the category, and then click the **Move to>>** button:

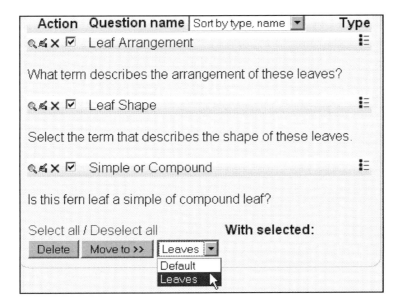

Create a Question

To create a new question, from the **Create new question** drop-down list, select the type for the next question:

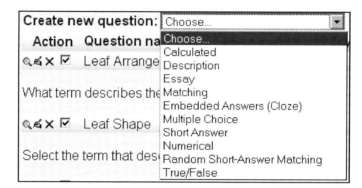

This brings you to the editing page for the question:

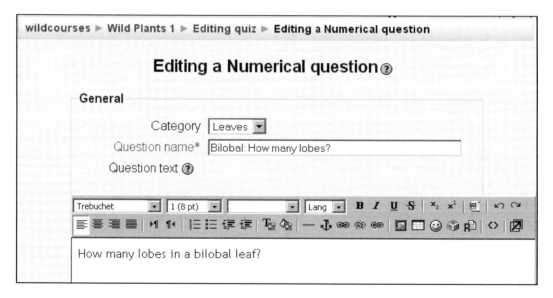

After you save the question, it is added to the list of questions in that category:

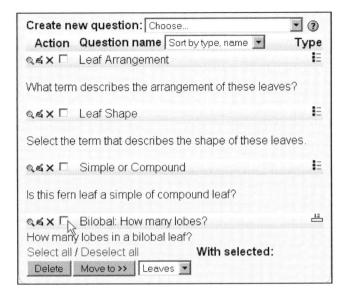

Question Types

The following chart explains the types of questions you can create, and gives some tips for using them.

Type of Question	Description and Tips for Using
Calculated	When you create a calculated question, you enter a formula that gets displayed in the text of the question. The formula can contain one or more wildcards, which are replaced with numbers when the quiz is run. Wildcards are enclosed in curly brackets.
	For example, if you type the question **What is 3 * {a}?**, Moodle will replace {a} with a random number. You can also enter wildcards into the answer field, so that the correct answer is **3 * {a}**. When the quiz is run, the question will display **What is 3 * {a}?** and the correct answer will be the calculated value of **3 * {a}**.
Description	This is not a question. It displays whatever web content you enter. When you add a description question, Moodle gives you the same editing screen as when you create a web page.
	Recall that under the **Quiz** tab, you can set page breaks in a quiz. If you want to break your quiz into sections, and fully explain each section before the student completes it, consider putting a Description on the first page of the section. For example, the Description could say 'The following 3 questions are based on this chart', and show the chart just once.

Type of Question	Description and Tips for Using
Essay	When the student is given an essay question, he or she uses Moodle's online rich-text editor to answer the question. However, if there is more than one essay question on a page, the rich-text editor appears only for the first essay question. This is a limitation of Moodle. To work around this, insert page breaks in your quiz so that each essay question appears on its own page. You enter page breaks under the **Quiz** tab.

Also, you might want to instruct your students to save their essay every few minutes. |
| Matching | After you create a matching question, you then create a list of sub questions, and enter the correct answer for each sub question. The student must match the correct answer with each question. Each sub question receives equal weight for scoring the question. |
| Embedded Answers (Cloze) | An embedded answers question consists of a passage of text, with answers inserted into the text. Multiple-choice, fill-in-the-blank, and numeric answers can be inserted into the question. Moodle's help file gives the following example:

Note that the question presents a drop-down list first, which is essentially a multiple choice question. Then, it presents a short answer (fill-in-the-blank) question, followed by a numeric question. Finally, there's another multiple-choice question (the Yes/No drop-down) and another numeric question.

There is no graphical interface to create embedded answers questions. You need to use a special format that is explained in the help files. |

Type of Question	Description and Tips for Using
Multiple Choice	Multiple choice questions can allow a student to select a single answer, or multiple answers. Each answer can be a percentage of the question's total point value.
	When you allow a student to select only a **single** answer, you usually assign a positive score to the one correct answer and zero or negative points to all the other, incorrect, answers. When you allow the student to select **multiple** answers, you usually assign partial positive points to each correct answer. That's because you want all the correct answers to total 100%. You also usually assign negative points to each incorrect answer. If you don't bring down the question's score for each wrong answer, then the student can score 100% on the question just by selecting all the answers. The negative points should be equal to or greater than the positive points, so that if a student just selects all the answers, he or she won't get a positive score for the question. Don't worry about the student getting a negative score for the question, because Moodle doesn't allow that to happen.
	In the Editing Quiz page, if you have chosen to shuffle answers, check all of the multiple-choice questions that you use in the quiz. If any of them has answers such as 'All of the above', or 'Both A and C', then shuffling answers will ruin those questions. Instead, change them to multiple-answer questions, and give partial credit for each correct answer. For example, instead of 'Both A. and C' you would say, 'Select all that apply' and then give partial credit for A. and for C.
Short Answer	The student types a word or phrase into the answer field. This is checked against the correct answer or answers. There may be several correct answers, with different grades.
	Your answers can use the asterisk, a wildcard. And, they can be case sensitive.
Numerical	Just as in a short-answer question, the student enters an answer into the answer field. However, the answer to a numerical question can have an acceptable error, which you set while creating the question. For example, you can designate that the correct answer is 5, plus or minus 1. Then, any number from 4 to 6 inclusive will be marked correct.
Random	When this type of question is added to a quiz, Moodle draws a question at random from the current category. The question is drawn at the time the student takes the quiz. During the same attempt, the same student will never see the same question twice, no matter how many random questions you put into the quiz. This means that the category you use for your random questions must have at least as many questions as the random ones that you add to the quiz.

Type of Question	Description and Tips for Using
Random Short-Answer Matching	Recall that a matching question consists of sub questions and answers that must be matched to each sub question. When you select Random Short-Answer Matching, Moodle draws random short-answer questions from the current category. It then uses those short-answer questions, and their answers to create a matching question.
	To the student, this looks just like any other matching question. The difference is that the sub questions were drawn at random from short-answer questions in the current category.
True/False	The student selects from two options: True or False.

Adding Feedback to Questions and Quizzes

Moodle enables you to create several different kinds of feedback for a quiz. You can create feedback for:

- The **entire quiz**, which changes with the student's score. This is called Overall Feedback, and uses a feature called Grade boundary.

- A **question**, no matter what the student's score is on that question. All students receive the same feedback. This is called General Feedback. Every question can have General Feedback.

The exact type of feedback that you can create for a question varies with the type of question.

Feedback for a Multiple-Choice Question

In a multiple-choice question, you can create feedback for any correct, partially correct, or incorrect response. If a response has a value of 100%, it is considered completely correct, and the student receives all of the points for that question. However, a response can have a value of less than 100%. For example, if a question has two correct responses, you could give each response a value of 50%. In this case, each response is partially correct. The student needs to choose both responses to receive the full point value for the question. Any question with a percentage value between 0 and 100 is considered partially correct.

A response can also have a negative percentage value. Any response with a percentage value of less than zero is considered an incorrect response.

Choosing a response with a value of 100% will display the feedback under **Feedback for any correct answer**. Choosing any response with a point value between zero and 100% displays the feedback under **Feedback for any partially correct answer**. Choosing any response with a zero or negative percentage displays the feedback under **Feedback for any incorrect answer**.

Any individual response to a question. Each response can display its own feedback. This type of feedback is called Response Feedback, or just **Feedback**.

The following screenshot shows **Overall feedback** with **Grade Boundaries**. Students who score **90 – 100%** on the quiz receive the first **Feedback – You're a geography wizard!**... Students who score **80 – 89.99%** receive the second **Feedback – Very good!**... Students who score **70 – 79.99%** receive the third **Feedback, Not bad.**... Below that, you can see the feedback for students who scored between **0** and **69.99%**.

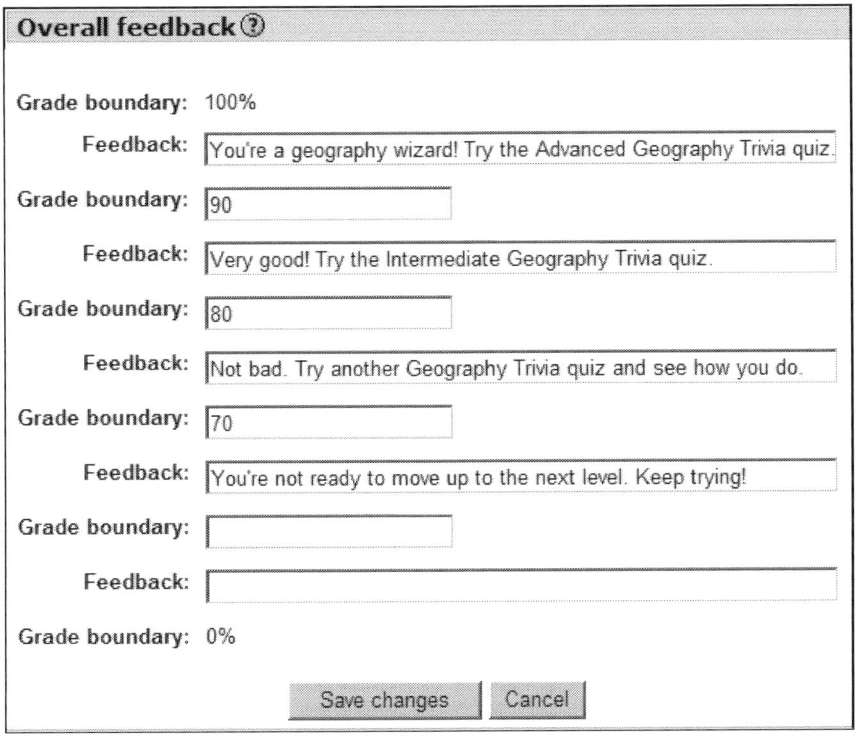

Overall feedback ⑦

Grade boundary: 100%

Feedback: You're a geography wizard! Try the Advanced Geography Trivia quiz.

Grade boundary: 90

Feedback: Very good! Try the Intermediate Geography Trivia quiz.

Grade boundary: 80

Feedback: Not bad. Try another Geography Trivia quiz and see how you do.

Grade boundary: 70

Feedback: You're not ready to move up to the next level. Keep trying!

Grade boundary:

Feedback:

Grade boundary: 0%

Save changes   Cancel

The screenshot on the next page shows a multiple-choice question that uses several kinds of feedback. You're seeing this question from the course creator's point of view, not the student's. First, you can see **General feedback – The truth is, most New Yorkers have never even thought about the "missing Fourth Avenue" issue.**. After the question is scored, every student sees this feedback, no matter what the student's score is.

Below that, in the next screenshot, you can see that **Choice 1** through **Choice 4** contain **Feedback** for each response. This feedback is customized to the response. For example, if a student selects **Sixth Avenue** the **Feedback** is **Nope, that name is taken. Sixth is also known as the "Avenue of the Americas."**.

At the bottom of the page, under **Feedback for any incorrect answer**, you can see the feedback the system gives if the student selects one of the incorrect responses. In this case, we use the feedback to tell the student what the correct response is.

There is not the feedback under **any correct answer** or **partially correct answer**. Those options are useful when you have multiple responses that are correct, or responses that are partially correct. In this case, only one response is correct, and all other responses are incorrect.

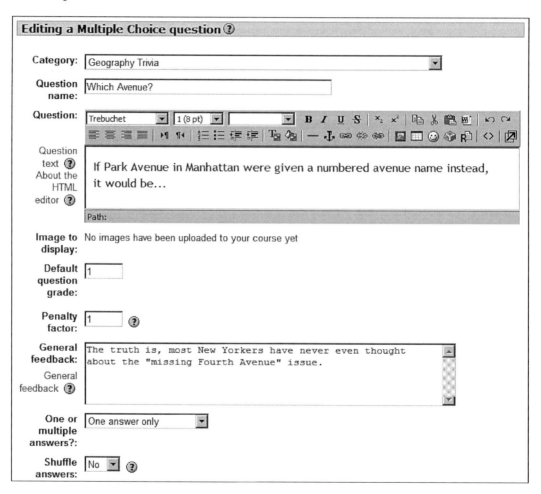

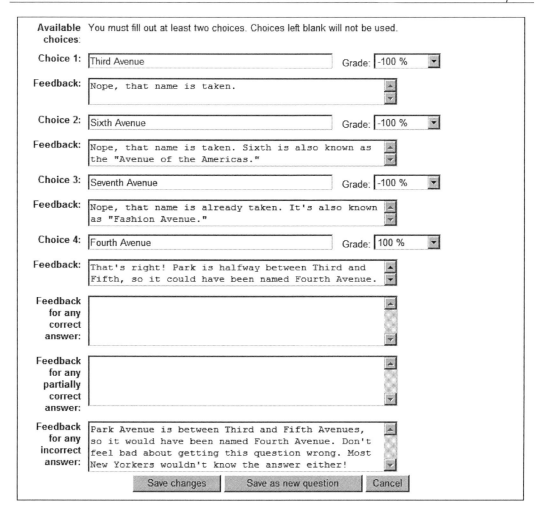

Feedback for a Numeric Question

The following screenshot shows feedback for a numeric answer question.

Note that the **General feedback** explains how the question is solved. This feedback is displayed to everyone after answering the question, even those who answered correctly. You might think that if the student answered correctly, he or she doesn't need this explanation. However, if the student guessed or used a method different from the one given in the **General feedback**, explaining the solution can help the student learn from the question.

In a numeric answer question, the student types in a number for the answer. This means that the student can enter literally any number. It would be impossible to create customized feedback for every possible answer, because the possibilities are infinite. However, you can create customized feedback for a reasonable number of answers. In this question, I've created responses for the most likely incorrect answers. After I've given this test to the first group of students, I'll need to review their responses for the most frequent incorrect answers. If there are any that I haven't covered, I'll need to add them to the feedback for this question.

In the following screenshot, note that each response has customized feedback. **Answer 1** is correct. **Answer 2** would be the result of switching between the two numbers, while trying to solve the problem. As this is a likely error, I've included feedback just for that answer, explaining the error that the student made. **Answer 3** is the result of interpreting **b(3)** as **b times 3** instead of **b cubed**. This is also a likely error, so I've included feedback for that answer. **Answer 4** is a wildcard, and applies if the student submitted any answer other than the three above.

| Answer 1: | 28 | Accepted error | | ± Grade: | 100 % |
| Feedback: | Correct. | | | | |

| Answer 2: | -180 | Accepted error | | ± Grade: | None |
| Feedback: | It looks like you transposed the two numbers. In the equation, you substituted 2 for "a" and 6 | | | | |

| Answer 3: | 30 | Accepted error | | ± Grade: | None |
| Feedback: | It appears that instead of calculating b cubed, you calculated b times 3. | | | | |

| Answer 4: | * | Accepted error | | ± Grade: | None |
| Feedback: | No, that answer is incorrect. | | | | |

Assemble the Quiz

After you have created categories and questions, you can go to the **Quiz** tab and begin adding questions to the quiz.

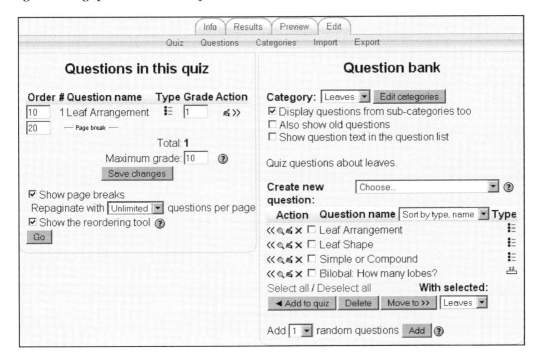

Most of the functions on this page are self-explanatory. However, here are some tips for using them.

Maximum Grade

The quiz's **Maximum grade** is the quiz's point contribution towards the course. In this example, the quiz is worth **10** points toward the student's total for the course.

The grade for each question will be scaled to the quiz's **Maximum grade**. For example, if this quiz had five questions worth **1** point each, but the **Maximum grade** is **10**, then each question will contribute **2** points to the student's total grade for the course.

Page Breaks

If you put all the questions of the quiz in one page, and if the student's browser refreshes or freezes before the quiz is submitted, he or she will lose the selected answers. To avoid this, use page breaks to put a few questions on each page, so your student can't lose more than a page of work.

Random Questions

Add random questions to the quiz using the **Add** button at the bottom right of this page. This will add random questions from the currently selected category. You can add random questions from several categories to the same quiz. In the following screenshot, I've added one random question from the **Leaves** category:

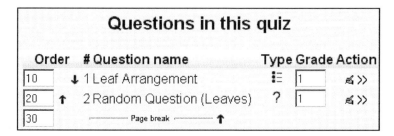

On the same attempt, the student will never see the same random question twice. However, the questions are reset between attempts, so a student can see the same question twice, if he or she attempts the same quiz twice.

Naming Questions

Every question has a name, as you can see in the previous screenshot. You can use the name of a question to convey meaningful information about that question. For example, 'Leaf Question 1' would not be a very descriptive name, but 'PrinciplesofBio-Chap8-Pg3' would tell you the source of that question. If you forget what a question says, you can always click on the 🔍 button next to the question, to preview it.

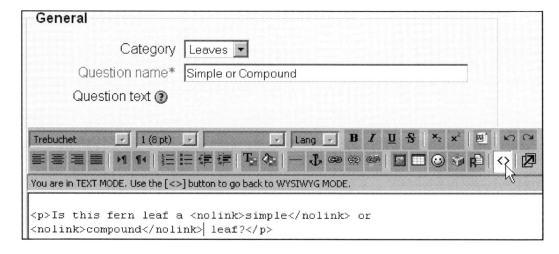

Preventing Glossary Auto-Linking in Quiz Questions

If you have a glossary in your course, glossary words that are used in quiz questions will link to their glossary entries. If you don't want students to have this resource when they take the quiz, then go to the glossary, and change the setting **Automatically link glossary entries** to **No**. Or, while typing a glossary word in a quiz question, using the online editor's HTML view, add the tag `<nolink> </nolink>` to the word, like the following:

Preventing an Open-Book Quiz

In most Moodle courses, quizzes are 'open-book' affairs. This is because when the student is taking a quiz, there is nothing to prevent the student from reading other parts of the course. If you want to prevent this, you can do so with some manual intervention.

The easiest way to prevent a quiz from becoming open-book is to put that quiz into a separate course topic, by itself. Then, hide all the other course topics. This can be done with a single click on each topic. Administer the quiz, and redisplay the topics afterward.

SCORM/AICC

SCORM stands for Sharable Content Object Reference Model. AICC stands for Aviation Industry CBT (Computer-Based Training) Committee. They are standards, not products or features. It is a collection of specifications that enable learning management systems to use content developed for each other. Almost all learning management systems support SCORM, so developing content that is SCORM-compliant enables that content to be ported onto many systems.

The SCORM module allows you to upload any standard SCORM or AICC package to include in your course.

The **Summary** is displayed when the student selects this activity from the course's Home Page.

To select the SCORM package that you want to import, use **Course package** and the **Choose** button.

If the package you imported is graded, select one of the **Grading methods**.

If **Auto-continue** is set to **Yes**, when the student finishes with one Sharable Content Object, the next one in the course displays automatically. Otherwise, the student must click a **Continue** button to proceed.

Enable preview mode enables the student to browse the content without taking the associated test. The content is marked as browsed.

As Sharable Content Objects display in the same window or a separate window, the **Width** and **Height** settings determine the size of the display area for the object, not the size of the window.

Survey

Moodle's survey consists of questions about the students' attitudes towards learning in general, and the course specifically, and about the students' experience with the course. Moodle enables you to create five different surveys, all of which are pre-created for you. The survey questions are designed to help you assess your students. The questions and choices in these surveys are set, and you cannot edit them. If the stock survey questions are not appropriate for your usage, you will need to repurpose a quiz into a survey.

Creating a Survey

To create a survey, add it to your activity and then select the **Survey type**. Set the **Group mode**, edit the introductory text, and the survey is complete. The questions are set for you.

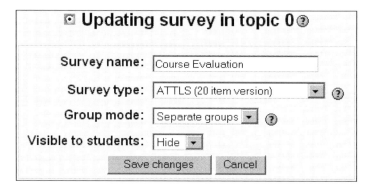

Survey Types

Moodle offers five different surveys, divided into three survey types.

COLLES

COLLES stands for **Constructivist On-Line Learning Environment Survey**. There are three surveys in this category. Each consists of 24 statements, to which the student indicates a level of agreement or disagreement. The questions ask about:

- The course's relevance to the student's interests and professional goals
- The level of critical or reflective thinking that the student applies to the material in the course
- The level of interactivity the student engages in, during the course
- The level of tutor support the student is receiving in the course
- The level of peer support that the student is receiving in the course
- The success of the student's tutor, and other students' interpretation of the interaction between them

The three COLLES surveys ask students about their preferred learning environment, the actual learning environment they are experiencing in the course, and a combination of the two.

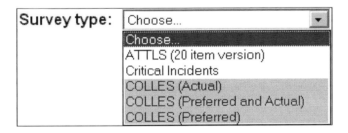

ATTLS

ATTLS stands for **Attitudes To Thinking and Learning Survey**. It consists of 20 questions that ask about the student's style of learning, discussion, and debate. For example, the survey asks about the student's attitude towards logic versus personal concerns—*I value the use of logic and reason over the incorporation of my own concerns when solving problems.*

The **ATTLS** questions are useful for measuring the student's attitudes in general, but not for measuring the student's perception of, or satisfaction with a course.

Critical Incidents

The **Critical Incidents** survey is different from the **COLLES** and **ATTLS** surveys in two ways:

- It is much shorter, has only five questions.
- Students answer by typing short responses instead of selecting from multiple choices.

This survey asks students how they feel about recent events in the course. The five questions in the **Critical Incidents** survey are:

1. At what moment in class were you most engaged as a learner?
2. At what moment in class were you most distanced as a learner?
3. What action from anyone in the forums did you find most affirming, or helpful?
4. What action from anyone in the forums did you find most puzzling, or confusing?
5. Which event surprised you most?

When to Use the Different Types of Surveys

At the beginning of a course, the **COLLES (Preferred)** survey can give you an idea of the students' preferred way of learning. This can help you design and present the course in the best way for your students. During the course, you can use a **COLLES (Actual)** survey to measure how well the course is meeting their needs. These are long surveys, so use them sparingly.

The **ATTLS** survey can also be used at the beginning of a course to help you understand the students' learning style. Remember that this survey is about the student, not the course. You might want to ask each new student in your learning site to complete an **ATTLS** survey before participating in any courses. Then, each teacher can check their students' **ATTLS** surveys, and know 'who they are dealing with' in their course.

As the **Critical Incidents** survey is short, and asks about recent events, you can use this survey after each topic or week. It provides a useful guide for making quick, small changes to a course in progress.

Choices

Moodle's choice is the simplest type of activity. In a choice activity, you create one question, and specify a choice of responses. You can use a choice to:

- Take a quick poll.
- Ask students to choose sides in a debate.
- Confirm the students' understanding of an agreement.
- Gather consent.

Before we look at how to accomplish this, let's look at the choice activity from the student's point of view, and then explore the settings available to the teacher while creating a choice.

Student's Point of View

From the student's point of view, a choice activity looks like this:

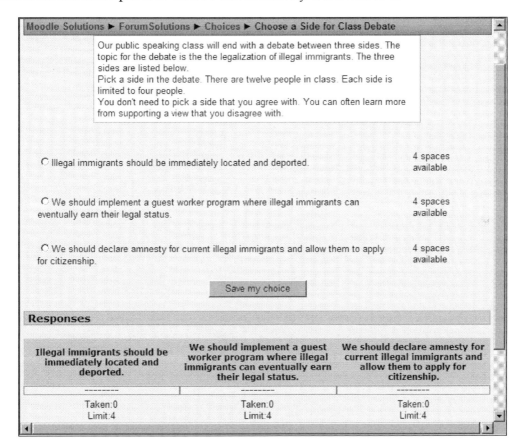

Note that at the bottom of the window, the student can see how many other students have chosen a response. There is also a limit to the number of students who can choose each response.

Teacher's Point of View

Before we discuss some of the uses for a choice activity, let's look at the settings available on the Editing Choice page. Then, we'll see how we can make creative use of these capabilities.

Number of Choices

When you first use the Editing Choice page, Moodle gives you space for five responses:

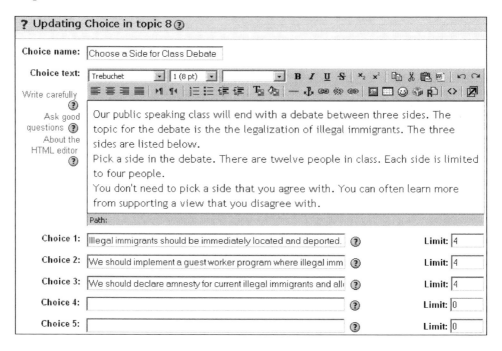

If you use all of the choices, and then save the activity, Moodle gives you two more blank choices when you return to the editing page. You can continue doing this until Moodle has created as many choices as you need.

Limit

The **Limit** next to each choice enables you to limit how many students can select that choice. In the previous example, no more than **4** students can select each choice. So after four students have selected **Choice 1**, that choice becomes unavailable. Limits must be enabled for the choice:

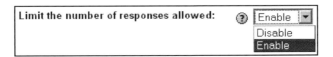

Time Limit

You can define a time period during which students are allowed to make a choice. If you don't set a time limit (if you leave the box unchecked), the choice is always available.

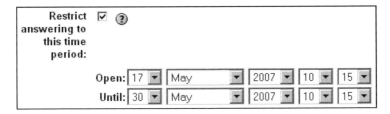

Publish Results

You can choose whether to reveal the results of the choice to the students, and if so, when:

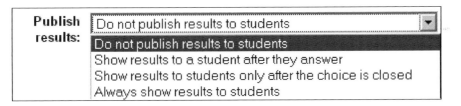

In the example at the beginning of this section, **Publish results** was set to **Always show results to students**. That is why the student could see how many students had chosen each response. If it had been set to **Do not publish results to students**, the activity would not have shown how many students had selected each response. Note that at the bottom of this page, the numbers, **Taken** and **Limit,** are no longer displayed:

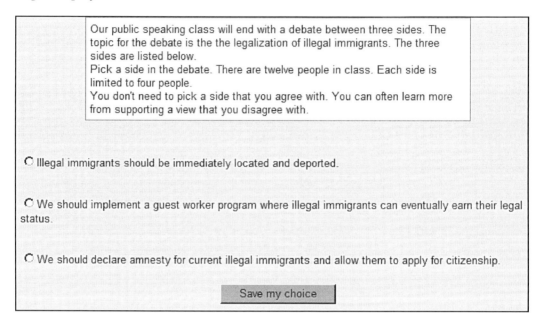

If you are going to limit the number of students who can choose a response, consider using **Always show results to students**. That way, the student can see how many others have chosen the response, and how many slots are left for each response.

Privacy

If you publish the results of the choice, you can then choose whether to publish the names of the students who have selected each response:

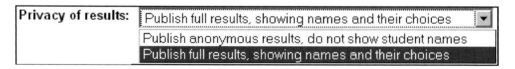

In the example at the beginning of this section, **Privacy of results** was set to **Publish anonymous results**. If it had been set to **Publish full results**, the student would have seen who had selected each response:

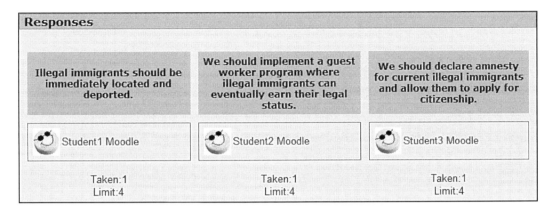

Allow Students to Change Their Minds

The setting **Allow choice to be updated** determines if a student can change his or her answer after submitting it. If this is set to **Yes**, a student can retake the choice activity until the activity is closed.

Summary

Moodle's assignments, journals, and lessons enable you to create course material that students interact with. This interaction is more engaging, and usually more effective, than courses consisting of static material that the students view. While you will probably begin creating your course by adding static material, the next step should usually be to ask, 'How can I add interactivity to this course?' Lessons can even take the place of many static web pages, as they consist of web pages with a question at the end of each page.

Survey and **Choice** give teachers the opportunity to assess students, their attitudes towards learning, and their satisfaction with a course. The **ATTLS** survey can become part of student's record, available to all teachers who have that student in a course. The **COLLES (Preferred)** survey can be used at the beginning of a course to assess the student's motivation and expectations, while the **COLLES (Actual)** can be used every few weeks to assess the students' satisfaction. Add a **Critical Incidents** survey after each topic or week, and a **Choice** as needed, and the result is a structured, ongoing conversation between the students and teacher.

7
Adding Social Course Material

Social course activities encourage student-to-student interaction. Peer interaction is one of the most powerful learning tools that Moodle offers. It not only encourages learning, but also exploration. It also makes courses more interesting, which increases student participation and satisfaction. This chapter teaches you how to add social resources to a course, and also how to make best use of them.

Chat

The Chat module creates a chat room where students can have real-time online chats. Online chat has some unique advantages over an in-person classroom discussion. Students do not need to deal with the fear of public speaking; transcripts can be edited and used as course material, and conversation can proceed at a leisurely pace that gives participants time to think. The key to using these advantages is preparation. Prepare your students by ensuring that they know chat room etiquette and also know to use the software. Prepare yourself by having material ready to copy and paste into the chat. And everyone should be prepared to focus on the goals and subject of the chat. More than any other online activity, chat requires that the teacher take a leadership role and guide the students to a successful learning experience.

When you add a chat room to a course, any student in the course can enter that chat room at any time. The chat room can become a meeting place for the students in the course, where they can come to collaborate on work and exchange information. If you give group assignments, or have students rate other students' assignments, consider adding a chat room to the course and encouraging students to use it.

The Editing Chat Page

The Editing Chat page is where you create and select settings for a chat:

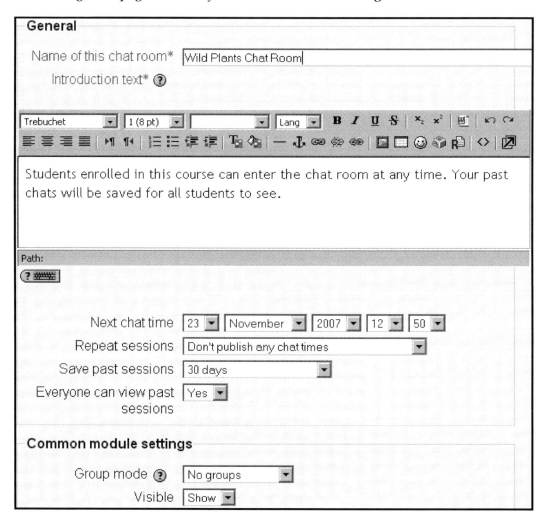

Let's take a look at the settings on the Editing Chat page:

Name

This is the name that students will see on the course's Home Page.

Introduction Text

When a student selects the chat, he or she sees the introduction text before clicking into the chat room:

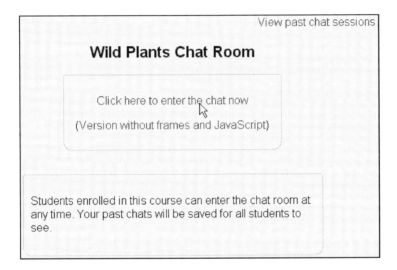

Next Chat Time and Repeat Sessions

This page looks like the following:

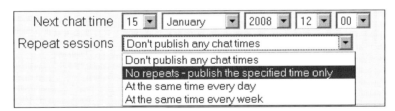

As stated in the beginning of this section, a student can enter that chat room at any time, as long as a chat is visible to them. Therefore, the settings for the **Next chat time** and **Repeat sessions** don't open and close the chat. Instead, these settings put a time and date for the chat on the class calendar.

This setting creates the result shown as follows:

Chat times are listed in the **Calendar** and **Upcoming Events** blocks. Note that chat is not restricted to these times; they are only announced as a way for people in the course to 'make a date' with the chat. Spontaneous chats have the best chance of happening if the course has a lot of students who frequent the course's Home Page. Also, consider adding the **Online Users** block, so that when students visit the site they will know who is online and can invite others into the chat room.

To make the chat room available only during designated times, you should make the person running the chat a teacher with editing privileges. Then, hide the chat room during off hours. When the chat is about to begin, the teacher can show the chat room.

Save Past Sessions and Everyone Can View Past Sessions

Past chats are saved. The **Save past sessions** setting enables you to set a time limit for saving chats. The settings for **Everyone can view past sessions** determines whether students can view past chats (**Yes**), or whether only teachers can view past chats (**No**).

Chat Security

The only security for a chat room is turning the group mode on, so that only students in a selected group can enter.

Remember that in the **Course Settings** page, you can set the **Enrolment duration** as **Unlimited**. This means that once a student is enrolled in the course, he or she is always enrolled until you manually unenrol the student. If you leave the course open to all students who were ever enrolled, consider segregating your chat by groups. Then, create a group that includes only the currently enrolled students. This prevents previous students from giving away too much in the chat room.

Forum

Forums are one of Moodle's most powerful features. A well-run class forum can stimulate thoughtful discussion, motivate students to become involved, and result in unexpected insights.

You can add any number of forums to a course, and also to the site's Front Page. Anyone with access to the course will have access to the forums. You can use Group mode to limit access to a forum to specific groups.

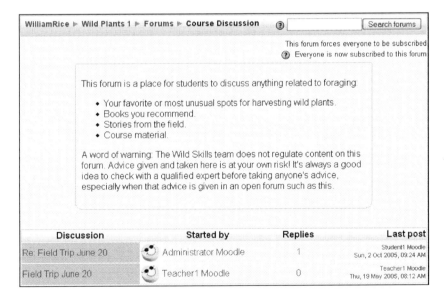

When a student enters a forum, the student sees the description entered during creation of the forum, as shown in the previous figure.

While writing a forum posting, the student uses the same online WYSIWYG editor you see when creating web pages in Moodle. Also, you can allow students to upload files into a forum. If you ask students to collaborate on assignments, or ask them to review each others' work, consider adding a forum specifically for discussing the assignment. Encourage the students to use the forum to preview each others' work and collaborate on the assignments.

Discussion Equals Topic

In the Moodle forum, discussions are the equivalent of topics or threads. When the setting for **Can a student post to this forum?** is set to **Discussions and replies are allowed**, students can create new topics and reply to existing topics. When set to **No discussions, but replies are allowed**, students can post to existing topics, but the teacher must create discussion topics. When set to **No discussions, no replies**, only the teacher can create discussions or post replies.

In Moodle **1.9+**, the settings for **Can a student post to this forum?** and **Discussions and replies are allowed** are now controlled under the **Roles | Override roles** sub-tab.

Using a Forum to Send Mass Emails

The last option, **No discussions, no replies**, is commonly used when you want to send mass emails to an entire class. Moodle does not have a module just for sending email announcements. So, when you want to send an email to everyone in a class (or in your site), you can create a **Forum** for the class (or site), and select **Yes** for **Force everyone to be subscribed?** With the forum locked down, only teachers can post messages. When the teacher posts a message, everyone who is subscribed to the forum receives the message via email. With everyone subscribed, the entire class will receive a copy of each posting by email.

Multiple Forums

Remember that a class can have as many forums as you want. If your course uses groups, you can use groups in the forum. Also, you can hide old forums and create new ones. This is useful if you run students through a course on a schedule. Just turning off the old forums and creating new ones enables you to refresh part of the course.

Forum Settings

The Editing Forum page is where you select settings for a forum. Let's look at how each of the settings affects the user experience.

General Settings

The **General** settings page looks like the following:

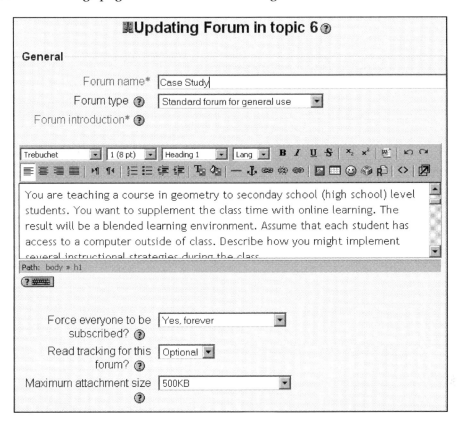

Forum Name

This is the name that students will see when the forum is listed on the course's Home Page.

Forum Type

In Moodle, you can create several types of forums. Each type can be used in a different way. The types of forums are:

Type of Forum	Description
Single simple discussion	The entire forum appears on one page. The first posting, at the top of the page, is the topic for the forum. This topic is usually created by the teacher. The students then post replies under this topic. A single-topic forum is most useful for short, highly focused discussions.
Standard	In a standard forum, anyone can start a new topic. Teachers and students can create new topics and reply to existing postings.
Each person posts one discussion	Each student can create one and only one new topic. Everyone can reply to every topic.
Q and A	This is like a single-topic forum, in that the teacher creates the topic for the forum. Students then reply to that topic. However, a student cannot see anyone else's reply until he or she has posted a reply. The topic is usually a question posed by the teacher, and the students' replies are usually answers to that question.

Forum Introduction

When the student enters a forum, he or she will see the **Forum introduction** at the top of the forum's page. This text should tell the student what the forum is about. You can also use this introduction to tell the student if he or she can rate posts by other students, and even to link to a document with more extensive instructions for using the forum. This is possible because the *Introduction* is a full-featured web page that can hold anything you can put on a web page.

Force Everyone To Be Subscribed?

Selecting **Yes** for **Force everyone to be subscribed?** subscribes all students to the forum automatically, even students that enroll in the course at a later time. Before using this settings, consider its long-term effect on the students who take your class.

If you re-use the same class for a later group of students, then the previous group will still be enrolled. Do you want previous students to be notified of new postings in the current class' forum? If not, there are several solutions such as:

- Don't force all students to be subscribed.
- Use groups to separate the current group of students in the class from previous groups.
- Create a fresh instance of the course for each new group.

Read Tracking For This Forum?

When turned on, this highlights the messages that the student hasn't read.

If students are subscribing to the forum via email, then this feature is less useful because it won't reflect the posts read via email.

Maximum Attachment Size

Students can attach files to forum postings. This sets the maximum size of a file that the student can upload.

Grade Settings

The **Grade** settings page looks like the following:

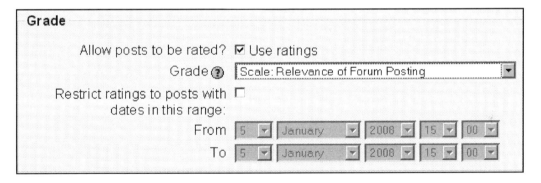

In a forum, a 'grade' is really a 'rating.' When you enable **Allow posts to be rated?**, you are really allowing the teacher to give each forum posting a grade. In the following screenshot, you can see the first posting in the forum that was made by the teacher. Below that, you can see the reply left by **Student1**. The student's reply was rated by the teacher. The student wanted to see who rated it and when it was rated, so he or she clicked on the rating and the small pop-up window got displayed:

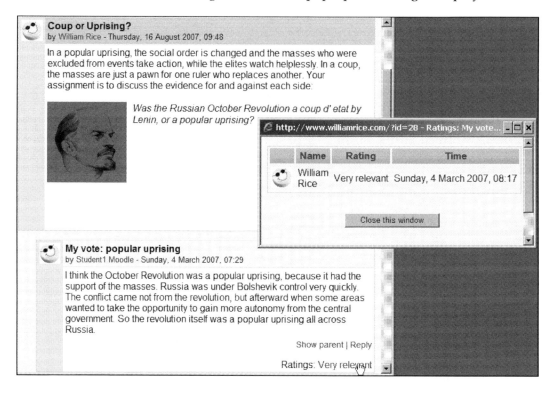

By default, only teachers and site administrators can rate forum postings. If you want the students to be able to rate postings in a forum, you must enable this for the forum. You do that with the Override Roles page. Before leaving the settings page, save your work.

To Enable Students To Rate Forum Postings

1. From the Editing Forum page, select the **Roles** tab.

2. Select the **Override Roles** sub-tab. Note that in version 1.9+ of Moodle, the site administrator must give teachers permission to access the **Override Roles** sub-tab.

3. From the list of roles, select **Student**.

4. Scroll down until, under **Forums**, you find the capability **Rate posts**.

5. Select the radio button in the second column, for **Allow**.

6. Select the **Save changes** button.

Post Threshold For Blocking Settings

This settings page looks like the following:

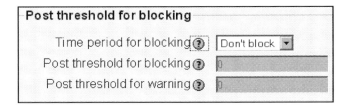

This setting helps you to prevent the forum from being taken over by a few prolific posters. Users can be blocked from posting more than a given number of posting in a given amount of time. As they approach the limit, they can be given a warning.

Glossary

The glossary activity is one of the most underrated in Moodle. On the surface, a glossary is a list of words and definitions that students can access. However, a course creator can allow students to add to a glossary. This transforms the glossary from a static listing of vocabulary words to a collaborative tool for learning.

You can use a glossary for building a class directory, a collection of past exam questions, famous quotations, or even an annotated collection of pictures.

Adding Glossary Entries

Selecting **Glossary** from the course menu displays the **Glossary** page. In this page, you can edit and browse the existing glossaries in your course. The following screenshot shows the **Browse** tab, where you can add a new entry:

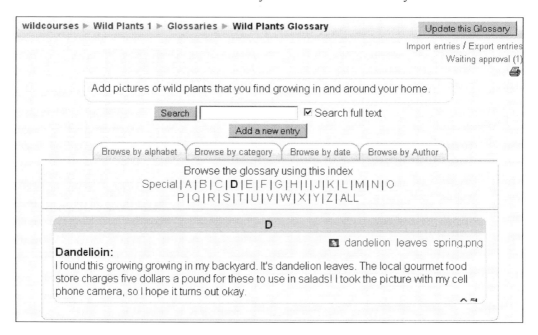

On this page, concept is the term that you are adding to the glossary. Keyword(s) are synonyms—the equivalent of a 'see also' in an index or dictionary. These terms will link to the same definition as the concept.

Create new glossary categories by clicking the **Add a new entry** button. This button appears under each of the tabs when you're browsing the glossary, so it's always available.

Categories are created under the **Browse Categories** tab. Click the button labeled **Edit categories** under that tab to create, delete, and rename categories.

You can also upload an optional file for each glossary entry. The **Import entries** link is in the upper right corner. The **Import** and **Export** links enable you to exchange glossaries between courses and even Moodle installations. You might want to begin a course with a small glossary, and let students add to it as they discover new concepts. If you want to do this, export the beginning glossary so that you have it available for the next course. The next time you teach the course, you can choose to export everything in the completed course except student information and the glossary. In the new copy, just create a new, blank glossary and import the starting glossary.

Also, note that the editing window enables you to include hyperlinks in the definition (the 🔗 icon). This can be used to link to freely available information on the Web, such as `http://www.wikipedia.org/`.

When you create a glossary, in the settings window you choose whether terms that students add are approved automatically, or whether they need the teacher's approval. In this example, the **Waiting approval** tab is unavailable because terms are automatically approved. If that settings were turned off, new terms would await the teacher's approval before being added. In the following screenshot, notice the link in the upper right corner for **Awaiting approval**:

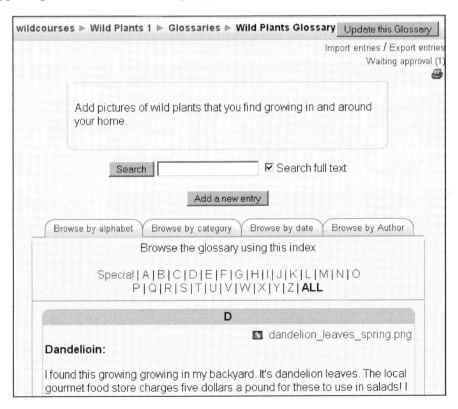

Global Versus Local Glossary

Under **Site Administration | Modules | Filters**, the site administrator can turn on **Glossary Auto-Linking**. When this is turned on, any word appearing in the course from a glossary is highlighted in gray. Clicking the word brings up a pop-up window with the word's glossary entry. By default, a glossary applies only to the course in which it resides. However, you can choose to make a glossary global, in which case the words from that glossary will be highlighted and become clickable wherever they are in your site. The work done in one course then becomes available to all the courses on your site. If your site's subject matter is highly focused (as in our example, **Wilderness Skills**), consider using a global glossary. If your site's subject matter is very broad, as in a university-wide learning site, you should use local glossaries to avoid confusion. For example, imagine you have a course on chemistry and another on statistics. Both use the word 'granular', but chemistry uses it to indicate a powdered substance while statistics uses it to indicate a fine level of detail.

Main and Secondary Glossaries

If you want students to be able to add entries to a glossary, you must make it a Secondary glossary. Only teachers can add terms to a Main glossary. A Secondary glossary has only the terms that the students and teacher add to. Since Moodle 1.7 and the introduction of roles, we have been able to override these settings and allow students to add entries to the Main glossary through the Override roles capabilities.

You can export terms one-at-time from a Secondary glossary to a Main glossary. So, you can create a Secondary glossary to which students will add terms. Then, you and/or the students can export the best terms to the Main glossary. Imagine a course with one Main glossary, and a Secondary glossary each time the course is run. The Main glossary would become a repository of the best terms added by each class.

You can add a Secondary glossary for each section in a course. For example, put a Secondary glossary into each topic or week. Then, you can create a Main glossary for the course that will automatically include all the terms added to each Secondary glossary. Put the Main glossary into Topic 0, the section at the top of the course's Home Page. An alternative to using Secondary glossaries is to use one Main glossary, and create categories within that glossary for each section in the course. This keeps all glossary entries in one place.

If you want the course to have only one glossary, and you want students to be able to add to it, make it a Secondary glossary. Even though the term 'Secondary' implies that there is also a primary or main glossary, this is not the case. You can have just a Secondary glossary (or more than one) in a course, without a Main glossary.

Ratings and Comments

You can give students the ability to rate glossary entries, just like they can rate forum postings. The question is, what do you want students to rate—the glossary entry's clarity? Its helpfulness? Your writing skill in creating the entry? You'll need to consider what you want students to rate, and create a custom scale that supports the rating. You determine who can rate glossary entries, and what scale to use, on the Editing Glossary page:

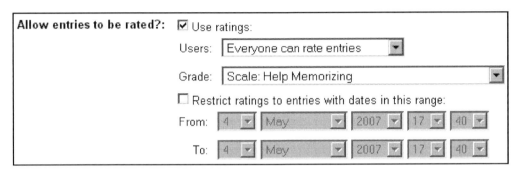

In the previous screenshot, the course creator is applying a custom scale called **Help Memorizing** to the glossary. Students will be able to rate each glossary entry on how helpful it is in memorizing the material. From the student's point of view, the result looks like the following:

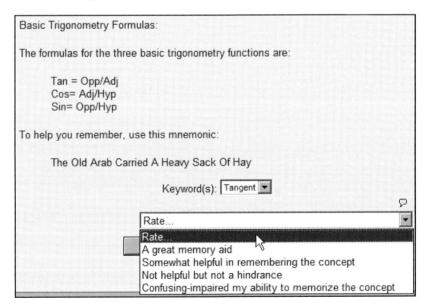

Wiki

The Moodle wiki module enables students to collaborate on a group writing project, build a knowledge base, and discuss class topics. As a wiki is easy to use, interactive, and organized by date, it encourages collaboration among the participants. This makes it a powerful tool for creating group knowledge. The key difference between a forum and a wiki is that when users enter a forum, they see a thread devoted to a topic. Each entry is short. The users read through the thread, one entry at a time. The result is that the discussion becomes prominent. In a wiki, users see the end result of the writing. To see the history of the writing, they must select a **History** tab. The result is, the end result of the writing becomes prominent.

Old wiki content is never deleted and can be restored. Wikis can also be searched, just like other course material. In the following section, we'll look at the settings on the Editing Wiki page and how they affect the user experience.

Using Wiki Type and Group Mode to Determine Who Can Edit a Wiki

A wiki can be open for *editing* by the entire class, a group, the teacher, or a single student. It can also be open to *viewing* by the entire class, a group, the teacher, or single student. Notice that the course creator determines who can *edit* the wiki, and who can see it, and that they are different settings. Setting who can edit the wiki is done using the **Type** drop-down box. Setting who can see the wiki is done using the **Groups** mode. For a matrix that explains all the options, select the 🔘 icon next to the **Type** drop-down box.

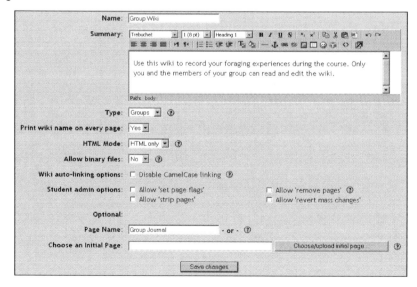

Making a wiki editable by only a single student appears to turn the wiki into a personal journal. However, the difference between a single-student wiki and a journal is that a journal can be seen only by the student and teacher. You can keep a single-student wiki private, or you can open it for viewing by the student's group or the entire class.

Wiki Markup Versus HTML Mode

The **HTML Mode** setting determines whether wiki authors use standard wiki markup or HTML code while editing. If you're using the HTML editor for other student activities, setting this to **HTML only** can simplify this activity for your students. They will get the familiar HTML editor, and don't need to learn the wiki markup language. However, if your students are accustomed to wikis, you may want to select **No HTML**. This enables them to use wiki markup, which is faster for experienced typists.

Enabling the Uploading of Binary Files

Allow binary files enables or disables the ability to upload non-text files to the wiki. The most common usage of binary files is pictures embedded on the wiki pages or attached to the wiki. Setting to **Yes** permits both. The size of the uploaded files is limited by a configuration setting, discussed in Chapter 3.

When to Use CamelCase Linking

CamelCase is the practice of writing compound words or phrases where the words are joined without spaces, and each word is capitalized within the compound. This is also known as **Bicapitalization**, **InterCaps**, and **MixedCase**. CamelCase is a standard identifier naming convention for several programming languages, and carried over into the standard Wiki markup language. It is also fashionable in the marketing of names of products and companies.

The original wiki, **WikiWiki**, the convention for creating hyperlinks was CamelCase. However, due to problems of syntax, some wikis (such as Wikipedia) switched to an alternative syntax that allowed any sequence of characters to be a link. If you're going to import older wikis into a Moodle wiki, you might want to enable CamelCase so that the older wiki's links import correctly. However, if you're not importing an older wiki, it is best to disable CamelCase because its usage has fallen into disfavor.

Student Admin Options

The Student Admin Options become available to students only if students are allowed to edit the wiki. If you enable these, but do not allow students to edit the wiki, they will have no effect.

Page Name

Notice that in the previous example, the name of the wiki is the rather uninspired 'Group Wiki'. If you leave the **Page Name** field blank, the name on the first page of the wiki will be taken from the name field. To override that, you can enter a page name in the **Page Name** field.

Choose Initial Page

When you first create a wiki, it is blank. Using **Choose an Initial Page**, you can create a starting page or pages for your wiki. These pages will be in place, and blank, when the student first enters the wiki. You can use these initial pages to give the students an outline for taking notes, a structure for group writing, or simply to keep the conversation on topic.

If there is one wiki for the entire class, when the first student enters the wiki, that student will see the starting page(s). If that first student edits any page, the next student who enters will see the edited version, and so on. If there is one wiki for each group in the class, then each group will get a 'fresh' wiki, with the starting page(s) that you created. And, if each student gets his or her own wiki, then each student will see those starting pages when they enter their wiki.

Detailed directions for creating a wiki's starting page(s) follow. The overall process looks like this:

1. Create a text file for the wiki's Home Page.
2. If desired, create additional text files for additional starting pages.
3. Upload text files to the course.
4. Create the wiki.
5. While creating the wiki, select the text file(s) for the initial page(s).
6. Test the wiki as a student.

Create a Text File for the Wiki's Home Page

For every initial page that you want your wiki to have, you must create and upload a text file. Later, we will deal with uploading and selecting the text files. First, we must deal with creating the text files for our wiki's initial pages. And before we create the text files that will become our initial pages, we must answer a question: HTML or wiki markup?

Wikis can use formatting commands called 'wiki markup'. The purpose of these commands is to enable an author to quickly format text, while typing, without needing to go to a menu. For example, to create a small headline (the equivalent of a Heading 3 in Word or your HTML editor), you would type `!Headline`. That would create a heading that looks like this:

Headline

To create a medium headline (Heading 2), use two exclamation points. For a large headline (Heading 1), use three. For example, `!!Heading` would look like this:

Heading

And `!!!Heading` would be largest of all:

Heading

If you wanted the starting page of your wiki to contain the first-level headings for an outline, and you wanted your wiki to be called 'Microscopy', you might create a text file called `Microscopy_` that contains this text:

```
!!!Microscopy and Specimen Preparation
[Lenses and the Bending of Light | Lenses_and_the_Bending_of_Light]
[The Light Microscope | The_Light_Microscope] [m3]
[Preparation and Staining of Specimens | Preparation_and_Staining_of_
Specimens]
```

If you chose that text file as the starting page for a wiki, the first time a student accessed the wiki, he or she would see this:

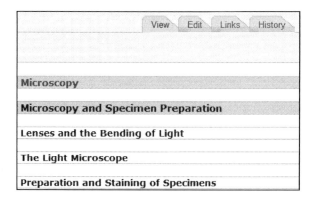

Note that the name of the text file, Microscopy, became the name of the page as well. Also note that the text preceded by ! ! ! became a top level heading. And the text inside square brackets became links.

In this example, we use wiki markup language for the text file that creates the wiki's initial page. This would be appropriate if we wanted the students to also use wiki markup when they edit the wiki. If you want to use HTML in your wiki, the text files that create your initial pages must be written with HTML. If you want to use wiki markup language, the text files must be written in wiki markup language.

At the initial page, the student would then select the **Edit** link and begin editing the wiki.

If Desired, Create Additional Text Files for Additional Starting Pages

You need to create and upload a text file for each initial page in the wiki. In our example, the text files for the starting page and the three topic pages would look like the following:

Microscopy.txt

!!!Microscopy and Specimen Preparation

[Lenses and the Bending of Light | Lenses_and_the_Bending_of_Light]

[The Light Microscope | The_Light_Microscope]

[Preparation and Staining of Specimens | Preparation_and_Staining_of_ Specimens]

Lenses_and_the_Bending_of_Light.txt

!!Lenses and the Bending of Light

```
!Refraction
!Focal Point
```

The_Light_Microscope.txt

```
!!The Light Microscope
!The Bright-field Microscope
!Resolution
!The Dark-field Microscope
```

Preparation_and_Staining_of_Specimens.txt

```
!!Preparation and Staining of Specimens
!Fixation
!Dyes and Simple Staining
!Differential Staining
```

After you've created a text file for each initial page that you want in your wiki, you are ready to upload them.

Upload Text Files to the Course

While creating the wiki, you select the text files that create the initial pages. You select them from the course's `Files` folder.

1. On your course's Home Page, from the **Administration** block, select **Files**.

2. In the resulting window, select the **New Folder** button.

3. Name the new folder. I prefer to use a similar name as the wiki.

4. Upload the text files to the folder. The result will look like the following:

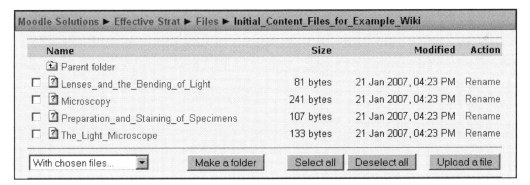

In the previous example, note that the files have underscores in their file names, for example, `The_Light_Microscope.txt`. The wiki starting page created from this text file will also have underscores in its name. Thus, it will be **The_Light_Microscope**.

Also notice in the previous example that the navigation bar (the 'breadcrumbs' at the top of the page) shows us the course name, then files, and then the name of the folder we created for our text files.

Create the Wiki

With the text files in place, now you can add the wiki to your course:

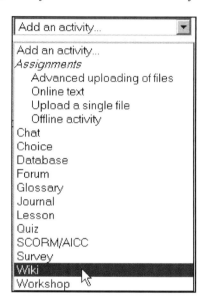

While Creating the Wiki, Select the Text Files for the Initial Pages

While creating the wiki, under **Choose an Initial Page**, click the **Choose/upload initial page...** button, and navigate to the folder where you stored the text files. This folder should contain only the text files for the starting pages.

From within the folder, select the text file for the starting page. That will become the Home Page of the wiki. Any other text files in that folder will become additional pages. In the following example, **Microscopy** becomes the Home Page for the wiki, and the other text files become additional starting pages.

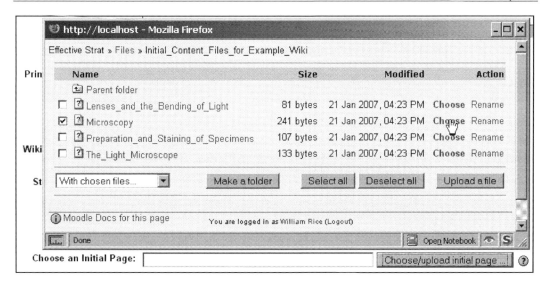

Note that I only needed to select **Microscopy**. **Microscopy** will be the wiki's first page. The other files in this directory automatically become initial pages. That is why it is important that this directory contain only text files for the starting pages in your wiki. Remember that earlier, we created a separate directory to hold just the text files for the initial pages. We did this to isolate the text files in their own directories.

Test the Wiki As a Student

When creating a course, it is helpful to keep two separate browsers running, such as Internet Explorer and Firefox. In one browser, create the course. In the other, log in as a student, and test as you create.

Log in as a student and view the wiki, to ensure that the starting pages have been created. But be aware that, once a student has viewed the wiki, you can no longer change the starting page. At that point, if you want a wiki with a different starting page, you must create a new wiki.

Workshop

A workshop provides a place for the students in a class to see an example project, upload their individual projects, and see and assess each other's projects. When a teacher requires each student to assess the work of several other students, the workshop becomes a powerful collaborative grading tool.

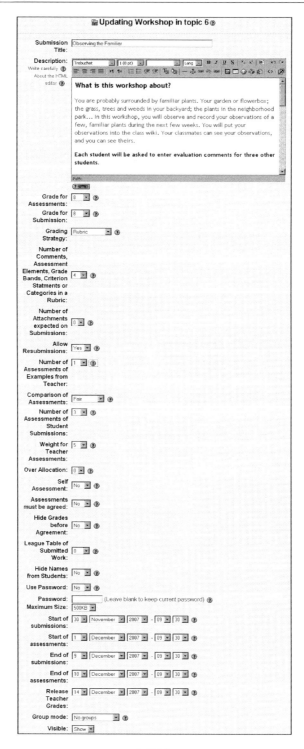

Workshop Strategies

Workshops can be ungraded, peer graded, instructor graded, or a combination of peer and instructor graded. Workshops enable you to create very specific assessment criteria for the graders to use. Also, workshops let you set the due dates for submitting work, and for grading work. You can use these and other features to build a strategy for making best use of workshops in your courses.

Peer Assessment of Assignments

One strategy for workshops is to have students assess each other's work, before submitting that same work as a graded assignment. For example, you could create a workshop where students assess each other's subject matter, outlines, and hypothesis for their term papers. Or they could assess each other's photos for specific technical and artistic criteria before submitting them to the instructor for grading.

Timing of Submissions and Assessments

Workshops enable you to set different due dates for submitting work, and for assessing other student's work. If you set the same due dates for both submission and assessment, many students might submit their work just before the submission deadline and they cannot all be assessed before the assessment deadline. Consider setting the submission deadline well before the assessment deadline. Then, before opening up the assessment ability to the students, examine the work submitted by them to ensure that it's close to what you expected or were trying to elicit from the students. You might even want to use the time between submission and assessment to refine your assessment criteria, in response to the work submitted.

Creating a Workshop

The fields in the workshop window give you many choices. No matter what you enter into each field, your many decisions can be summed up as:

- What will you have each student do? Create a file offline and upload it to the workshop? Write a journal entry? Participate in an online chat? Perform some offline activity and report on it via email or wiki? While the workshop window enables the student to upload a file, you can also require any other activity from the student.

- Who will assess the assignments? Will the teacher assess all assignments? Will students be required to assess other students' assignments? Will each student self-assess his or her work?

- How will the assignments be assessed? You can determine the number of criteria upon which each assignment is assessed, the grading scale, and the type of grading.

- When will students be allowed to submit their assignments? The assignment becomes available as soon as you show it. However, you can require students to assess an example before being allowed to submit their own work, and you also set a deadline for submission.

All the fields that we'll discuss henceforth are variations of these questions. The online help does a good job of explaining how to use each field. Instead of repeating how to use each field here, we will focus on how your choices affect the student and teacher experience.

Workshop Fields

The workshop activity is the most complex tool currently available in Moodle. Workshops are designed so that a student's work can be submitted and offered for peer review within a structured framework. Workshops provide a process for both instructor and peer feedback on open-ended assignments, such as essays and research papers. There are easy-to-use interfaces for uploading assignments, performing self-assessments, and peer reviews of other students' papers. The key to the workshop is the scoring guide, which is a set of specific criteria for making judgments about the quality of a given work. There are several fields under workshop. They will be explained in the following sections. They provide a place for the students in the class as well as the teachers to make the best use of Moodle.

Title and Description

Your students will see and click on the **Title**. The **Description** should give instructions for completing the workshop. If you want to make printer-friendly instructions, you can upload a .pdf file to the course files area, and put a link to the document in the workshop description.

Grade for Assessments and Grade for Submission

These two fields added together determine the maximum points a student can earn for a workshop. **Grade for assessments** is the grade that the student receives for grading other submissions. This grade is based on how close the assessment a student completes is to the average of all assessments for that same submission. For example, say Student A submits his or her work. Students B, C, and D assess the work and give scores of 10, 9, and 5 respectively. The average assessment is 8, so students B and C would receive higher marks for their assessments as compared to student D. In essence, the **Grade for assessments** is the 'grade for grading'.

Grade for submission is the maximum number of points a student can be given by the grader. If you choose **Not Graded** for the **Grading Strategy**, these grades are irrelevant.

The submission grade can come from the teacher or other students. If the field **Number of Assessments of Student Submissions** is set to something greater than zero, then students assess each other's work. If it's set to zero, then only the teacher is assessing the work.

Making the maximum grade a multiple of the number of assessment elements enables the students to interpret their grades more easily. For example, suppose a workshop is assessed on five elements; for each element, the assessor will choose from the following four statements:

1. The workshop does not meet this requirement in any way (0 points).
2. The workshop meets this requirement partially (1 point).
3. The workshop meets this requirement (2 points).
4. The workshop exceeds this requirement (3 points).

You could assign a point value of zero for each A, one point for each B, two points for each C, and three points for each D. Then, each element would be worth a maximum of three points. With five elements, the workshop would have a maximum grade of 15. This would make it easier for the student to interpret his or her grade.

Grading Strategy

A workshop assignment is quite flexible in the type of grading scheme used. It can be one of the following:

Not Graded

When this is selected, students can comment upon each assessment element but do not select a grade. The teacher can grade the students' comments. In that case, the workshop is transformed from one where students grade each other to where the teacher grades each student's comments.

This may be especially useful when you want to have a structured discussion about the material that you present to the students. As the course creator, you can present the students with material uploaded to the workshop, or use the workshop's description to direct the students to the material they must assess. After the students view the material, they enter the workshop and leave comments according to the elements presented. As the workshop presents the students with evaluation elements, and it requires that they complete each element, your discussion would be more structured if you used a wiki or a forum.

Accumulative

In the **Accumulative** grading strategy, the grade for each element is added to arrive at the accumulated grade. This style of grading enables you to present the reviewer with a numeric scale. You can also present the reviewer with Yes or No questions, such as 'Does this workshop meet the requirement?' Or, you can present the reviewer with a grading scale, such as 'Poor, Fair, Good, and Excellent'. If you do use a Yes or No or a grading scale, you will assign a point value to each response. Consider informing the reviewer of the value of each response. For example, instead of just writing:

- Poor
- Fair
- Good
- Excellent

Consider writing:

- Poor (1 point)
- Fair (2 points)
- Good (3 points)
- Excellent (4 points)

Error Banded

When you choose this option, students evaluate a workshop using a series of Yes or No questions. Usually, you create questions to evaluate whether the workshop met a requirement, such as 'Does the student present a variety of opinions?'

When writing an error banded question, make sure that it can be answered using only Yes or No. A sign that you need to revise your question is the presence of the word 'or'. For example, don't write 'Did the student describe the plant well enough to distinguish it from others, or, is there still a doubt as to which plant the student is describing?' Such a question cannot be answered Yes or No.

Making Best Use of Error Banded Questions

The answer to an error banded question is sometimes very clear, and sometimes subjective. For example, the question 'Did the student describe the plant well enough to distinguish it from others?' is subjective. One reviewer might think the student did an adequate job of describing the plant, while another might think otherwise. Error banded questions can be a good way to perform subjective peer evaluations of the students' work.

If the work requires a more objective evaluation, such as 'Did the student include all five identifying features covered in this lesson?' you may not need a workshop. That kind of objective evaluation can be performed easily by the teacher using an assignment.

Criterion and Rubric

For a criterion grading scale, write several statements that apply to the project. Each statement has a grade assigned to it. The reviewers choose the one statement that best describes the project. This single choice completes the review. The rubric grading scale is the same as the criterion, except that reviewers choose a statement for multiple criteria. The following is a screenshot of an assessment element:

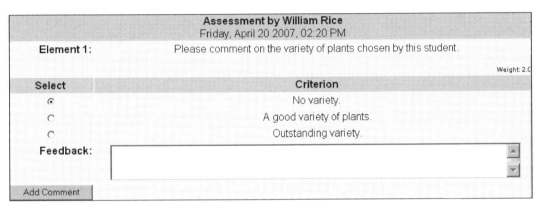

For a rubric, you would create several of these elements, and the reviewers would select a statement for each of them. For a criterion scale, you would create only one of these:

Number of Comments, Assessment Elements, Grade Bands, Criterion Statements, or Categories in Rubric

This field determines how many elements will be evaluated. No matter which number you select, the reviewers will always be presented with a general comments field into which they can type text. If you set this field to zero, reviewers will see only the general comments field.

Allow Resubmissions

The name of this field implies that a student can replace a previous submission with a new one. Actually, if you turn this option on, students can submit more than once, but all previous submissions are retained. Also, the latest submissions are not likely to be evaluated any more than the earlier submissions. Each submission is equally likely to be assigned to a reviewer.

This has implications for the course management. For example, suppose for the field, **Number of Assessments of Student Submissions**, you select 3. Half way through the course, you run a report showing that most students have completed their three assessments (they have evaluated three other students' work). Then, students begin resubmitting their work. These resubmissions will be distributed at random among the reviewers who have assessments left. As course manager, you need to determine if there are enough assessments left to cover the resubmissions.

The system keeps the highest grade of all the assignments submitted by the student (the highest grade is the largest teacher-peer combined score).

Number of Assessments of Examples from Teacher

Setting this field to a number greater than zero forces the students to assess that many number of example projects from the teacher. The student must comment upon and grade the example. The student's assessment can be graded by the teacher. The student cannot submit her or his work until she or he has gone through the example the teacher provided.

Comparison of Assessments

Work is often assessed by both the teacher and students. The work being assessed can be examples provided by the teacher, or work submitted by the students. In either case, it can be assessed by both the teacher and the student.

When a student assesses a piece of work, the assessment can be graded. For example, suppose the teacher is conducting an online digital photography class. The teacher supplies a photo and asks the students to rate the photo's contrast, brightness, focus, and so on. The students can be graded on their assessments. (Did they notice the overexposed area on the subject's cheek? Did they notice that the eyes were a little out of focus?) Moodle grades a student's assessment by comparing it to the teacher's assessment of the same work. The closer the student's assessment agrees with the one given by the teacher, the more points the student earns.

How close to the teacher's assessment must the student's be to earn a good grade? That is determined by this setting. When **Fair** is selected, random guessing will usually give a score of zero, or close to zero. The other settings range from **Very Lax** to **Very Strict.** You can change this setting on the fly, and evaluate its effect on student grades.

Number of Assessments of Student Submissions

This field determines how many other projects each student is asked to review. If there are more submissions than the allowed assessments, the reviewer will get only the number set in this field. Some projects will not be reviewed.

Weight for Teacher Assessments

This value can range from zero to ten. If set to zero, the teacher's assessment for a piece of work carries no weight for the student's grade. If set to 1, the teacher's assessment carries the same weight as the student's assessment of that piece of work. If set to 2, the teacher's assessment counts as much as two student assessments, and so on. If students have consistently over or under-graded assignments in a workshop, this setting can be used by the teacher to raise or lower the overall grades.

Over Allocation

As students submit or upload their work to a workshop, Moodle allocates it to other students for assessment. The field **Number of Assessments of Student Submissions** determines how many submissions each student is required to assess. Ideally, everyone will submit their assignments on time, and the students will have plenty of time to evaluate each other's work. For example, suppose there are ten students in the class, and the **Number of Assessments of Student Submissions** is set to **3**. This means that each of the ten submissions is assessed three times. Moodle assigns the assessments as the work is submitted.

However, if a student submits work late, the students who are going to evaluate the late person's work will need to wait before they can complete their assessments. Let's suppose one student doesn't submit his or her work by the deadline. This means that the class is three assessments short. As Moodle assigns the assessments evenly, three students will end the class one assessment short. Shall we penalize these students for not completing the required three assessments?

In our example, **Over Allocation** is set to zero, and each submission is evaluated three and only three times. If we set **Over Allocation** to one, and the deadline arrives, Moodle will over allocate some work to the students who still need to complete assessments. In this example, Moodle will randomly choose three pieces of work that have already been assessed three times, and assign them to the three students who are missing an assessment. These pieces of work will then be over allocated by one assessment each. Moodle allows a maximum over allocation of two.

Self Assessment

If this is set to **Yes**, each student is asked to evaluate his or her own work. This is in addition to the number of student submissions that the student is asked to evaluate.

Assessments Must Be Agreed

If this is set to **Yes**, then an assessment made by one student can be viewed by the other reviewers of the same work. If the other reviewers disagree, the evaluation process continues until they agree or until the assignment's closing time is passed. This can be a useful tool for determining how clear your evaluation elements are. If there is a lot of disagreement among reviewers of the same work, revisit your evaluation elements and the instructions you give the reviewers.

Hide Grades Before Agreement

If this is set to **Yes**, the numeric parts of a project's evaluation are hidden from other reviewers. The reviewers can see each other's comments, but not the grades they've assigned. The grades will appear after the reviewers agree with each other.

League Table of Submitted Work

This creates a list of the best-rated assignments in this workshop. If it is set to zero, no list is created.

Hide Names from Students

When set to **Yes**, this hides the names of the students whose work is being evaluated. Note that the names of students are never hidden from the teacher. Also, if a teacher assesses a student's work, the teacher cannot do so anonymously. This only hides the names of students who submitted work from the students who are evaluating the work.

Use Password and Password

You can use these fields to password-protect the assignment.

Maximum Size

This field sets the size limit for project files uploaded to the workshop.

Start and End of Submissions/Assessments

These fields determine when the workshop opens and closes. On the closing date, if any hidden grades appear, students can no longer upload files and evaluate others' work.

Release Teacher Grades

You can use this field to withhold the teacher's assessments until a given date.

Group Mode

Just as in other activities, this determines if access is segregated by group.

Visible

This field shows the workshop or hides it from students.

Summary

Moodle offers several options for student-to-student and student-to-teacher interaction. When deciding which social activities to use, consider the level of structure and amount of student-to-student, student-to-teacher interaction you want. For example, chats and wikis offer a relatively unstructured environment, with lots of opportunity for student-to-student interaction. They are good ways of relinquishing some control of the class to the students. A forum offers more structure because entries are classified by topic. It can be moderated by the teacher, making it even more structured. A workshop offers the most structure, by virtue of the set assessment criteria that students must use when evaluating each other's work. Note that as the activities become more structured, the opportunity for students to get to know each other decreases.

You may want to introduce a chat and/or forum at the beginning of a course, to build 'esprit de corps' among the students, then move into a collaborative wiki, such as a group writing project. Finally, after the students have learned more about each other and are comfortable working together, you might use a workshop for their final project.

8
Welcoming Your Students

When prospective students enter your site, what will they see? Will it be a welcome page, with some explanation of your site? Sample courses that are open to the public? Or a secure Login Page? Each of these is possible, by itself, and in combinations as well. In this chapter, you will determine what kind of welcome page prospective and existing students receive.

First Impression—Login Page, Front Page, or Your Page?

In Chapter 2, you have learned that the site variable **Forcelogin** can be used to force users to log in to your site. If this is set to **Yes**, all users see the Login Page as soon as they hit your learning site.

The Login Page does not present much of a welcome for prospective students. It is not a very good sales tool for your site. If you want to welcome prospective students with more information about your learning site, consider using the Front Page, or a page of your own design as the welcome page to your site. To do this, you only need to set **Forcelogin** to **No**. Then, when people hit your site, they will automatically see the Front Page:

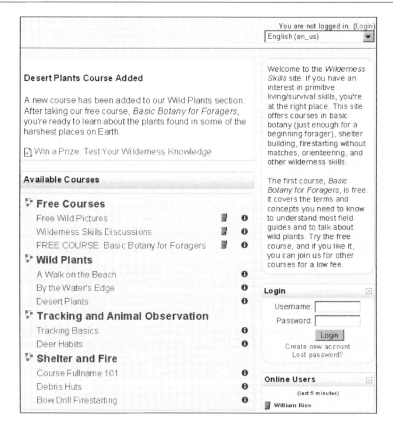

Another alternative is to use your own web page as the Front Page to your site. This page can be your sales pitch, and contain a link to the Front Page or Login Page of your Moodle site. If you select this option, you need to know how your web hosting service handles `*.htm` and `*.php` pages.

By default, when a user hits an Apache web server's directory, the server displays the page `index.html` or `index.htm`, if it's present in the directory. If neither of these is present, the server displays `index.php`. Moodle's Front Page is `index.php`. This behavior is controlled by a line in the Apache server's configuration file. Here's a default configuration for the Apache version 2.0 web server:

```
DirectoryIndex index.html index.htm index.php index.php4 index.php3
index.cgi index.pl index.html.var index.phtml
```

This means that if you put a file called `index.html` in Moodle's directory, the visitors coming to your Moodle site will see `index.html` instead of Moodle's Front Page, which is `index.php`. This enables you to construct the exact welcome page you want, unconstrained by Moodle's Front Page or Login Page layout. From the welcome page, you can link up to Moodle's Front Page, (`index.php`). You can test this behavior by putting `index.html` in your Moodle directory, and hitting that directory with your web browser. If `index.html` doesn't display, talk to your webmaster about modifying the directory index line to put `index.html` before `index.php`.

You might want the colors on `index.html` to match those used in your Moodle site. If you're proficient with reading HTML code, and using CSS, you can see which colors your Moodle site uses by looking in `/theme/themename/config.php`, where `themename` is the name of the theme you're using.

Customizing the Login Page

Moodle's Login Page displays directions for creating a new user account in the right column:

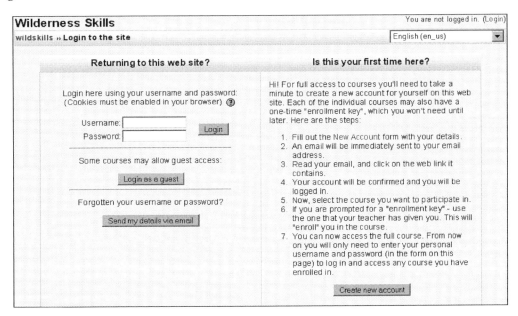

The contents of this page will change based upon the authentication methods that you enable. For example, notice that the directions on the page displayed above tell the user how to register for an account. These directions appear if email-based self registration is enabled. If that method is turned off, then these directions would be replaced with something else.

Moodle 1.9 enables you to customize the directions that appear in the Login Page. You can customize this under **Site Administration | Users | Authentication | Instructions**.

In Chapter 3, during the configuration, you learned that Moodle stores almost all its text messages in language files. Each language has a separate directory, such as `\moodle\lang\en` for British English, and `\moodle\lang\es` for Spanish (Español). In the previous screenshot, the user has selected the language as U.S. English, so Moodle will use the text files found in `\moodle\lang\en_us`.

The `moodle.php` file holds the text displayed in the right column. Search `moodle.php` for the line that begins as `$string['loginsteps']=`. This line holds the HTML code displayed in the right column of the Login Page. By editing this line, you can put whatever HTML code you want in that column.

Customizing the Front Page

The Front Page of your Moodle site can do two things. It can do either, or both of these:

- Display a list of courses, and/or course categories, enabling visitors to jump to a selected course or category.

- Act as a course in itself, by displaying anything that a course can display.

Anything that can be added to a course can be added to the Front Page, so that the Front Page can become its own course. In the following example, the Front Page does both of these:

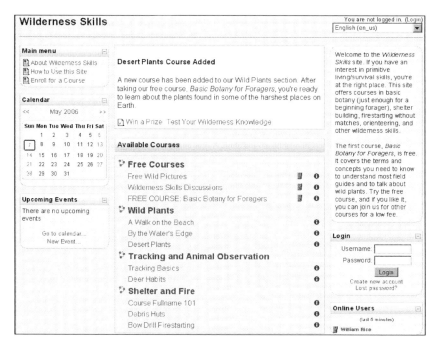

Desert Plants Course Added is a label in Section 1 of the Front Page, as is the text below it. The link below that is a quiz that was added to this section.

Available Courses is the result of choosing to display course categories on the Front Page. This is done with the **Front Page format** variable on the **Site Settings** page. For more about this, refer to Chapter 2.

Note that the upper left block displays the title, **How to Use this Site**. In the default installation, this was labeled **Main Menu**, because it is the main menu block. You can add anything to the main menu block that you can add to a course.

In my course, we added three web pages using the **Add a resource** drop-down menu. We also edited the title of the block. In the /lang/en/moodle.php file, the line $string['mainmenu'] = 'Main Menu'; was changed to $string['mainmenu'] = 'How to Use this Site'. In the newer vesions of Moodle, you can edit these strings from the page **Site Administration | Language | Language Editing**.

Front Page Blocks

In Chapter 4, you saw how blocks can be added to a course to enhance the user experience. Any block that can be added to a course can also be added to the Front Page. Some blocks behave slightly differently when they appear on the Front Page. Other blocks can be added only to the Front Page; they cannot appear in courses. Each subsection below talks about how to add a standard block to the Front Page, and how to make best use of that block.

Activities

The **Activities** block lists all of the types of activities available in the Front Page. If the type of activity is not used on the Front Page, the link for that type of activity is not presented. When this block is on the site's Front Page, clicking on a type of activity gives a list of the activities on the Front Page , and not for the entire site. In the following screenshot, clicking **Resources** will display a list of all the static course material that has been added to the Front Page.

Keep in mind that the people taking your Front Page course might be first-time users. That is, the Front Page might be the first Moodle course your visitor has ever taken. The Activities block is not entirely intuitive for a first-time user. One reason is because it uses terminology that is specific to Moodle, such as assignments, choices, lessons, and resources. At this point, your visitor doesn't know what these things are. Another reason the **Activities** block may be confusing to a first-timer could be because it probably lists the activities out of order. The activities are listed in alphabetical order, no matter in which order they appear on the Front Page. Moodle encourages exploration, and only the Lesson activity enforces an order on the student. However, you may want to orient your new student before allowing them this freedom.

Site Administration Menu

Only teachers and site administrators can see the **Site Administration** block. It is hidden from students. For that reason, there is very little disadvantage to having this block displayed. It appears on the Front Page and each course's Home Page, by default. Consider keeping it unless you have a specific, compelling reason to hide it. For more about the Site Administration menu, see Chapter 3 on Configuration.

Calendar

Workshops, assignments, quizzes, and events, all have dates; so all of them appear on the **Calendar**.

In the previous screenshot, the colored block next to each of the event types indicates how that type is displayed on the **Calendar**. To turn off the display of that event type, click the eye next to the event type. The colored block will disappear, and the event type will be taken off the **Calendar**. **Global events** are events that a site administrator adds to the Front Page. **Course events** are events that an administrator or teacher adds to a course. **Group events** are events created by a teacher that are open only to the group of which the student is a member. **User events** are created by the user. They are personal events, viewable only by the user.

The display of events in a calendar is specific to the user. If a user hides a type of event, that setting is applicable only for that user. For example, if you are a teacher, and you hide global events in the calendar, you are hiding them only on your calendar. Your students can still see the global events on their calendars.

The type of people who will have access to the Front Page determines which event types you want to display on the Calendar. If your Front Page is open to anonymous, unregistered viewers, you must decide if you want to reveal global events to them. Will these events act as good sales tools, and inspire people to sign up for your site? Or, will revealing these events betray your users' confidence? Usually, showing global events to anonymous users is a good sales tool, without revealing anything confidential about the enrolled users. Course, group, and user events are not visible to anonymous visitors.

Front Page Description

When you view a course, the **Course Summary** block displays the course summary from the course's **Settings** page. When you view the Front Page, the Front Page description block displays the **Site Description** from the **Site Settings** page.

Like all blocks, the Front Page description appears in the left or right column. Research shows that readers notice items placed in the upper right corner of a web page more than those in other positions. If it's important for new visitors see this block, consider placing it there.

Welcome to the *Wilderness Skills* site. If you have an interest in primitive living/survival skills, you're at the right place. This site offers courses in basic botany (just enough for a beginning forager), shelter building, firestarting without matches, orienteering, and other wilderness skills.

The first course, *Basic Botany for Foragers*, is free. It covers the terms and concepts you need to know to understand most field guides and to talk about wild plants. Try the free course, and if you like it, you can join us for other courses for a low fee.

Also, remember that this block is essentially a full-featured web page. The editing window for creating this text is the same one that Moodle gives you for creating web pages. You can use text styles, graphics, even embedded multimedia objects, or JavaScript in this block. The Front Page description is your first and best chance to convince visitors to go beyond the Front Page. Use it well.

In addition to appearing on the Front Page, the **Site Description** also appears in the `meta` tag of your site. The following figure is the source code for the Front Page of the example site. Note that the **Site Description** appears in the meta tag amed `description`..

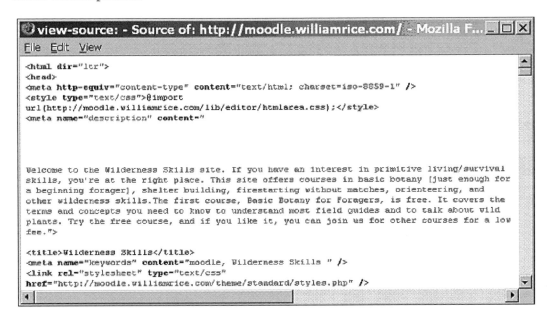

Most search engines use the `description` meta tag to classify your site. In some cases, the first words in this meta tag appear in search results. When you write the **Site Description**, make sure that the first few sentences are search-engine friendly. Imagine that these are the sentences which someone will see, when your site is displayed in search engine results. Also, don't be afraid to use text styles, graphics, and other web page features in the description.

Courses

For guests and site administrators, the **Courses** block displays links to the course categories. Clicking a link takes the user to the list of courses. For teachers and students who are logged in, this block displays a list of **My courses**.

Recall that on the **Site Settings** page, you can choose to display a list of course categories, or a list of courses. Either of these will appear in the centre of the page.

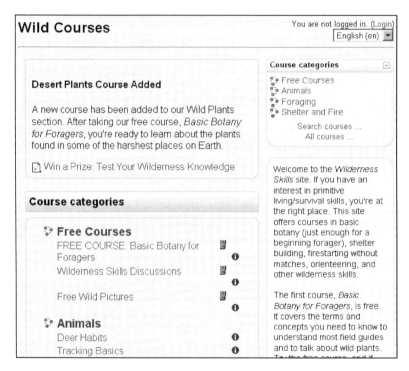

In the last figure, I've displayed the Courses block (which actually displays as **Course categories**), and also displayed the list of courses using the setting from the **Site Administration** menu. Of course, these lists are redundant. However, this gives you the chance to compare the two methods of listing your courses, side by side. Note that displaying the courses in the centre of the page makes them much more prominent. If you use the Courses block instead of displaying the course list in the centre of the page, consider including some text on the Front Page that instructs visitors to choose a course category from the Courses block, when they are ready to enter a course.

Latest News

By default, the Front Page has a News forum. The **Latest news** block displays the most recent postings from this forum.

Even if the forum is renamed, this block displays the postings. The number of postings displayed in this block is determined under **Site Administration | Front Page | Front Page settings | News items to show**.

Login

The **Login** block is available only for the site's Front Page.

After the user logs in, this block disappears. If a visitor is not logged in, Moodle displays small **Login** links in the upper-right corner and bottom-center of the page. However, the links are not very noticeable. The Login block is much more prominent, and contains a message encouraging visitors to sign up for an account.

The main advantage to the Login block over the small Login links is the block's greater visibility. However, if you want to make the Login link in the upper-right larger, look in Moodle's index.php file for this line:

```
$loginstring = "<font size=2> <a href=\"$wwwroot/login/index.php\">"
.get_string("login")."</a></font>";
```

Change <font size=2> to a larger number. This increases the font size of the Login link.

If you want to edit the message displayed in the Login block, look for the string `startsignup` in the the `moodle.php` file, in the language folder. In my example site, I'm using the language **en_us**, so I look in the file `/lang/en_us/moodle.php` for this line:

```
$string['startsignup'] = 'Start now by creating a new account!';
```

I can change the message to something else, such as **Click here to sign up!**.

Main Menu

The **Main menu** block is available only on the site's Front Page. Anything that can be added to a course can be added to this block, as you can see from the pull-down menus labeled **Add a resource...** and **Add an activity....**

In my example site, I use the **Main menu** to convey information about the site and how to use the site. I want visitors to be able to easily get instructions for enrolling and using courses. Perhaps I should change the name of this block to **How to Use this Site**. I can do that by looking in the language folder for the `moodle.php` file, for the following line:

```
$string['mainmenu'] = 'Main Menu';
```

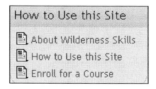

Change **Main menu** to whatever you want displayed for the name of the menu. In newer vesions of Moodle, you can also edit these strings from the page, **Site Administration | Language | Language Editing**.

Online Users

The **Online Users** block shows who is on the site at a given time. Every few minutes, the block checks who is on the site. You set the number of minutes under **Site Administration | Modules | Blocks | Manage Blocks | Online Users | Settings**.

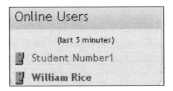

Note that the users can be anywhere on the site; the block does not tell you where. Also note that it tells you who is on the site now. It is not a complete list of everyone who is registered on the site.

When a visitor clicks on a user's name in this block, Moodle displays the user's profile. However, if the setting **Force users to login for profiles** is selected (under **Site Administration | Security | Site policies**), then the visitor must create an account, and log in to see the user's profile.

People

When the **People** block is added to the site's Front Page, it lists the users enrolled on the site.

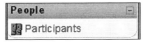

When it's added to a course, it lists the users enrolled in that specific course. If the site or course uses groups, it provides a link to those groups.

Recent Activity

When the **Recent activity** block is added to the site's Front Page, it lists all the student and teacher activity on the Front Page, since the user's last login.

If someone is logged in as a guest user, this block displays the guest's activities since the last time he or she logged in. If guest users are constantly coming to your site, this block may be of limited use to them. One strategy is to omit this block from the site's Front Page, so anonymous users don't see it, and add it only to courses that require users to log in.

Search Forums

The **Search Forums** block provides a search function for forums. It does not search other types of activities or resources. When this block is added to the site's Front Page, it searches only the forums on the Front Page.

This block is different from the **Search courses** link that automatically appears in the **Courses** block. The **Search courses** field searches course names and descriptions for the search terms, while **Search Forums** searches forum posts.

Upcoming Events

The **Upcoming Events** block is an extension of the Calendar block. It gets event information from your Calendar. By default, the Upcoming Events block displays a maximum of 10 upcoming events. It looks ahead a maximum of 21 days.

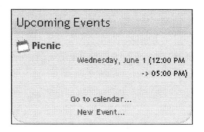

In the older versions of Moodle, these limits are set in the `/blocks/calendar/lib.php` file, in the following lines:

```
define ('CALENDAR_UPCOMING_DAYS', 21);
define ('CALENDAR_UPCOMING_MAXEVENTS', 10);
```

To change these preferences in a **Moodle version 1.9** and above, you can use the regular Moodle interface:

1. Click on the name of the month in the Calendar.

2. In the resulting **Detailed Month View** page, click the **Preferences...** button in the upper-right corner.

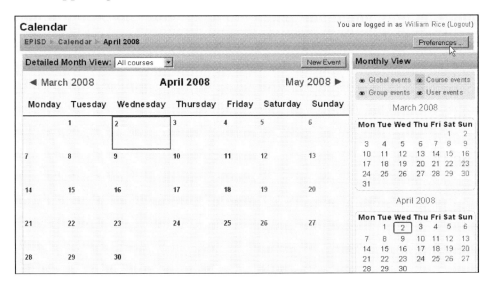

3. Change the preferences, and save.

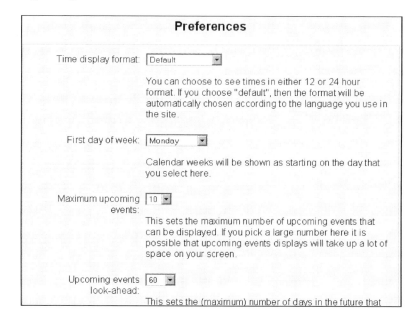

Combining Anonymous, Guest, and Registered Access

There are three ways by which you can gain access into Moodle: through Anonymous, Guest, or Registered access. However, you need to know which kind of user access is best for your learning site. As the different kinds of access can be applied to the site, and individual courses, you can combine them to create the effect you want. This is explained in the following section.

Security Options Available to You

Moodle's security options enable you to choose the kind of user access that is best for your learning site. From the moment that a web browser hits your Moodle site till the point where a student has enrolled in a course, the following are the options:

* Add your own introductory page, `index.html`, to the Moodle directory. When browsers first visit your site, instead of seeing Moodle's Front Page they'll see `index.html`. This enables you to create the exact first impression you want, without the limitations imposed by Moodle's layout.

- Enable anonymous access, or require login to the Front Page. Which option you use depends upon the purpose of the Front Page. If the Front Page sells your site, you will probably want to allow anonymous access. If the Front Page educates registered users on how to use your site, you will probably need to ask for registration.

- Enable or disable guest access for individual courses. If you want anonymous visitors to be able to sample your courseware easily, create a course category for free courses, and put that prominently on the Front Page. Enable guest access without an enrollment key for these sample courses. Then, you can restrict access to your core courses to registered users only.

- Enable or disable enrollment key for individual courses. You pass the enrollment key to your students outside of Moodle. This gives you another way to authenticate students. You can issue the enrollment key, one at a time, after you have confirmed a student's identity and/or they have paid for the course. In that case, in the course settings, you would select not to allow guest access, and to use the enrollment key. Then, only registered users with the enrollment key could access the course. Another option is to allow guests into the course with the enrollment key. In that case, the students would remain anonymous because they haven't registered, but there would still be some control on who can access the course. For example, suppose you have a course to help emergency workers deal with the stress of their jobs. You might want to give students the option of remaining anonymous, by allowing guest access. However, you don't want the entire world to be able to access the course. So, you could distribute the enrollment key to the users via their agency's email, or a memo in their inboxes, or some other means that ensures that only the intended audience gets the enrollment key.

- Segregate courses into groups. Remember that for each kind of activity, you can turn the **Group Mode** on and off. This offers an even finer layer of security than just regulating access to courses. You can allow open access to a course's introductory information, and then turn the **Group Mode** on, for the paid activities in the course.

Look and Feel

You can brand your learning site with your own colors, fonts, styles, logo, and text messages.

Themes—Customize Colors and Styles

In Moodle, the theme determines the colors and font styles that your site uses. To choose a theme, select **Site Administration | Appearance | Themes | Theme selector**. The choices you see there are standard themes that come with Moodle. On your server, you will find the files for these themes in /theme. Compare the theme names available in the **Themes** page with the directories you see on the server:

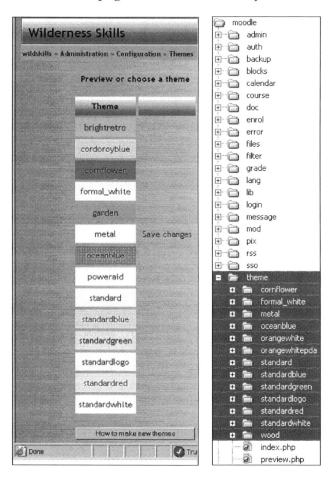

Instead of modifying a standard theme, duplicate the theme that is closest to what you want, and modify the duplicate. Also, check http://moodle.org/ for other themes that you can use. For example, the theme called *Kubrick* gives Moodle a look similar to the default installation of the **WordPress** blogging software. With this theme, your site is hardly recognizable as a Moodle site.

The following sections show you how to achieve some of these customizations.

Custom Logo

Not every theme uses a logo. For example, the theme **Standard** does not, but **standardlogo** does. The easiest way to include a customized logo in your Moodle site is to copy a theme that uses a logo, and then replace that theme's `logo.jpg` file with your own.

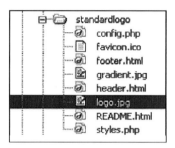

Custom Header and Footer

Inside the `Theme` folder, you will find the files `header.html` and `footer.html`. These are displayed as the header and footer on each page. Note that the Home Page (Front Page) of your site uses a header different from that in the inside pages. If you want to use the same header on the inside pages and the Front Page, you'll need to customize both headers.

Customizing the Header

The lines that you need to customize in `header.html` are copied below. I have added the line numbers. You will not find these in the code, and do not need to add them. I will refer to the line numbers as we discuss how to customize the code:

```
1.        if ($home) {   // home page ?>
2.    <div id="header-home">
3.    <h1 class="headermain"><img alt="[ REPLACE ME ]" src="<?php
      echo $CFG->wwwroot.'/theme/'.current_theme()
      ?>/images/logo.jpg" width="457" height="64" /></h1>
4.        <div class="headermenu"><?php echo $menu ?></div>
5.    </div>
6. <?php } else if ($heading) {//This is what gets printed on any
   other page with a heading.
```

```
7.   ?>
8.        <div id="header-home">
9.        <h1 class="headermain"><img alt="[ REPLACE ME ]" src="<?php
          echo $CFG->wwwroot.'/theme/'.current_theme()
          ?>/images/logo.jpg" width="457" height="64" /></h1>.
10.            <div class="headermenu"><?php echo $menu ?></div>.
11.       </div>
```

Recall that I said that the header for the site's front page is different from the header for all other pages. Line 1 tests whether you are on the front page. If you are, then lines 2 through 5 create the header. If you are not on the site's front page, lines 6 through 11 create the header. The only real difference between these two headers is in line 10, which creates the breadcrumb menu at the top of each page:

wildcourses ▶ Wild Plants 1 ▶ Assignments ▶ The Plants Around You

Notice that lines 3 and 9 specify the width and height of the logo:

```
<h1 class="headermain"><img alt="[ REPLACE ME ]" src="<?php echo $CFG-
>wwwroot.'/theme/'.current_theme() ?>/images/logo.jpg" width="457"
height="64" />
</h1>
    <div class="headermenu"><?php echo $menu ?></div>
    </div>
<?php } else if ($heading) {   // This is what gets printed on any
other page with a heading
?>
    <div id="header-home">
<h1 class="headermain"><img alt="[ REPLACE ME ]" src="<?php echo $CFG-
>wwwroot.'/theme/'.current_theme() ?>/images/logo.jpg" width="457"
height="64" />

</h1>
```

If you use a different graphic for your logo, you'll want to change these values to fit the new graphic.

If you want to add some text to the header, place it between the `<h1>` tags:

```
<h1 class="headermain"><img alt="[ REPLACE ME ]" src="<?php echo $CFG-
>wwwroot.'/theme/'.current_theme() ?>/images/logo.jpg" width="457"
height="64" />add your text here
</h1>
    <div class="headermenu"><?php echo $menu ?></div>
```

```
    </div>
<?php } else if ($heading) {  // This is what gets printed on any
other page with a heading
?>
    <div id="header-home">
<h1 class="headermain"><img alt="[ REPLACE ME ]" src="<?php echo $CFG-
>wwwroot.'/theme/'.current_theme() ?>/images/logo.jpg" width="457"
height="64" />add your text here

</h1>
```

Perhaps the most useful technique for customizing your site's header is to make one change at a time, save it, and then preview that one change in your browser. Repeat this till you get the effect that you want.

Customizing the Footer

The `footer.html` file is even simpler and easier to customize as compared to the header. There are two lines that you will see at the bottom of each page in your site. On the Front Page of your site, you will see the following:

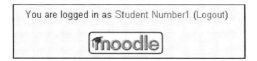

Note that the footer displays your login name, and a link to the official Moodle.org site.

On every other page of your site, you will see the following:

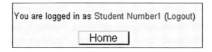

Note that you still see your login name, but instead of a link to the Moodle.org site, you see a link to the Home Page of your site. These two lines are created by the following lines of code in `footer.html`:

```
<?php echo $loggedinas ?>
<?php echo $homelink ?>
```

You can edit, delete, or add to this, as you wish. However, remember that if you remove the menu from the header `<?php echo $menu ?>`, and also remove `<?php echo $loggedinas ?>` from the footer, the user will not get any login confirmation message. You should keep at least one of these on the page. You can also insert HTML code before, between, or after these two lines. That content will show up on every page in your site.

Custom Icons

Icons for your Moodle site are in the directory `/moodle/pix`. Subdirectories inside `/pix` organize the icons based on their purpose:

- `/moodle/pix/c` holds course icons. For example, it holds the icons that appear before course names, event names, and groups.

- `/moodle/pix/f` mostly holds icons for the various file formats. For example, it holds icons for text files, videos, and Excel files.

- `/moodle/pix/g` holds the pictures that teachers upload to their personal profiles. The default Moodle installation has two files in this directory: a large and a small happy face.

- `/moodle/pix/i` holds Moodle's navigation and function icons. For example, there are icons for the edit function, to hide and show items, and to show the news.

- `/moodle/pix/m` holds icons for currency.

- `/moodle/pix/s` holds icons for smilies—angry, sad, wink, and so on

- `/moodle/pix/t` holds icons that appear in a teacher's functions: backup, delete, hide, and restore.

- `/moodle/pix/u` holds pictures that students upload to their personal profiles. The default Moodle installation has two files in this directory—a large and a small happy face.

You can replace any of these icons with your own. However, if you change the size of an icon, you should preview the results on several pages to ensure that the icon still fits in the space given by Moodle.

Custom Strings

In this and the earlier chapters, you saw that you can edit strings from the page, **Site Administration | Language | Language Editing**.

If you're using an older version of Moodle, editing strings in the `/lang/en/moodle.php` file enables you to customize the messages, prompts, and box names that Moodle displays. If you look in the folder `/lang/en`, you will see many other files in that directory. These files contain strings for Moodle's additional modules. For example, `/lang/en/forum.php` contains strings for forums, such as `$string['deleteddiscussion'] = 'The discussion topic has been deleted.'`. If you want to customize a string, and you're unsure where to find it, use your HTML editor (or even your word-processor) to search the files in the language directory for that string.

Summary

First impressions are as important for a learning site, as for a job interview. By customizing your site's Front Page, and opening access to sample learning material, you can give potential students the best impression. Customizing your site's logo, header, footer, icons, and strings requires a slightly higher level of technical skills, but results in a site that conveys your unique brand.

9

Features for Teachers

Moodle offers several features that are of special interest to teachers. These features focus on determining how well your students are progressing through a course. Reports and logs show you who has done what on your site or in your course. And grades not only tell you how well your students are scoring, but can also be curved and weighted very easily.

Reports and Logs

Moodle keeps detailed logs of all activities that users perform on your site. You can use these logs to determine who has been active in your site, what they did, and when they did it.

Moodle has a modest log viewing system built into it. You can see the logs under **Administration | Reports**. These reports enable you to look at the raw logs for a course. However, for sophisticated log analysis, you need to look outside of Moodle. The following section will help you with the tools you need to view and analyze your site logs.

The Reports Page

The following is a screenshot of the **Reports** as it appears in Moodle's **Logs** page:

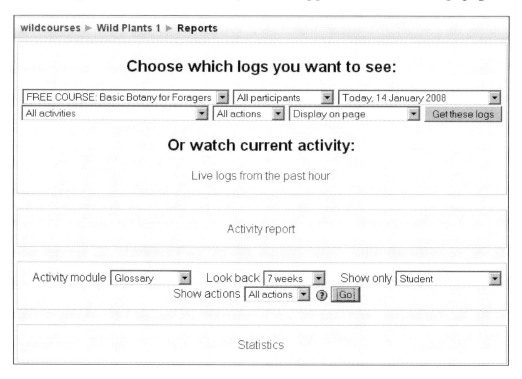

You can use this page to display three different kinds of information. From top to bottom, they are:

1. Raw logs
2. Activity report
3. Site statistics

Let's look at each separately.

Viewing Logs

Notice that Moodle's display of the log files can be filtered by course, participant, day, activity, and action. You can select a single value for any of these filters:

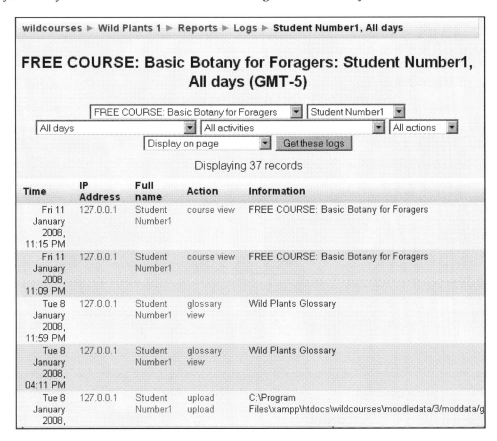

You cannot select multiple values for any of these variables. That is, you cannot select two courses from the first drop-down list, then four participants from the second, and a few days from the third. If you want a more sophisticated view of the logs, you must use a tool other than Moodle's built-in log viewer. Fortunately, you can download the logs as text files and import them into another tool, such as a spreadsheet. To download the logs, use the last drop-down list on the page:

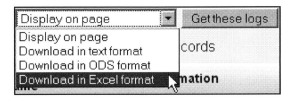

For example, you could use Excel's data menu to format, chart, and analyze the data. A complete discussion of Excel's data functions is beyond the scope of this book, but there are many sources of help for these functions. The following figure is an example of a table created in Excel from imported data. I've sorted the data by participant ('Full name'), so that at a glance, I can see which users are most active:

	A	B	C	D	E	
1	Course	Time	IP Address	Full name	Action	Information
2	FreePics	2007 February 24 19:34	82.27.68.16	LisaMarie Alexandria	course view	Free Wild Pictures
3	FreePics	2007 January 16 19:43	82.27.73.24	LisaMarie Alexandria	course view	Free Wild Pictures
4	FreePics	2007 January 16 19:23	82.27.73.24	LisaMarie Alexandria	resource view	Common Burdock in the Spring
5	FreePics	2007 January 16 19:23	82.27.73.24	LisaMarie Alexandria	course view	Free Wild Pictures
6	FreePics	2007 January 16 19:23	82.27.73.24	LisaMarie Alexandria	course enrol	Deer Habits
7	Debris Huts	2007 February 18 16:43	86.136.132.	Bradford Sorens	course view	Debris Huts
8	Debris Huts	2007 February 18 16:43	86.136.132.	Bradford Sorens	course enrol	Debris Huts
9	Bow Drill	2007 February 18 16:43	86.136.132.	Bradford Sorens	course view	Bow Drill Firestarting
10	Bow Drill	2007 February 18 16:43	86.136.132.	Bradford Sorens	course enrol	Debris Huts
11	Tracking Basic	2007 February 18 16:42	86.136.132.	Bradford Sorens	user view all	
12	Tracking Basic	2007 February 18 16:41	86.136.132.	Bradford Sorens	course view	Tracking Basics
13	Tracking Basic	2007 February 18 16:41	86.136.132.	Bradford Sorens	course enrol	Debris Huts
14	Water's Edge	2007 February 18 16:40	86.136.132.	Bradford Sorens	course enrol	Debris Huts
15	Water's Edge	2007 February 18 16:40	86.136.132.	Bradford Sorens	course view	By the Water's Edge
16	FreePics	2007 February 18 16:31	86.136.132.	Bradford Sorens	course view	Free Wild Pictures
17	FreePics	2007 February 18 16:31	86.136.132.	Bradford Sorens	resource view	Wild Plant Pictures
18	FreePics	2007 February 18 16:31	86.136.132.	Bradford Sorens	course view	Free Wild Pictures
19	FreePics	2007 February 18 16:31	86.136.132.	Bradford Sorens	course enrol	Debris Huts

Viewing Activity Reports

An activity report offers a user-friendly view of the activity in a single course. While the logs show complete information, an activity report just shows the course items, what was done in each item, and the time of the latest activity for that item:

Notice that by default, an **Activity report** shows the activity of all participants in a course. If you want to see the activity for just a single participant:

1. Your course should have the **People** block displayed. From the **People** block, select **Participants**:

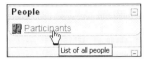

2. From the list of participants, select the one for which you want an activity report:

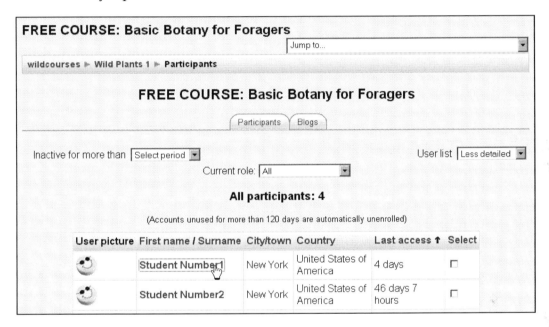

3. From the student's page, select the **Activity reports** tab. A report shows the student's activity in the current course:

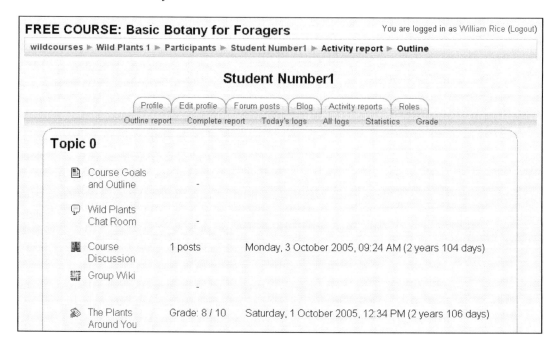

Site Statistics

If you run a website, you might be familiar with using site statistics to track the usage of your site. These statistics are recorded by the web server and displayed using a statistics analyzer. In Moodle, if you enable site statistics, Moodle will record statistics about each course and the site, just as your web server records statistics about your website. Moodle will also produce graphs to display the statistics, similar to a statistics analyzer.

The statistics page shows how many hits the different pages in your Moodle site have. You can look at the hits for a given day or hour. The statistics page does not show which users visited these pages. For that, you will need to use the site logs.

If you enable the site statistics, Moodle will record activity as it happens. Then at a time that you specify, Moodle will process the statistics to generate the graphs and charts on the statistics page. For a very active site, this processing can take a long time. Therefore, you should specify a time when the site is not busy serving students. Also, you do not want the statistics processing and backup routines to run at the same time, so you should schedule them a few hours apart.

To Enable Site Statistics

Select **Site administration | Server | Statistics**.

1. Click the **Enable statistics** check box.

2. Using the **Run at** field, set the time to start processing. This should be a time when the site is not being used by students.

3. Use the **Max runtime** field to set the length of time the processing will run. If you also use automated course backups, you might want to make sure the statistics processing ends before the backups begin.

4. Click the **Save changes** button.

Using Scales for Feedback, Rating, and Grading

In Moodle, you can use scales to rate or grade forums, assignments, quizzes, lessons, journals, and workshops. These scales can be used by anyone who is grading or evaluating a student's work. For example, if a workshop is being graded by other students, then the students use the scale selected by the teacher to grade that workshop. Being able to apply a scale to so many types of activities is a powerful way to make your courses more interactive and engaging.

Moodle comes with two pre-existing scales. One is called 'Separate and Connected Ways of Knowing'. This scale enables students to describe an item as connected to other knowledge in the course, or separate from the other knowledge. It isn't useful as a way to grade students, but instead is used to stimulate discussion about the item.

The other built-in scale that Moodle offers is numeric. You can assign a maximum number of points, from 1 to 100, to an item. Whoever is rating or grading the item selects a numeric grade from a drop-down list.

Moodle also enables you to create custom scales. This is covered in the subsequent subsection. But first, let's see how to apply a scale to an activity, and how to use that scale to grade a student's submission.

Applying a Scale to an Activity

In the next screenshot, I've added a grading scale to a journal activity. I could have selected **No grade**, **Separate** and **Connected Ways of Knowing,** or any number from **1** to **100**. I chose to give this journal entry a maximum point value of **10**:

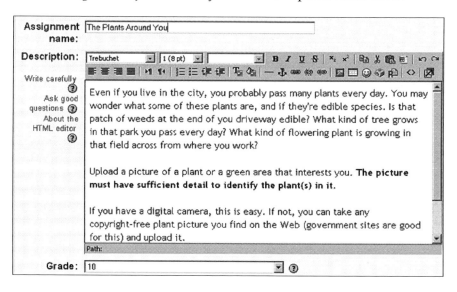

When a teacher views this journal assignment, the teacher clicks the **Grade...** button to display a pop-up window where the teacher can view the uploaded file, write a comment, and select the numeric grade:

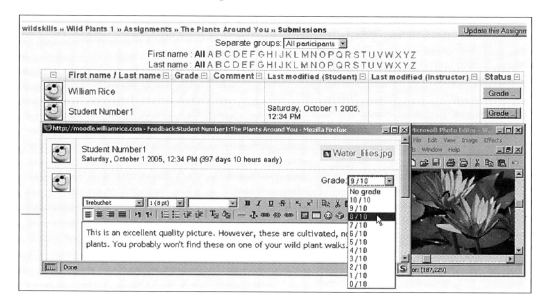

If **No grade** was selected for this assignment, only the comments would be available. The drop-down list of grades would not appear.

Establishing Custom Scales

The site administrator can create custom grading scales that are available to all teachers. A teacher can also create a custom scale to be used in the course in which it is created. A custom scale consists of a list of choices that you enter in an ascending order.

For example, you can create a scale for students to rate forum posts that reads **1-Does not apply to our discussion topic, 2-Partially applies to our discussion topic, 3-Mostly applies to our discussion topic, 4-Totally on target for our discussion topic**:

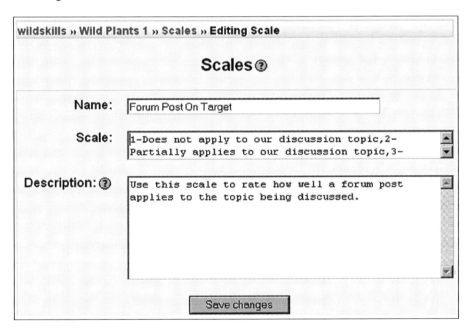

To reach the **Scales** page, select **Scales** from the **Administration** block. Then click the **Add a new scale** button. That will display a window like the one shown in the previous figure.

Grades

Moodle offers a very flexible reporting tool for grades. When you combine the ability to customize grading scales with Moodle's extensive grading tools, you have a powerful way to view the progress of your students. As a teacher, you can categorize graded activities, assign ranges to letter grades, use weighted grades, and hide/reveal grades to students. If Moodle doesn't have the reporting capabilities you want, you can download grades in text-only or Excel format and use a spreadsheet to chart and analyze them.

Anything that can have a scale applied to it can be graded—forums, assignments, quizzes, lessons, journals, database, and workshops.

Remember from the previous section on scales that grades can be assigned by both teachers and students.

Viewing Grades

To access grades, select the course whose grades you want to see, and then select **Grades** from the **Administration** block. This displays a summary of the grades for that course:

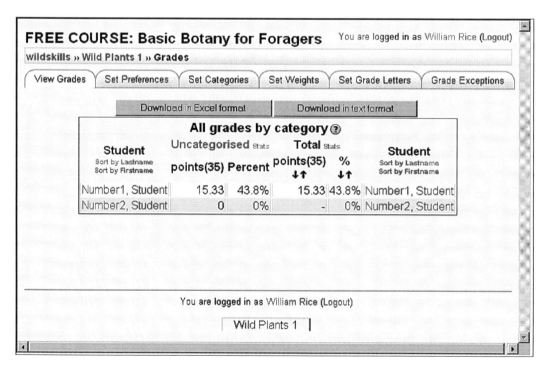

Notice that Student 2 has not completed any of the assignments in this course. Student 1 has earned a total of **15.33** points out of a possible **35**. We know that all of the grades are **Uncategorised**, because that is the only category with a link. To investigate the grades further, click the **Uncategorised** link and the detailed grades will display:

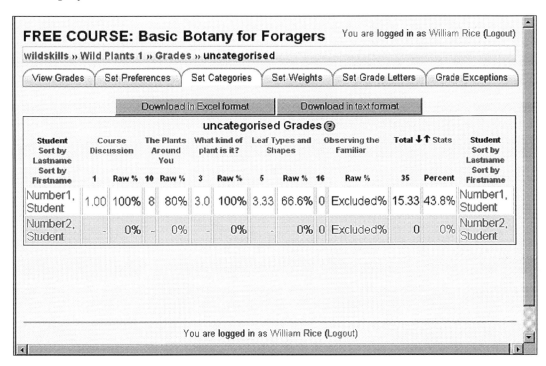

Now you can see why Student 1's overall grade is so low. For the assignment **Observing the Familiar**, the student has a grade of **0** out of a possible **16** points. We know the student has not completed that assignment because **Excluded** displays where the percentage would be. If the student has completed the assignment but earned zero points, then **0%** would display instead.

Categorizing Grades

Each of the graded activities can be put into a category. Note that you put activities into categories, not students. If you want to categorize students, put them into groups. Categorizing the graded activities in a course enables you to quickly see how your students are doing with various kinds of activities. If you do not assign an activity to a category, by default it belongs to the category **Uncategorised**. The following screenshot shows a course that uses the default categories of **Student-graded**, **Teacher-graded**, and **Uncategorised**. These are built into Moodle, and the system automatically assigns activities to the correct category as you create the activities:

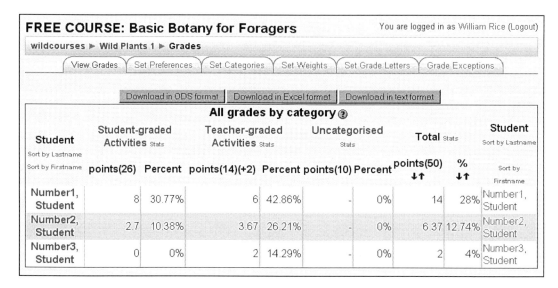

Creating and Viewing Categories

In the next example, the **Set Categories** tab has been selected. This is where you would assign and create grade categories for the activities in your course:

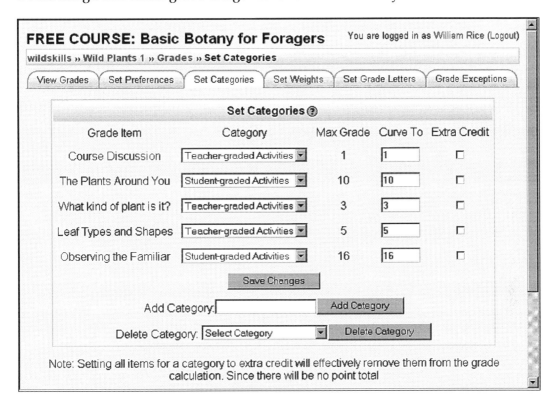

The most important point here is to determine what kind of question you want to answer when you examine student grades, and create categories that enable you to answer that question. For example, 'How do my students do on quizzes versus more interactive activities, like workshops and forums?' To answer that question, create a category just for quizzes, and you can answer that question just by viewing the grades. Or, 'How do my students do on offline activities versus online activities?' To answer that question, create online and offline grading categories. And remember, these categories are not 'written in stone'. If your needs change, you can always create and assign new grading categories as required.

Using Extra Credit

You can designate any activity as extra credit under the **Set Categories** tab. In this example, I'm setting the **Course Discussion** as **Extra Credit**:

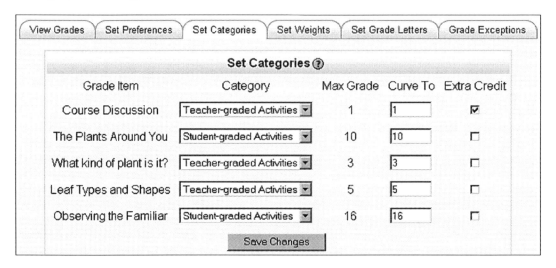

In an earlier screenshot, you saw that the category **Teacher-graded Activities** had a total of **9** points possible. Now that the **Course Discussion** has been designated as **Extra Credit**, this category has a total of **8** points possible:

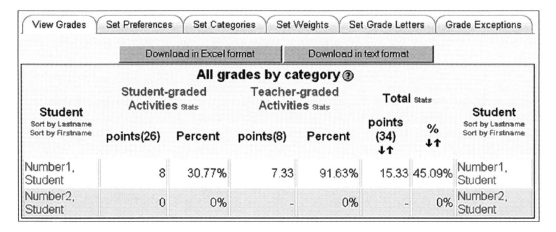

While it may be tempting to create a category just for extra credit activities, Moodle recommends against making all of the activities in a category extra credit. This might cause errors in the program, and might cause those activities to not even register. Instead, use the extra credit setting on selected activities.

Grading on a Curve

The **Set Categories** tab gives you the ability to grade any activity on a curve. This means that instead of the activity receiving the total number of points set in the activity's **Settings** page, it receives the number of points that you enter under the **Set Categories** tab. In this example, I've assigned the three-question quiz **9** points. Each question in the quiz now contributes three points to the total grade:

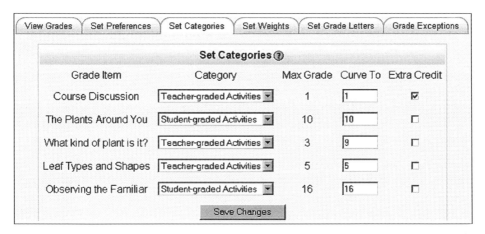

Looking under the **View Grades** tab, you can see that now the total number of **points** for **Teacher-graded Activities** has changed from 9 to **15**:

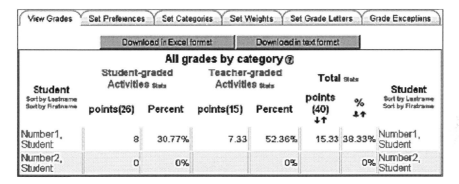

When to Use Curve and When to Use Weight

Grading on a curve is a convenient way to compensate for a single activity that proved too easy or too difficult. For example, if all of your students did poorly in a quiz, you could curve the quiz to a lower number of points, or even give it zero points. Your students could still see their quiz grades, but the zero points would eliminate them from their total grade.

Note that giving a single activity a zero point value is different than hiding it.

Under the **Set Weights** tab, you can hide an entire category of activities so that their grades are not displayed to the students, and are not used in the total calculation. A curve affects just a single activity, and still enables students to see their grades.

Use a curve when you want to adjust the amount that a *single activity* contributes to the total. Use weighting (covered in the next subsection) when you want to adjust the amount that an *entire category* contributes to the total.

Compensate for a Difficult or Easy Category by Weighting Grades

The **Set Weights** tab contains several settings to help you adjust how much a category contributes to the point total. You can use these settings to compensate for an especially difficult or easy category.

Weight

You can assign a weight to a grade category. By default, a weight of **100** is applied to the **Uncategorised** category. This doesn't mean that none of the other categories count towards the total. It means that each category is outweighed:

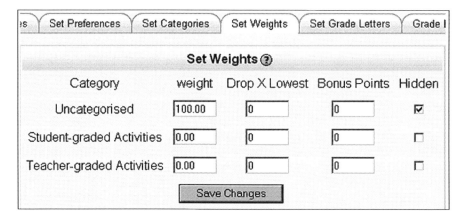

Hide Ungraded Activities

Under the **Set Weights** tab, selecting the **Hidden** checkbox removes a category from display and also from grade calculation. This is an easy way to add items to the grade calculation only after they have been graded. Just keep an activity hidden until you've graded it. After grading, unhide the activity. It then becomes visible to the students and is used in the grade totals.

Dropping the Lowest Scores in a Category

Weighting is intended to enable you to adjust the scores in an entire category of activities, when those activities have proven too difficult or too easy. One way to do this is giving a category a lower or higher weight than the others. Another way to improve the scores in a difficult category is to use **Drop X Lowest** to drop the lowest scored activities from that category's grades. Before using this feature, make sure every activity in that category has the same point value. The setting will work when the activities have different values, but the results become meaningless. For example, in the next screenshot, you can see that there are three **Teacher-graded Activities**, each with a different point value. If you use **Drop X Lowest** to drop the lowest-scored activity from that category, the score for Course Discussion would almost always be dropped because a perfect score of 1 would still be lower than a bad score in **What kind of plant is it?** or **Leaf Types and Shapes**.

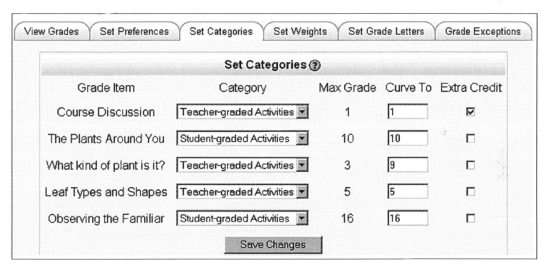

Giving Bonus Points

The **Set Weights** tab enables you to give all bonus points to every student's total grade in a category. This is a good way to compensate for a category of activities that was too hard. The bonus points show up on the **View Grades** tab. Note the **+2** displayed for the **Teacher-graded Activities**:

Student Sort by Lastname Sort by Firstname	Student-graded Activities Stats		Teacher-graded Activities Stats		Total Stats		Student Sort by Lastname Sort by Firstname
	points(26)	Percent	points(14) (+2)	Percent	points (40) ↓↑	% ↓↑	
Number1, Student	8	30.77%	9.33	66.64%	17.33	43.33%	Number1, Student
Number2, Student	0	0%	2	14.29%	2	14.29%	Number2, Student

All grades by category ⑦

Points, Percents, and Letter Grades

The **Set Grade Letters** tab enables you to determine the percentages that apply to each letter grade. Moodle comes with suggested values. You can change these at any time, for any course. Note that your change applies only to the course with which you are working:

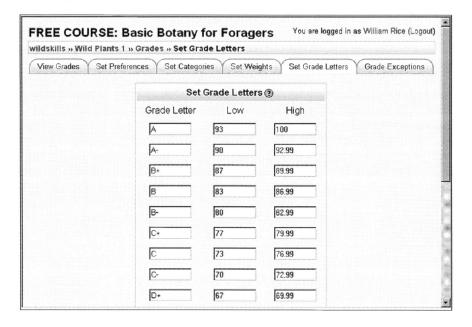

In this screenshot, I used the traditional letter grades. I could have entered any text under **Grade Letter** instead. For example, instead of **A**, I could have entered **Excellent** and instead of **B**, I could have entered **Above Average**, and so on.

To display letter grades to students and teachers under the **Set Preferences** tab, select those who can view the letter grades.

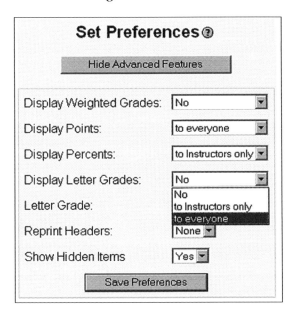

In the same window, select who can view the points and percentage scores. Take special note of the setting for **Show Hidden Items**. If this is set to **Yes**, even though a category has been hidden, it will show to the students. You probably want to keep this set to **No** because if you're hiding a category, the intent is that students will not see it. The setting **Letter Grade** determines whether letter grades are calculated based on raw percentages or weighted percentages.

For example, you could choose **No** for **Display Weighted Grades**, and let students see their true percentages. Then, select **Use Percent** for **Letter Grade**, so that students can see what grade they've earned after the weighting is taken into account.

The Teacher Forum

Each course can have a **Forum** for the teachers in that course. This is especially useful when several teachers collaborate on a course. To create a teacher-only forum, add a normal forum and then hide it. Teachers can view hidden course activities while students cannot.

If you are the course creator or a teacher in the course, when you enter the **Teacher forum** you see several links in the upper-right corner:

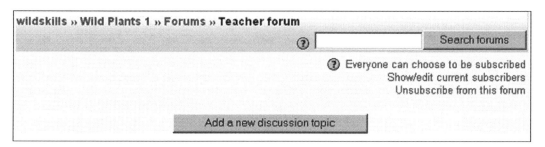

The line **Everyone can choose to be subscribed** means that right now all teachers in this course can choose to be subscribed to the forum or not. Subscribers receive email notices when someone posts to the forum. Clicking on this link forces all teachers of this course to be subscribed to the forum. It is one of Moodle's quirks that not only can the course creator force all the teachers to be subscribed, but so can any teacher of this course.

The links for **Show/edit current subscribers** and **Unsubscribe from this forum** do exactly what they say.

Roles

The next chapter, *Extending and Administering Moodle*, discusses the use of roles in your Moodle site. While creating, editing, and assigning roles is technically an 'Administrator' function, as a teacher and course creator, you will usually be the one to do this. So even if you're not the administrator for your Moodle site, I encourage you to read the section on *Roles* in the next chapter.

Summary

Whether in a classroom or online, managing a successful course requires two-way communication between the teacher and students. Constantly monitoring a course's logs and grades gives you an early indication that a class may need a midcourse correction. You can use questions, surveys, and chats to discover specific problems and challenges the students are facing. After bringing the course back on track, custom grading scales, extra credit, and curves can help you to equalize the grades. When teaching online, make a habit of often checking the logs and grades.

10

Extending and Administering Moodle

In the previous chapters, you worked with Moodle's standard modules. For example, assignments, forums, glossaries, lessons, quizzes, surveys, and other course features are all made possible by modules. These standard modules are installed with Moodle. You can also install modules that you get from the official `http://www.moodle.org/` site, and from other sites. We'll cover adding new modules in this chapter. We'll also cover duplicating courses on your site, and importing course material from other Moodle sites. Finally, we'll take a look at how Moodle uses roles to determine who can do what on your site.

Add-On Modules

New modules are constantly being developed. To keep abreast of the latest developments, take an occasional look at the Modules and plug-ins database, on `http://www.moodle.org/` where you get most modules. And even if you're not a programmer, contributing feedback and documentation to the modules in progress is a great help in their development.

Getting Modules

The following screenshot shows you the **Modules and plugins** page from moodle. org. Notice that the page lists the version of Moodle required, and whether the module is standard, third party, or contributed. Clicking the icon all the way to the right takes you to that module's page. On that page, you will find all the forum postings dealing with that module. You will also be able to download that module.

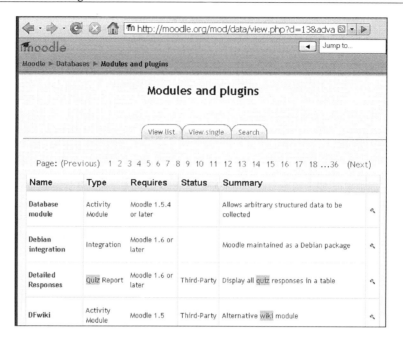

Installing Modules

In the previous screenshot, you can see the /mod directory in the Moodle installation. Under that directory is a subdirectory for each module:

Installing a new module is a simple process:

1. Download the module from http://www.moodle.org/, or whichever site supplies you with the module.
2. Copy the module files into the /mod directory, so that the module now lives in its own subdirectory.
3. Make sure all students and teachers are logged out of the site.
4. Log in to your site as the administrator, and go to the **Site Administration** menu.
5. Select **Server | Maintenance Mode**. While in this mode, only administrators can log in and use the site.
6. Moodle will search for new modules. When it finds one, it displays a message saying that it is building new module tables. At this point, it is adding tables to the database to accommodate the data that the new module will generate.
7. Click the **Continue** button to return to the **Maintenance** page.
8. Select the link to disable **Maintenance Mode**.

9. Select the link for **Modules | Activities**. You will see a list of installed modules. The one that you just installed should be on that list.

Managing Modules

The main tasks for managing modules are hiding/showing them, changing their settings, and deleting them. All these tasks are accomplished from the **Site Administration | Modules | Activities | Manage Activities** page:

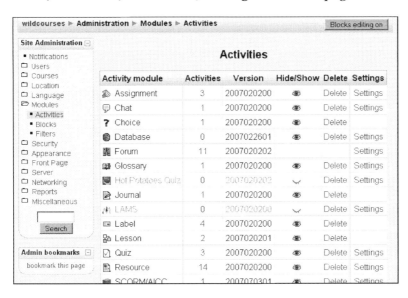

An open eye icon indicates that the module is available. A closed eye icon indicates that the module is installed but hidden. So course creators cannot use that module or activities created with it. Click the eye icon to open and close it.

Clicking **Delete** will delete the module's settings, and everything created with the module, from your site's database. However, it will not delete the module code from the /mod directory. If you do not delete the module's directory from /mod, the next time you access the **Administration** page, the module will reinstall itself.

Note that every module doesn't have a **Settings** link. If a module does have settings, then what you choose on that page will affect all the activities created with the module.

You might need to determine if you have the latest version of the module installed. To do this, download the latest version from http://www.moodle.org/, or wherever you obtain the module from. Usually, the module is in a ZIP archive. Unzip the readme.txt file, and look for the version number at the top of that file. Compare it to the version you have installed to determine if you're using the latest.

Backing Up, Restoring, and Duplicating Courses

Moodle enables the administrator to automatically back up all the courses in your site. And as your site's Front Page is essentially a course, it gets backed up as well. In addition to automated backup, Moodle also enables you to back up a course manually, on demand. Whichever method you use, you can specify the location of the backup files. You can use the following backup files to:

- Restore your courses in case of a computer failure or human error
- Import your courses into another site
- Keep old versions of courses stored, without having to keep them in your working Moodle site

Moodle also enables you to duplicate courses and parts of courses on your site. So, if you want a 'fresh' copy of one of your courses, you can get one with a few clicks.

In this section, you'll see how to back up, restore, and duplicate your courses.

What Gets Backed Up?

When Moodle creates a backup of your site, it backs up each course individually. The only difference between a site-wide backup and a course backup is that the former includes every course automatically, saving you the time of backing up each course, one at a time. The following screenshot shows the result of a site-wide backup:

Remote Site	Modified	Size
⊟ 🗁 moodle/		
⊞ 🗁 lib	9/30/2005 5:20 PM	
⊞ 🗁 moodle	9/30/2005 5:03 PM	
⊟ 🗁 moodledata	10/20/2005 4:43 PM	
⊞ 🗁 1	10/19/2005 6:51 PM	
⊞ 🗁 4	10/1/2005 5:25 PM	
⊞ 🗁 cache	10/20/2005 3:35 PM	
⊞ 🗁 sessions	10/21/2005 2:53 PM	
⊞ 🗁 temp	10/20/2005 4:43 PM	
⊞ 🗁 users	9/30/2005 5:23 PM	
📄 backup-bow_drill-20051020-1143.zip	10/20/2005 4:43 PM	3KB
📄 backup-debris_huts-20051020-1143.zip	10/20/2005 4:43 PM	3KB
📄 backup-deer-20051020-1143.zip	10/20/2005 4:43 PM	3KB
📄 backup-desert_plants-20051020-1143.zip	10/20/2005 4:43 PM	2KB
📄 backup-discussion-20051020-1143.zip	10/20/2005 4:43 PM	3KB
📄 backup-freepics-20051020-1143.zip	10/20/2005 4:43 PM	4KB
📄 backup-on_the_beach-20051020-1143.zip	10/20/2005 4:43 PM	3KB
📄 backup-tracking_basics-20051020-1143.zip	10/20/2005 4:43 PM	3KB
📄 backup-water_s_edge-20051020-1143.zip	10/20/2005 4:43 PM	3KB
📄 backup-wild_plants_1-20051020-1143.zip	10/20/2005 4:43 PM	12KB
📄 backup-wildskills-20051020-1143.zip	10/20/2005 4:43 PM	7KB

Note that the name of each backup file includes the name of the course, and the date/time of the backup. The last file, **backup-wildskills-20051020-1143.zip,** is the Front Page of the site. This is another example of how the Front Page of your site is essentially just another course.

Each of these `.zip` files contains an `.xml` file. The `.xml` file includes all the information in the course: web pages, forums and their entries, assignments, and so on. It also contains the graphics and uploaded files that are part of the course.

Where were those graphics and uploaded files stored on the server? Take a look at the following screenshot:

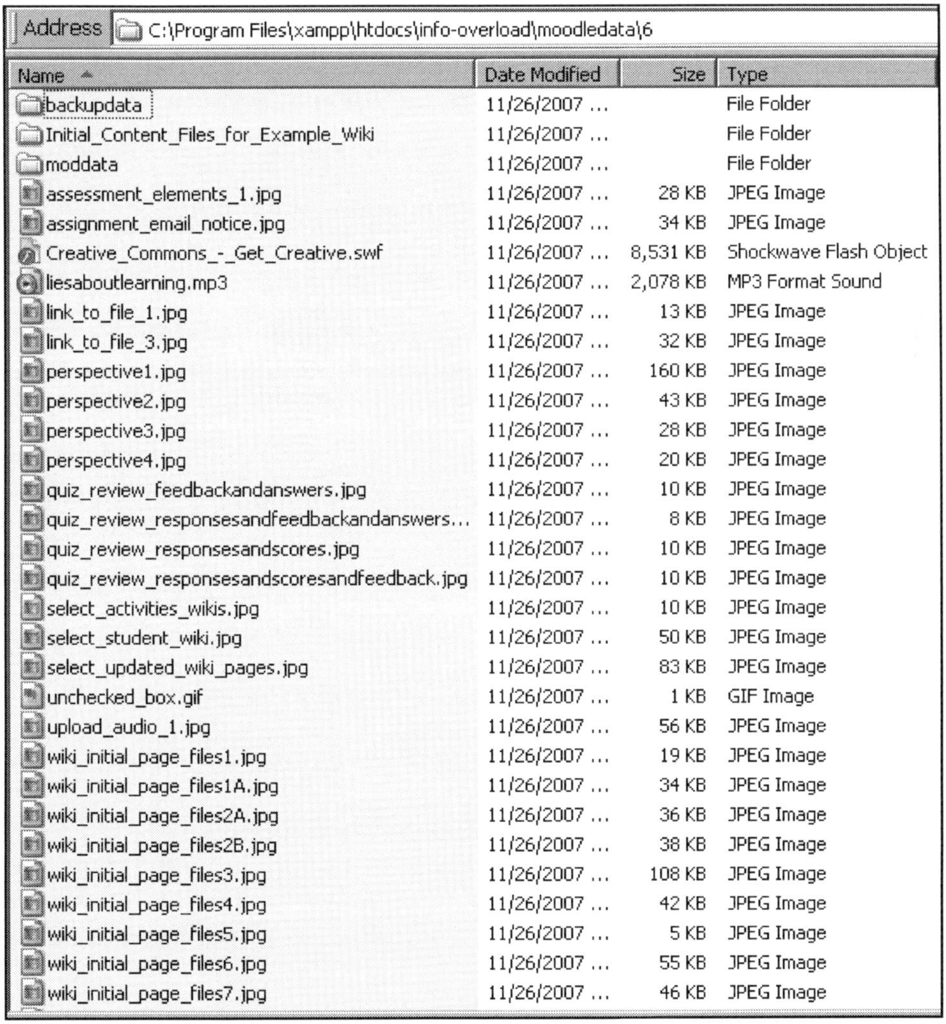

This is the data directory for a course called 'Effective Strategies'. The parts of the course that were **created with Moodle** are stored in the Moodle database—the text on web pages, forums and forum postings, wikis, and text that was entered into the wikis, quizzes, the students who are enrolled in the course, the students' grades, and more. The data directory holds parts of the course which were **created outside of Moodle** and uploaded to the course, such as graphics that the teacher added to web pages created in Moodle, graphics that the students uploaded on their forum postings, audio files, and Flash files. When you back up a course, all the course's components—the parts that are stored in the Moodle database and the parts that are stored in the course's data directory—are put into the backup file. The following is a screenshot of the .zip file which was created when I backed up this course:

Note that the backup file contains the same files as the course's data directory. Also note an extra file in the backup called moodle.xml. This file contains all the course information that resides in the database. So the files from the course's data directory and the information from the database are brought together here in the ZIP file.

You can take this `.zip` file and use it to restore your course in case of disaster. You can also use the file to restore this course to another Moodle site. Or, you can just store the .ZIP file offline, which will enable you to create an archive of the course without keeping it in your live site.

Moodle Backup versus Database Backup versus Directory Backup

From the previous screenshot, you can see that the Moodle backup, whether it's site-wide or for a single course, creates a `.zip` file for each of your courses. If you have to restore your entire site, you would have to reinstall the Moodle software, and then restore each course, one at a time.

If you back up the entire Moodle database, your backup will include everything in the Moodle backup files plus site settings. However, it will not include graphics and files that students submitted, which are stored in the Moodle data directory. If you needed to restore your entire site, you would have to reinstall the Moodle software, import the database, and then restore the Moodle data directory.

If you back up all the software directories on your Moodle server, and the Moodle data directory, plus the Moodle database, in that case you are taking a complete snapshot of your entire site. For disaster recovery, this is the best option. This is not something that you can do with Moodle. You must work with your system administrator or host to accomplish this.

Automated Backup of Your Site

Teachers and administrators can back up an individual course on demand. For a site-wide backup, you do not manually back up your entire Moodle site on demand. Instead, you use the **Site Administration | Courses | Backup** page to determine when your site gets backed up, what features are backed up, and where the backup files are put. Site-wide backup are automated. Teachers who want to ensure that a course is backed up, or those who want to take a snapshot of a course at a certain time, can use the manual backup feature. We will cover backing up and restoring individual courses later in this chapter.

The following screenshot shows the backup settings for my demo site:

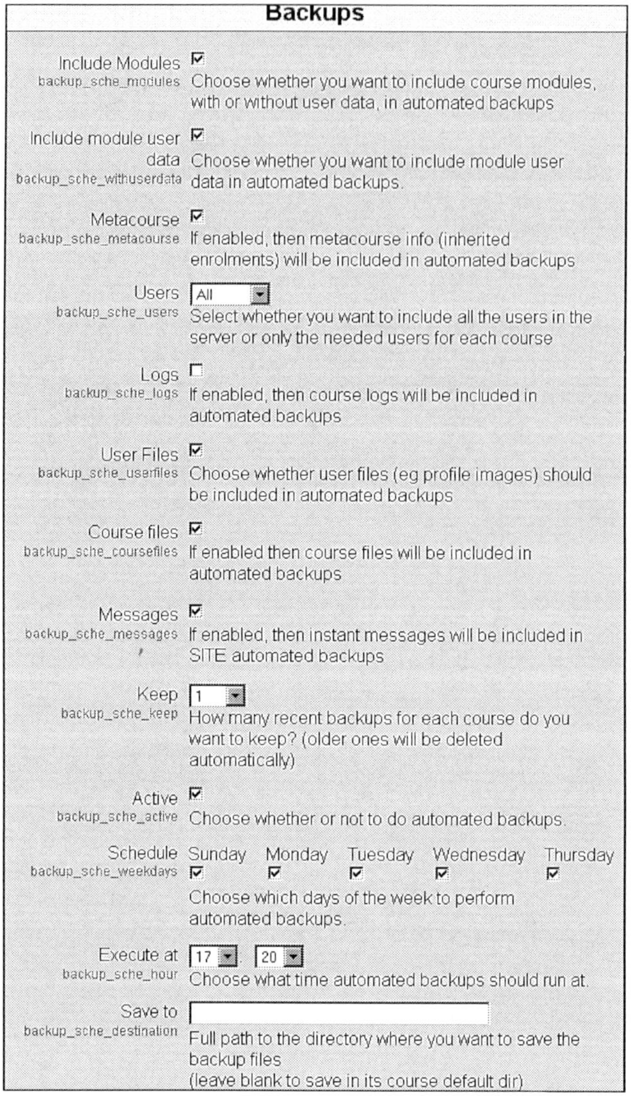

The one setting on this page that seems most obvious, **Execute at**, needs some further explanation. That setting actually causes the backup to happen not at the exact time you specify, but at the first cron job after the designated time. Recall that the Moodle cron job runs at the times specified during the Moodle installation. If your cron job runs every minute, then you'll need to wait only one minute past the designated time for the backup to occur. In the previous screenshot, the backup is set to run at 5:20pm. If my cron job runs every hour on the hour, the next backup will happen at 6pm.

Choosing a Backup Location

Note the directory name at the bottom of the screen. It specifies the location of the backup files on the server. Moodle is designed to back up the files on the same server which hosts the software.

However, if you're using a UNIX or Linux server, you can work with your system administrator to place the files almost anywhere, even on a different computer. ***nix** operating systems enable you to create aliases for other directories and devices. These aliases are called **symlinks**. If you've been given your own user directory on the Moodle server, or some other machine, you can ask your system administrator to create a symlink to your directory. Then, you specify the symlink as the backup location.

Backing Up the Database

To back up the Moodle database, you can use SQL database commands or a tool such as phpMyAdmin, which many hosting services supply. If your site is hosted by your institution, you can work with your system administrator to establish an automated backup routine.

Using phpMyAdmin to Back Up the Database

phpMyAdmin is one of the most popular database managers installed on commercial hosting services. Like Moodle, it is written in the PHP programming language, is open-source software, and is freely available. If your institution is hosting Moodle, it also has the capacity to host phpMyAdmin. Consider asking your institution to install it so that you can directly manipulate the Moodle database.

Backing up the Moodle database consists of exporting all the data to a single file. To do this in phpMyAdmin, select the database, and then select the **Export** function:

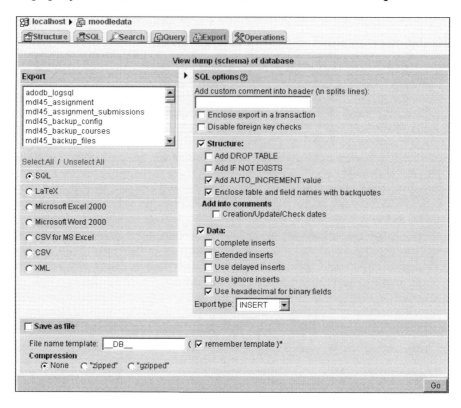

In this example, because the entire database is being backed up, **Select All** has been chosen. This selects all the tables in the database.

For a file format, **SQL** is selected. If the site crashes, reinstall all the software, and import this file into a MySQL database. As the ultimate destination of this file is a SQL database, a format that matches has been selected.

The options in the right side column will probably have no effect on your export and import (backup and restore). In other situations, they might be relevant. But when you are planning on using the export to fill an empty database with the same structure as the original, those options can be skipped.

Selecting **Save as file** results in the export being downloaded to your local computer:

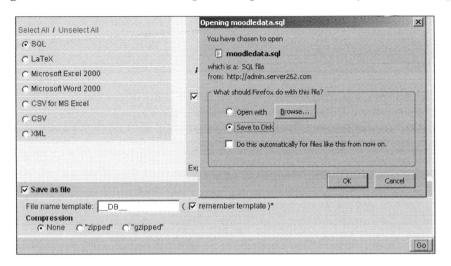

Here are some sample lines from my database export:

```
-- -----------------------------------------------------

--
-- Table structure for table 'mdl_choice_options'
--

CREATE TABLE 'mdl_choice_options' (
  'id' int(10) unsigned NOT NULL auto_increment,
  'choiceid' int(10) unsigned NOT NULL default '0',
  'text' text,
  'maxanswers' int(10) unsigned default '0',
  'timemodified' int(10) NOT NULL default '0',
  PRIMARY KEY  ('id'),
  UNIQUE KEY 'id' ('id'),
  KEY 'choiceid' ('choiceid')
) TYPE=MyISAM AUTO_INCREMENT=4 ;
--
-- Dumping data for table 'mdl_choice_options'
--

INSERT INTO 'mdl_choice_options' VALUES (1, 1, 'Yes, I''ve tried
edible plants found in the wild.', 0, 1120577795);
```

```
INSERT INTO 'mdl_choice_options' VALUES (2, 1, 'No, not yet.', 0,
1120577795);
INSERT INTO 'mdl_choice_options' VALUES (3, 1, 'Sort of. They were
plants that you can find in the wild, but I bought them from a
store.', 0, 1120577795);
```

Note that the export file contains SQL commands such as CREATE and INSERT. These are the commands that create the database tables and fill them with data. If you ever need to import this data, use phpMyAdmin's **SQL** tab:

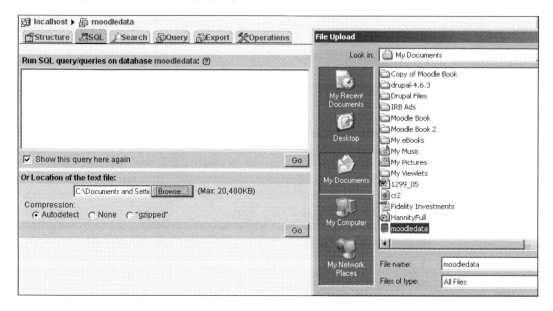

The export file already contains all the SQL commands, so you don't need to enter any into the query area. Instead, just browse, select the file, and then click the **Go** button. Note that during a normal Moodle installation, the Moodle software creates the database tables. If you restore your database using this method, it is the SQL file, and not the Moodle software which creates the tables.

Backing Up the Moodle Directories

While installing Moodle, we created a directory for the application and a directory for data files. Backing up these directories is as simple as copying them into another computer. In the following screenshot, I'm using DreamWeaver to download these directories from my hosting service to my local computer:

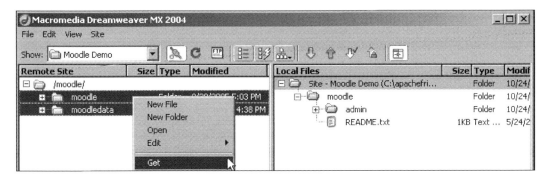

Create a Disaster Recovery Plan

As I mentioned earlier in this chapter, if you back up all the software directories on your Moodle server, and the Moodle data directory, plus the Moodle database, you are taking a complete snapshot of your entire site. For disaster recovery, this is the best option.

Set Moodle to automatically back up the entire site to the data directory overnight. Keep a week's worth of backup. This is not for disaster recovery, but to give you an easy way to restore any course to the condition it was in a few days ago.

Work with your system administrator to set up automated backup routines that will periodically copy the Moodle application directory, data directory, and export of the database to a different server or your local computer.

Duplicate a Course with Import

Moodle enables you to create a fresh copy of any course on your site with just a few clicks. This copy will not have any of the student enrolment or contributions of the original. However, it can have files that the teacher uploaded to the course.

You can also duplicate a course using the **backup and restore** function, which is discussed below. Import is faster and easier than backup and restore. However, it has some limitations. An import does not capture blocks or topic summaries, which backup and restore do. Some teachers prefer using backup and restore for duplicating courses, and import for grabbing pieces. Read this section and the next on backup and restore, and you should be able to make an informed decision about which to use.

To create a duplicate of a course:

1. Add a new course. You will still need to fill out the **Course Settings** page and assign a teacher, just as if you were creating a normal course.

2. Once inside the new course, from the **Administration** panel, select **Import**.

3. Moodle displays a page that enables you to select the course that you want to use as a template for the new one. You can search for and select any course in the system. Select the old course, and then click **Use this course**.

4. The next window displays all the content types in the course. Select and deselect the appropriate content types, and click the **Continue** button. If you choose to import the course files, you will also bring in any file that would be uploaded to the course by the teacher or course creator. You will not bring in any student files. Select **Continue**. When the import is complete, you're taken to your new course.

5. Make appropriate modifications to the new course.

6. Consider putting old courses into a category such as 'Closed Courses' and closing that category to students. This makes it easier to ensure that you don't accidentally leave an old course open. Or, you can create a subcategory under each category called 'Closed Courses', and move old courses there.

Especially for Teachers—Backing Up and Restoring an Individual Course

Many teachers prefer to make their own backup copies of their courses. They can save these backup on the Moodle site, their local PCs, a USB flash drive, or anywhere else they have access to. This is a good way to ensure that your course material is safe, and to take a snapshot of your course in time.

To Back Up a course

1. As a teacher, enter the course that you want to back up.

2. From the **Administration** menu, select **Backup**. The Course backup page is displayed.

3. On the left side of the page, select the types of activities and resources that you want to back up. Note that you can select a single occurrence of an activity or resource, or all the activities/resources of that type.

4. On the right side of the page, select whether you want to include user data. If you include no user data at all in your backup, all student records are left out of the backup. If you include user data, then the students' and teachers' contributions to the activities, and the history of their usage, will be included.

5. At the bottom of the page, select **additional settings**.

6. The **Users** setting determines if you will back up the enrolment information for the course. That includes the usernames and profiles of the students and teachers. Note that if you chose to include user data in your backup, the users who are enrolled in the course will also be backed up. You can't have user data without a user.

7. The **Logs** setting determines if the course logs are backed up. These logs show who did what, and when, in the course.

8. The **User files** setting determines if files contributed by the students of the course are backed up. Note that user data is different from user files. For example, a forum posting is user data. A file attached to a forum posting is a user file. An assessment made by a student during a workshop is user data. A file uploaded by a student during a workshop is a user file.

9. The **Course files** setting determines if files uploaded to the course's **Files** folder (accessed from the **Administration** block) are backed up.

10. Select the **Continue** button.

11. Enter a **Name** for the backup file. You can use any name, but it should end with `.zip`.

12. Scroll down the page and examine the activities and resources that will be backed up. This can be an important check to ensure that you are backing up the course, and the version of the course, that you intend doing.

13. Select the **Continue** button.

14. The backup will run. When you see, at the bottom of the page, the message **Backup completed successfully**, click the **Continue** button.

15. The Files page for that course is displayed. Among the course files you will see the backup file that you just made.

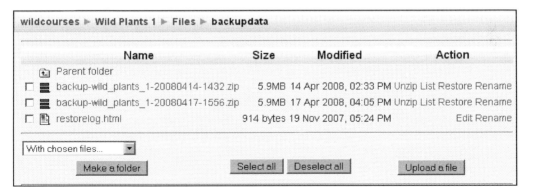

If you have the disk space on your server, leaving several iterations of your backup file on the server enables you to roll back your course to a given date. Notice that Moodle appends the file name with the date, month, day, and time the backup was made.

16. You can download the backup to your local computer for safe keeping. Like most files on the Web, if your right-click on the file name, you can choose to save the file to your local computer.

To Restore a Course

1. As a teacher, enter the course that you want to back up.

2. From the **Administration** menu, select **Restore**. The **Files | backupdata** page is displayed. This is where the backup for that course is automatically stored.

3. For the backup file that you want to use, click the **Restore** link.

4. At the confirmation message, click the **Yes** button.

5. On the resulting page, click the **Continue** button. A page with restore settings and a list of course material displays. On this page, you can select which items to restore and how to restore the course.

6. Use the **Restore to:** setting to restore the items to a new course, or an existing course. If you select **New course**, you will create a new course from the backup data.

7. If you select **Existing course, deleting it first**, then the course that you select as the backup target will be emptied and all the material replaced with the backup data.

8. If you select **Existing course, adding to it**, then the activities and grades that are in the backup file will be added to the selected course. If the selected course has activities of the same name and type, they will not be overwritten. They will only be duplicated. And the grades for the duplicated activities will be added to the gradebook. If the target course contains identically named students, they will not be duplicated.

9. The **Category**, **Short name**, and **Full name** settings take effect only if you are creating a new course from the backup data. If you are restoring to an existing course, these settings are irrelevant.

10. The restore process will start.

11. Select the **Start date** for the course.

12. On the left side of the page, select the types of activities and resources that you want to restore. Note that you can select a single occurrence of an activity or resource, or all of the activities/resources of that type.

13. On the right side of the page, select whether you want to include user data. If you include a user's data in your restore, that data is added to the logs and gradebook of that user.

14. At the bottom of the page, select **additional settings**.

15. The **Metadata** setting determines if this course will become a metacourse. If the original course was not a metacourse, then this is automatically set to **No**.

16. The **Users** setting determines if the enrolled students and teachers will be restored.

17. The **Logs** setting determines if the course logs will be restored.

18. The **User files** setting determines if files uploaded by users will be restored. Note that user data is different from user files. For example, a forum posting is user data. A file attached to a forum posting is a user file. An assessment made by a student during a workshop is user data. A file uploaded by a student during a workshop is a user file.

19. The **Course files** setting determines if files uploaded to the course's **Files** folder (accessed from the **Administration** block) are restored.

20. Use the **Role mappings** to equate roles in the course to roles in your site. If you backed up the course from this site, or if you are using Moodle's standard roles, you probably don't need to do anything with these settings.

21. Select the **Continue** button.

22. If you chose to restore the backup to an existing course, you will be given a list of all courses on the site to which you have access. Select one as the target for the backup.

23. At the confirmation page, click the button, **Restore this course now!.** The restore process will start.

24. After the restore is complete, click the **Continue** button. You are taken to the restored course.

Resetting Courses, and Continual Improvement

The **Administration** block for each course contains a link to **Reset** that course. Resetting a course empties a course of all user data, while retaining the activities and other settings. You can combine **Backup**, **Restore**, and **Reset** to continually improve the quality of your courses.

Often while teaching a course, you will make improvements and corrections to the material. When the course is finished, you are left with better material than when you started. At that point, you might want to use **Import** to bring the material over to a new course for the next session. However, remember that **Import** doesn't bring over blocks or topic summaries, while **Backup** and **Restore** does. So use **Backup** and **Restore** to create a fresh course. Then, **Reset** the restored course. Now the improved course is ready for a new batch of students.

Roles

Throughout this book, we have been using the term 'role' to mean a user's set of permissions on the site. For example, we've seen the roles of Student, Teacher, and Administrator in action as we created a site, created courses, and test course materials. To fully understand roles and to use them, we need to define a few more terms. Then, we'll explore what Moodle's built-in roles can and cannot do, ways to make best use of the built-in roles, and editing roles.

Terminology

Before we explore the use of roles in Moodle, let's define some terms that Moodle uses while working with roles.

Role

A role is a user's set of permissions. A user's role can change according to where the user is in your site. For example, a user might be a Teacher in one course, and a Student in another. Or, a user might be a Student in the course, but perhaps the Teacher wants that student to act as a mentor and leader for some other students in a forum discussion. So the Teacher could give that user the role of Teacher, but only in the forum. In all other parts of the course, the user would have the role of a Student.

If that user's role changes as they move through the system, the user's permissions change.

Context

Your context is your place in the system. Are you on the Home Page of a course? Then your context is **course**. Are you in wiki? Then your context is **wiki**. Are you looking at a student's profile? Then your context is **user**.

The highest context in a Moodle site is the **Core system**. Below that is **Course category**, and below that is the **course**. And below the **course**, are the various activities that you can add to a course (**assignment**, **forum**, and so on).

Capability

A capability is a specific Moodle feature or action. For example, posting to a forum is a capability. Adding an activity to a course is also a capability. The following is a screenshot of the Define Roles page, for the role of **Teacher**. The left column lists the capabilities in the site. The right columns show the **Permissions** for each capability. We'll define 'permission' next. For now, look at the name and variable for the capability. If you want an explanation of any capability, you can click on the name, and a Moodle documentation page explaining the capability will be displayed.

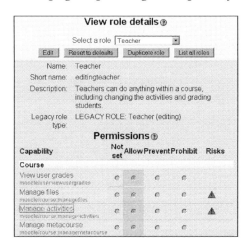

The previous screenshot shows some of the capabilities for a **Course**. That is, it shows some of the tasks that can be performed in a course. The context is course.

Viewing grades, uploading files, and adding activities are some of the tasks. There are many more, but I have edited the screenshot to compress it. Note the capability called **Manage activities**. This capability is what enables a user to add activities to a course.

Permission

In the previous screenshot, the permissions are **Not set**, **Allow**, **Prevent**, and **Prohibit**. You can see that all of the capabilities in the screenshot are set to **Allow**. In Moodle, each of the permissions has a specific meaning.

Not set is equal to the permission, **Inherit**, that many other systems use. It means inheriting the permission from the higher context. So if you're in a course, and a capability has the permission **Not set**, you don't really know if the role has that capability. You need to go up one level in the site and look at the permission there.

In general, permissions in Moodle trickle down from a higher context. That is, the higher overrides the lower context.

Allow does exactly what it says. Keep in mind that you are allowing the capability in that context. Just because you are allowed to manage files in a course that you teach, doesn't mean that you are allowed to manage files site-wide.

As stated above, permissions from a higher context flow down when **Not set** is selected. **Allow** will explicitly allow a capability, even if it's forbidden at the higher context. **Prevent** will forbid a capability, even if it's allowed at the higher context. Of course, you could **Prevent** a capability at a higher context (such as the site) and then someone could **Allow** that capability at a lower context (such as in a course).

Prohibit is like **Prevent**, except that it can't be overridden at a lower context. So if the site administrator wanted to ensure that someone with the role of **Non-editing teacher** could never approve the creation of new courses, the administrator would set that capability to **Prohibit** at the site level:

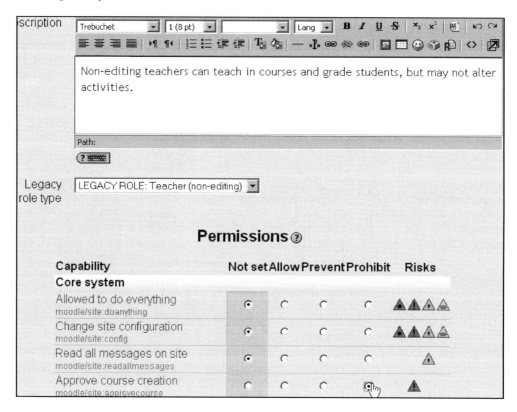

Moodle's Built-In Roles

Moodle's default installation has seven roles. You can edit these roles, and create additional roles. They are described in the following table.

Role	Description
Administrator	This role can do anything in any course on the site. If the same person who is an Administrator also teaches, I strongly suggest that the person use different logins for the different roles of Administrator and Teacher.
Course creator	This role can create new courses and teach in them. By default, the role of Teacher can edit and teach a course, but not create a new one. Course creator can create, edit, and teach courses.
Teacher	This role can do anything within a course, including editing the course. Note that if this role is assigned at the site level, that is, from the site's Front Page, the user will be a Teacher for every course on the site.
Non-editing teacher	This role can teach in a course, but not edit the course. So a Non-editing teacher can assign grades for an activity, but can't change the activity.
Student	This role gives the user access to a course and the ability to participate in its activities.
Guest	This role is for users who have not been enrolled in a course. As you saw earlier in the book, some sites forbid guest access while others allow it. Also, guest access can be forbidden/allowed on a per-course basis. If guests are allowed, they usually cannot enter any text anywhere or see the grades of enrolled students.
Authenticated user	All logged in users have this role in addition to any other roles that they have been assigned.

Assigning a Role

Recall that a role is assigned at a specific level, or in a specific context. So, you can assign someone the role of course creator at the site level, the course category level, or the course level. Each would have a different effect, as stated in the table below:

If you assigned the role of Course Creator in this context...	The user would be able to...
Site	Create and teach courses anywhere on the site, and in any category.
Course Category	Create and teach courses only in the category in which the user was given the Course Creator role.

If you assigned the role of Course Creator in this context...	The user would be able to...
Course	Edit and teach only the course in which the user was given the Course Creator role. A Teacher can also edit a course. If you wanted to give editing rights to a user for just one course, it would make more sense to assign the role Teacher.

As you can see from the table above, a course creator can perform the same actions at different levels, according to the context in which that role is assigned.

Not every role can assign every other role. In general, the more powerful roles can assign users to the less powerful roles. A site Administrator can assign all other roles. A course creator can assign teachers, non-editing teachers, students, and guests. Note that the course creator can only make those assignments in the context where he or she is a course creator. So, if you're a course creator in a specific course category, you can assign teachers to the courses only in that category. Teachers can assign non-editing teachers, students, and guests.

To Assign a Role to Someone at the Site Level

1. From the **Site Administration** menu, select **Users | Permissions | Assign system roles**:

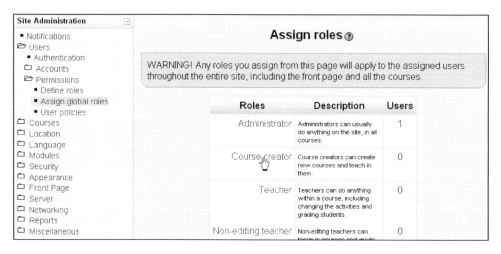

2. Select the role which you want to assign.

3. From the list of **potential users** on the right, select the user(s) to whom you want to assign the role. You can use *ctrl+click* to select multiple users. If your site has too many users to list, use the **Search** field at the bottom of the window to narrow the list.

4. Click the left-facing arrow to assign the user to the role:

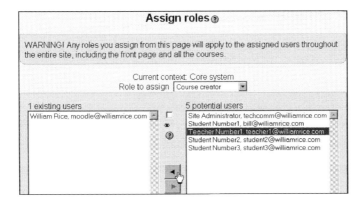

To Assign a Role to Someone Within a Course Category

1. From the **Site Administration** menu, select **Courses | Add/edit courses**:

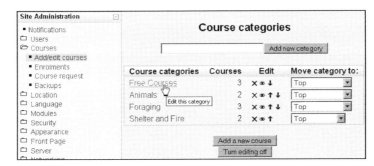

2. Select the course category in which you want to assign the role. In the previous example, the user has selected **Free Courses**.

3. On the resulting course category page, select the **Assign roles** link:

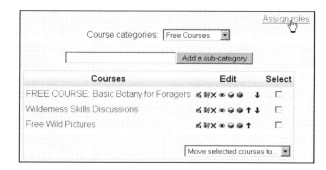

4. The **Assign roles** page is displayed. Select the role which you want to assign.

5. From the list of **potential users** on the right, select the user(s) to whom you want to assign the role. You can use *ctrl+click* to select multiple users. If your site has too many users to list, use the **Search** field at the bottom of the window to narrow the list.

6. Click the left-facing arrow to assign the user to the role.

To Assign a Role to Someone Within a Course (That Is, Enroll a Student or Assign a Teacher)

The following are the steps:

1. From the course's Home Page, select **Assign roles** under the **Administration** block:

2. Selecting this link takes you to the **Assign roles** page:

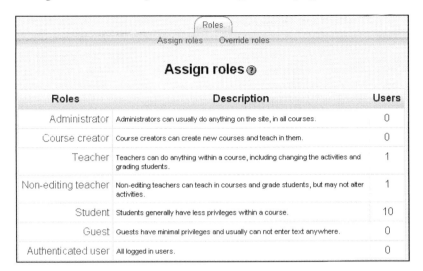

3. Select the role to which you want to assign the user. The page will change:

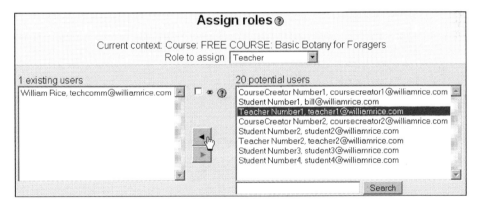

This screen lists all authenticated users in the system. Any authenticated user can be given any role in the course.

Note the drop-down list next to **Role to assign**, near the top of the page. You don't need to leave this page to assign different roles in the course.

4. In the right column, select the user(s) to whom you want to assign a role. If the user isn't listed, you can use the **Search** box to find the user. To select multiple users, use *Ctrl+click*.

5. Click the left-facing arrow to assign the selected user(s) to the role.

Editing a Role's Capabilities

When you want to know if a given role has a capability, you can look up the capability on the **View role details** page, or you can log in as a user with that role and test it. I prefer to do both. To get to the **View role details** page, select **Site Administration | Users | Permissions | Define roles**. If you want an explanation for a capability, click on it and you will be taken to the Moodle documentation site page for that capability. In the following screenshot, you can see the URL of the documentation page for the capability, **Backup courses**.

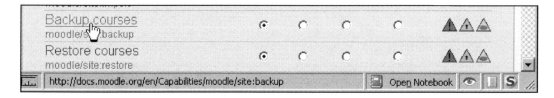

As stated earlier, you can edit a role by adding and removing capabilities. The edits you make are for the context in which you edited the role. So if you edit a role at the site level, you have change that role for every user on the site. If you edit a role in a course, you have changed the role only for that course. And if you edit a role in an activity, you have changed the role only for that activity in that course.

Before you edit a role, you should look up and understand the capabilities that the role already has. The following directions will help you to do that.

To Edit a Role's Capabilities

- Go to the context in which you want to edit the role.
    - ° If you want to edit the role for the entire site, go to your site's Front Page.
    - ° If you want to edit the role for a course, go to the course's Home Page.
    - ° If you want to edit the role for an activity, go to the activity's editing page and look for a button that reads, **Update this ....** The button will probably be in the upper right corner of the page:

    Update this Wiki

    - ° If you want to edit the role for a course category, from the **Site Administration** menu, select **Courses | Add/edit courses,** and then select the course category.

- What you do next depends upon the context in which you want to edit the role. In general, you want to get to the **Assign roles** page.

    ○ If you're editing the role for the entire site, then, select **Users | Permissions | Define roles** from the **Site Administration** menu, in the site's Front Page.

    ○ If you're editing the role for a course, then from the course's Home Page, select **Assign roles** under the **Administration** block.

    ○ If you're editing the role for an activity, select the **Roles** tab:

    ○ If you're editing the role for a course category, then, select the link **Assign roles** (it's in the upper right corner of the page) from the course category page.

The result should be that you are on the **Assign roles** page whatever be the context you have chosen. In this example, the user is in the **Assign roles** page for a wiki:

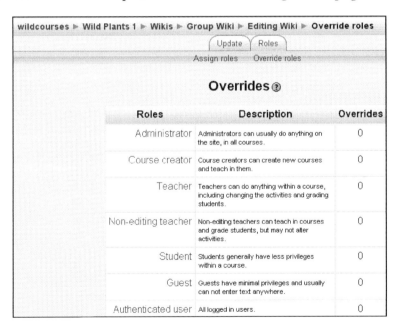

wildcourses ▶ Wild Plants 1 ▶ Wikis ▶ Group Wiki ▶ Editing Wiki ▶ Override roles

Update   Roles

Assign roles   Override roles

Overrides ⊙

Roles	Description	Overrides
Administrator	Administrators can usually do anything on the site, in all courses.	0
Course creator	Course creators can create new courses and teach in them.	0
Teacher	Teachers can do anything within a course, including changing the activities and grading students.	0
Non-editing teacher	Non-editing teachers can teach in courses and grade students, but may not alter activities.	0
Student	Students generally have less privileges within a course.	0
Guest	Guests have minimal privileges and usually can not enter text anywhere.	0
Authenticated user	All logged in users.	0

- Select the link for **Override roles**.
- Select the role that you want to edit. In the following screenshot, the user is editing the role of **Non-editing teacher** in the context of a wiki:

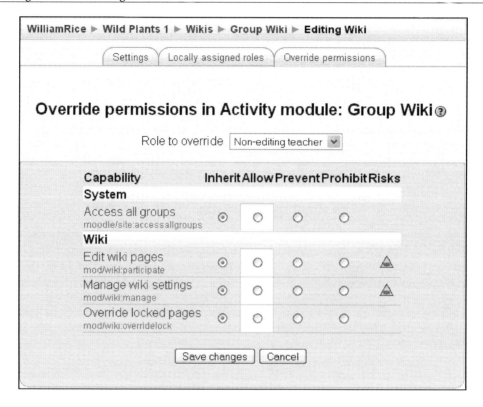

- Note that only some capabilities can be edited for the role. As the context changes, so do the capabilities that can be edited. If you want to change a capability for the Non-editing teacher that isn't listed here, you'll need to go up one level to the course context and edit the role there. Of course, if you edit a role at the site level, all capabilities are available for editing.

- If you're unsure what a capability does, click on it to go to the official Moodle.org documentation page for more details on that capability:

- Select the new values for the capabilities that you want to edit—**Inherit, Allow, Prevent,** or **Prohibit**.

- **Save** your changes.

- Test the results!

Recommendations for Working with Roles

Modifying roles can have significant, and sometimes unexpected effects upon your site. This is especially true when we modify roles at the site level. Before you start modifying and creating roles, consider the following recommendations.

- Some site administrators begin modifying roles even before they have built any courses. If you have experience with other roles-based systems, such as a content management system—Plone or Drupal, you might have a good idea of how you want to set up roles in Moodle. It is tempting to look at the capabilities of each role and immediately start modifying them according to your needs. However, don't customize or create roles until you've used the site and have evidence that the standard roles don't work the way you want. The standard roles have been developed with input from many users. Thousands of sites use them as is. Explore them thoroughly before customizing your roles.

- Don't modify standard roles at the site level. Make a copy of the standard role, and then modify the copy. This way, you always retain the standard role in case you need it. This is common practice for any role-based software. It's much safer to modify roles at the course and activity level.

- On the Roles page, there are very few reasons when you may have to use the setting, **Prohibit**. The effect of using this setting can be significant and unexpected. So, use it with caution.

Summary

Expanding your Moodle site with additional modules is a powerful tool for customizing and differentiating your e-learning site. Don't be afraid to add modules beyond those that come with the standard Moodle installation package. If you're worried about the stability or compatibility of add-on modules, you can easily install another Moodle instance just for testing new modules. Work with your system administrator to establish a backup and recovery routine. Add-on modules, Moodle upgrades, and upgrades that your web hosting service makes to their software can bring down your site and/or corrupt your data. A complete software and data backup is a smart investment.

Editing and creating roles gives you fine control over your user's privileges. Before doing this, use the official documentation to research each of the capabilities you are considering adding or removing from a role. And, try editing those roles in the context of a test course, so you can thoroughly test the effects of your edits on the user experience.

Index

Packt Open Source Project Royalties

When we sell a book written on an Open Source project, we pay a royalty directly to that project. Therefore by purchasing Moodle E-Learning Course Development, Packt will have given some of the money received to the Moodle Project.

In the long term, we see ourselves and you—customers and readers of our books—as part of the Open Source ecosystem, providing sustainable revenue for the projects we publish on. Our aim at Packt is to establish publishing royalties as an essential part of the service and support a business model that sustains Open Source.

If you're working with an Open Source project that you would like us to publish on, and subsequently pay royalties to, please get in touch with us.

Writing for Packt

We welcome all inquiries from people who are interested in authoring. Book proposals should be sent to authors@packtpub.com. If your book idea is still at an early stage and you would like to discuss it first before writing a formal book proposal, contact us; one of our commissioning editors will get in touch with you.

We're not just looking for published authors; if you have strong technical skills but no writing experience, our experienced editors can help you develop a writing career, or simply get some additional reward for your expertise.

About Packt Publishing

Packt, pronounced 'packed', published its first book "Mastering phpMyAdmin for Effective MySQL Management" in April 2004 and subsequently continued to specialize in publishing highly focused books on specific technologies and solutions.

Our books and publications share the experiences of your fellow IT professionals in adapting and customizing today's systems, applications, and frameworks. Our solution-based books give you the knowledge and power to customize the software and technologies you're using to get the job done. Packt books are more specific and less general than the IT books you have seen in the past. Our unique business model allows us to bring you more focused information, giving you more of what you need to know, and less of what you don't.

Packt is a modern, yet unique publishing company, which focuses on producing quality, cutting-edge books for communities of developers, administrators, and newbies alike. For more information, please visit our website: www.PacktPub.com.

Building Powerful and Robust Websites with Drupal 6

ISBN: 978-1-847192-97-4   Paperback: 330 pages

Build your own professional blog, forum, portal or community website with Drupal 6

1. Set up, configure, and deploy Drupal 6

2. Harness Drupal's world-class Content Management System

3. Design and implement your website's look and feel

4. Easily add exciting and powerful features

5. Promote, manage, and maintain your live website

Building Websites with Joomla! 1.5

ISBN: 978-1-847191-05-2   Paperback: 292 pages

The best-selling Joomla! tutorial guide updated for the latest 1.5 release

1. Learn Joomla! 1.5 features

2. Install and customize Joomla! 1.5

3. Configure Joomla! administration

4. Create your own Joomla! templates

5. Extend Joomla! with new components, modules, and plug-ins

Please check **www.PacktPub.com** for information on our titles